HAZEL

To my mother Barbara
And my late father Michael

HAZEL
A Life of Lady Lavery
1880-1935

❧

Sinéad McCoole

THE LILLIPUT PRESS
DUBLIN

First published in 1996 by
THE LILLIPUT PRESS LTD
62–63 Sitric Road
Dublin 7, Ireland
www.lilliputpress.ie

Reissued with amendments 2015

A CIP record for this title is available from The British Library.

ISBN 978 1 84351 6439

The Lilliput Press receives financial assistance from
An Chomhairle Ealaíon/The Arts Council of Ireland.

Design by Jarlath Hayes
Reset by Susan Waine in 11.5 on 15 Galliard
Printed in Spain by GraphyCems

Contents

Plates are between pages 20 and 21, 52 and 53, and 116 and 117

Preface

Had it not been for Hazel's portrait as the colleen of Irish banknotes, her features and even her name would be now forgotten in a land which has never accounted gratitude amongst its theological virtues. – Shane Leslie[1]

THIS RUEFUL assessment of history's short and selective memory provides the most obvious rationale for a biography of Hazel, Lady Lavery. Her role as a social diplomat during the Anglo-Irish Treaty negotiations and their aftermath has frequently been dismissed. Social history by its nature is difficult to document, which may account in part for Hazel's absence from the dominant historical narrative of the period. As the truth about the lives of the founding fathers of the Irish state comes into fuller perspective, those marginalized at their expense – such as Hazel Lavery – regain their stature.

There has been persistent interest in chronicling Hazel's life, starting with Hazel herself, who wished to publish her correspondence but was prevented by illness. Those letters, many of them published here for the first time, reveal both the breadth of Hazel's social connections with the leading writers, artists and statesmen of the day, and the depth of her political commitments.

Her husband, the painter Sir John Lavery, was to write in his autobiography *The Life of a Painter* (1940):

Hazel left behind a trunk full of letters and mementoes of those days. It is not for me to disturb them ... But neither in paint nor in words do I feel I could ever do justice to Hazel. Her rare beauty of face and character must have been known personally to be believed, and so upon the things nearest to me I will write least.[2]

In 1940 Sir John wrote to the novelist Louie Rickard, 'Of all Hazel's friends it was to you in her last sad months that her love and thoughts went – I know that if a record of her life was to be written it would have been you she would have chosen to write it.'[3] The Irish playwright Lennox Robinson approached John after Hazel's death seeking to compile a book he intended to call *Letters to Hazel,* but John denied him permission.[4] Osbert Sitwell wished to pen Hazel's life but his ambition never came to fruition.[5] Shane Leslie also toyed with the idea. He wrote, 'Many, who were enchanted by her on earth, hoped they would be allowed to write her biography.'[6] Lady Lavery's only child, Alice, believed that she could set down her mother's life story, but found the cares of family life encroached upon her desire to write.[7] She also questioned her ability: 'What could I write about that has not already been told, and much better, by someone else, but for my own amusement, or my children's, I might make an attempt one day.'[8] Shane Leslie suggested to Alice that their stories of Hazel should be put 'in a sealed envelope' for the benefit of 'the historian of 2000',[9] but this never happened. John himself produced a particularly durable monument to Hazel's life in the form of over forty portraits, but in his own rambling, somewhat inaccurate autobiography, the frequent references to Hazel are tantalizingly brief.

In the 1950s Lady Audrey Morris, who had known Hazel, began a biography. For eleven years she assembled a huge volume of documentation and recorded contemporary reminiscences, but many of those interviewed refused to have their statements published. The suggestion of Hazel's romantic involvement with major political figures, particularly the Irish nationalists Michael Collins and Kevin O'Higgins, would have been especially controversial. Leslie wrote to Lady Audrey:

... it is an excruciatingly difficult book to write especially as so much ms. material has disappeared ... much is quite impossible to tell. Remember Miss Collins is alive and the widow of Kevin O'Higgins. If Hazel's correspondence with those Irishmen Collins and Kevin were published or even their relations were truly portrayed there would be woe in Dublin and much protestation.[10]

Restrictions were imposed by Alice and the manuscript was never published. This biography has made extensive use of Lady Audrey's invaluable research, in which the voices of Hazel's contemporaries are preserved. In quoting from letters, I have left intact aberrant spelling, punctuation and syntax, without comment, except where these impede comprehension.

This work originated in research undertaken for a Master's thesis entitled 'Lady Lavery, Her Salon, and its Role in the Emergence of the Irish Free State' for the Department of Modern Irish History at University College Dublin. When I began my research in 1990, only fragmentary archival material could be found. I located Hazel's daughter, Alice Gywnn, then living in Co. Meath, but it was only possible to interview her three times before her death in April 1991. When scholars had approached Mrs Gwynn earlier, she claimed she had burnt all her mother's papers. However, after her death a large cache of letters and scrapbooks came to light in the attic of Rosenalis, to which I was kindly granted access. Hazel had created her own remarkable archive of correspondence, newspaper clippings, photographs and other documents; this work is largely based on these sources. All uncredited drawings, letters and photographs used here come from the scrapbooks. Hazel deliberately shaped the record other life. Conspicuous by their absence are the letters from family and friends not in the public sphere. The Lady Lavery Collection will no doubt provide the foundation for a fuller study in future.

Shane Leslie's words now seem prophetic:

In due time this biography or rather illustrated souvenir will reach the record. ... No one, English or Irish, who shared in those times, would now care to be without some kind of biography of Hazel. In the matter of her friendships and admirers, future historians will insist on being frank, as history in due time has always allowed them.[11]

Acknowledgments

THIS BOOK is the culmination of over five years' work and would not have been possible without the help of a number of individuals, particularly those who saw the potential of this subject long before I began to write. Most of all I am indebted to Lady Lavery's descendants who allowed me unlimited access to the Lady Lavery Collection. They afforded me hospitality on many occasions. Sadly, Hazel's daughter, the late Alice Gwynn, did not live to see the publication of her mother's biography, but I am happy in the knowledge that she knew I would write it.

I am grateful to the Hon. Edwina Epstein for allowing me to quote from an unpublished biography of Lady Lavery by her late mother, Lady Audrey Morris. The material gathered by Lady Audrey in the 1950s, and her insights into the personality of Lady Lavery and the period in which she lived, were invaluable.

I must particularly thank Dr Margaret MacCurtain O.P. for her encouragement. Her women's documents course at University College Dublin sowed the initial seeds of this study.

For their advice and source material I am grateful to Eoghan Harris, Fr Brian Murphy O.S.B., Dorothy Ramm, Mary B. Hotaling, Thomas J. O'Gorman, the late Terence de Vere White, the late Sherrif Harold Ford and his wife Lucy, Lady M. E. Ford, Kenneth McConkey, Liam O'Gradaigh and Deirdre MacMahon.

ACKNOWLEDGMENTS

I am indebted to the staff of the libraries and archives I consulted in Ireland, England and the United States. I extend my gratitude to Edburne Hare and the staff of The Masters School at Dobbs Ferry, New York; Seth Lampton of the Yale Club Library, New York; Barbara Parness at the Saranac Free Library;the staff of the New York Public Library and the New York Historical Society; the staff of the N ewbury Library of Chicago; the Chicago Historical Society; Dale Louiso of St Chrysostom's Church, Chicago; the staff of the Harry Ransom Humanities Center at the University of Texas at Austin, in particular Barbara Smith-La Borde; Nicholas B. Scheetz of Georgetown University Library, Washington D.C.; the staff of the British Library; the staff of the British Newspaper Library at Collingdale; the Tate Gallery Archive, London; the Public Record Office (England); Father lan Dicky of the Westminster Diocesan Archives, London; Dr S.B. Kennedy of the Ulster Museum, Belfast; Seamus Hel-ferty and the staff of the University College Dublin Archive; Dr Meehan and the staff of the manuscript department of Trinity College Dublin; the National Archive (Ireland); the National Library of Ireland; Rachel O'Flanagan of All Hallows College Archive, Dublin; and Pat Cooke of Kilmainham Gaol Museum.

A number of people kindly granted me permission to quote letters, personal papers and published material. I wish to thank Martyn McEnery for allowing me to quote the writings of Lady Lavery and Mrs Alice Gwynn. For use of the Lady Gregory papers I acknowledge the Henry W. and Albert A. Berg Collection, New York Public Library, Astor, Lenox and Tilden Foundations; Tim Healy for permission to quote his grandfather; Tarka King for permission to quote his grandfather Sir Shane Leslie and his mother Anita Leslie King; Mary Semple for permission to quote Hugh Kennedy; the Society of Authors for permission to use unpublished material from George Bernard Shaw and Lytton Strachey; Peters, Fraser and Dunlop for permission to quote Evelyn Waugh; the board of Trinity College, Dublin, for permission to quote the R.E. Childers and Thomas Bodkin papers; Kit Orpen Casey for permission to use her father's letters; Oliver D. Gogarty for permission to quote his father; and Kevin Rafferty C.M., Rector of All Hallows College, Dublin, for allowing me to quote from Fr Leonard's papers. I regret that I was unable to contact those in possession of Ramsay MacDonald's copyright.

I cannot say enough about the assistance given by my family: my sister Fiona, who was my dedicated proofreader; my mother, who brought me up to believe I could accomplish anything to which I set my mind; my brother Ciaran, who supplied technical expertise; and my fiancé Eamon Howlin, for supporting me throughout. Joe and Mary Talbot, the closest of friends, who helped me while I was researching and writing in America. For their editorial suggestions I thank Ann Marie Bennett, Caria Briggs, Jackie Clarke, Isabel Donnellan, Dolores Doyle, Anne Gormley, Bernard Guinan, Dr Brian Kennedy, Michael Kennedy, Donal and Marguerite Lynch, and Harriet O'Carroll. For their hospitality to me in New York and Chicago, I thank Patricia and Ned Trudeau, the late Dr Frank Trudeau and his wife Ursula, Kathleen Daniel, and John and Francis Shovlin. To those I have inadvertently overlooked, I extend my gratitude and apologies.

I am grateful to the staff of the Hugh Lane Municipal Gallery of Modern Art, Dublin – in particular Barbara Dawson, Christina Kennedy, Dara O'Connell, Maime Winters and Liz Foster – and to the staff at The Lilliput Press – Antony Farrell, Vivienne Guinness, Brendan Barrington and Amanda Bell – for their support of this project.

PUBLISHER'S NOTE

The Lilliput Press is especially grateful to Eoghan Harris and David Dickson for their editorial advice.

I

'The Most Beautiful Girl in the Midwest'
[1880-1903]

She had much Irish blood, but she was primarily an American. On the whole American women ... are amazingly different from the others .... Their eyes are large and have a certain age-old gaze about them that makes one think that these women belong to the most ancient rather than the youngest of nations. Hazel was one of this kind.[1]

EDWARD JENNER MARTYN and his wife Alice found it difficult to choose a name for their first child. The birth certificate issued for their daughter, born 14 March 1880 at 514 North Avenue in Chicago, bears no name at all. For the census in June they had settled on the name of Elsa.[2] However, Elsa's large brown eyes, which were to inspire artists and poets, prompted her parents to change her name to Hazel.[3]

Like many of his generation, Edward Martyn had left his home town of Attleboro, Massachusetts, and travelled west to seek his fortune. Chicago, on the shores of Lake Michigan, was a vibrant commercial metropolis, the centre of trade between the east coast and the advancing frontier of the western prairies. It had been almost completely rebuilt after the Great Fire of 1871, and by the turn of the century the city boasted the most important maritime port in the USA and the world's greatest railroad centre.

Edward Martyn was first employed by Hugh McLennan & Co., a Canadian grain and commission firm.[4] In 1875 he left the company to work as a messenger boy for Armour & Co., which, under the new management of Philip Danforth Armour, was to become the leading meat-packing firm in the country.[5]

Alice Louise Taggart was twenty-one when she married Edward Martyn, ten years her senior. She was the only surviving child of John Perkins and Susan Taggart, New Yorkers who had settled in Ripon, Wisconsin, where they owned a successful hardware business.[6] By 1879 Edward Martyn's ability had been recognized and rewarded, and he had become one of Armour's chief advisors.[7] The Martyn household was a happy one. Alice was affectionately known as 'ha ha', and Hazel's earliest memory was the sound of her mother's laughter.[8]

Although Hazel greew up with her Taggart grandparents, it was her Martyn ancestry that intrigued her. The Martins had ruled territory near Galway city on the west coast of Ireland between 1235 and 1300.[9] They were descendants of Oliver Martin, a follower of the Norman conqueror Strongbow. After the Reformation a variation of the surname, Martyn, was commonly used. Although Edward Martyn's ancestors settled in America in the seventeenth century,[10] and his antecedents were in fact among the earliest settlers from Dorset, he instilled in his daughter a love of Ireland.[11] Hazel never forgot her father's stories of how the Martyns had fought in rebellion.[12] She treasured a bronze engraving of the Martyn coat of arms and often quoted the family motto, '*Sic itur ad astra*' – 'Such is the way to immortality'.

In November 1887 Alice Martyn gave birth to a second daughter, Dorothea Hope. Dorothy, as she became known, was a pretty baby, with brown eyes like her father and sister, although her complexion was much darker. Even with the arrival of a second child, Hazel remained the dominant character in the family. Mr and Mrs Martyn idolized their vivacious elder daughter, who was already showing artistic and musical ability, and Dorothy was destined to spend her life in Hazel's shadow.

By 1890 Armour & Co. was the largest meat company in the city, known for turning 'bristles, blood, bones, and the insides and outsides of pigs and bullocks into revenue'.[13] Edward Martyn was now Philip Armour's right-hand man and Vice-President and Director of the Union Stock Yard and Transit Company of Chicago. One business associate recalled, 'Wherever anything went wrong, Martyn was always the man to look after it.'[14]

Mrs Martyn and her daughters lived far from the squalor of the stockyards. They moved several times over the years, although never more than a few blocks from Hazel's north-side birthplace. They lived at 71 Maple Street and 452 Dearborn Avenue before finally settling at 112 Astor Street in 1893, one of the most prestigious addresses in the city. The neighbourhood had been built on tracts of lake-side swamp land that had been drained and developed by the hotel magnate Potter Palmer.

The Palmers, the Wallers and the Hodges, prominent society families, became the Martyns' closest friends. From 1890 the Martyn name featured in the 'Blue Book', the social register of Chicago which listed the city's four hundred 'gold coast' families. Edward had little opportunity to enjoy his success, as he spent much time travelling within the United States and to Europe on business.[15] Hazel's imagination was fired by her father's accounts of his travels.

In 1893, when Hazel was thirteen years old, the World's Columbian Exposition was held in Chicago, bringing European treasures and millions of visitors to her home town. Exhibits included Columbus's contract with Ferdinand and Isabella, jewellery from Russia and Gobelins tapestries from France. Years later Hazel recalled that nothing had encouraged her zest for wide horizons more than this spectacle.[16]

Early on, Hazel was taught at home by her mother. Her social education began with dance classes at Bourniques. She received instruction in music and drawing[17] and was an avid reader. Her father once caught her with one of Louisa May Alcott's books, *The Rose in Bloom* (1876), in which the heroine is forced to choose

3

between suitors. Mr Martyn thought the novel too *risque* and forbade Hazel to finish it. Her riposte appeared in verse:

> When I'm dead and in my tomb,
> You'll wish you'd given me *The Rose in Bloom*.[18]

When Hazel outgrew her mother's tutoring she was sent to Sleboth-Kennedy School at Bellevue Place, a private establishment catering to north-side society families, where she became one of the most popular girls.[19] Her 'most intimate friend' was Ethel Hooper, the daughter of Dr Henry Hooper, a well-known Chicago physician; another friend was Marie Truesdale, whose family was one of the wealthiest in the city.

In her early teens Hazel moved on to Kemper Hall, a boarding-school for girls in Kenosha, Wisconsin. This tree-girt brick mansion facing Lake Michigan was a former home of Governor Durkee.[20] Founded in 1870 and named in memory of the Reverend Jackson Kemper, the first missionary bishop of the American Episcopal Church, the school was only an hour from Chicago by train. Hazel must nevertheless have felt far from home, as there were no breaks during the school term and only one week's holiday at Christmas.[21]

The school was run by the Sisters of Saint Mary, an Episcopalian order. Mother Margaret Clare, the headmistress, believed that the sisters' aim should be 'not simply to teach but to inspire'.[22] Kemper Hall had a strict daily regimen. According to the 1874 Rules Book pupils rose at 6 a.m. and were to be in their dormitories by 9 p.m. Every girl was required to take a walk before breakfast, and the school organized competitions to encourage physical exercise. Students were divided into the houses of Lancaster and York, and wore the appropriate rose-badges.[23] Competition was not confined to the sporting field; Hazel's most abiding memory was winning the title of 'The Most Beautiful Girl in the Midwest'.[24]

Why Hazel left Kemper Hall is not recorded, but by 1896 her name was on a waiting-list for a place at Miss Masters, a finishing-school in Dobbs Ferry-on-Hudson, New York. It was not uncommon in Chicago society for girls to be sent east, as the midwest was thought to lack the refinement of the established east-coast upper class. Hazel's application stated that she was 'exceedingly desirous of joining the school during that winter' and that she would 'go at a few hours' notice if a vacancy should occur'.[23]

Miss Masters School was established in 1877 by the widow of the Reverend Francis Masters and her two daughters.[26] Eliza B. Masters, the eldest daughter, was head of the school and its guiding force. The school followed Episcopalian and Presbyterian religious practices and the application form questioned whether the prospective pupil was a Church communicant. Bible-study classes and visits to the chapel were compulsory. This religious focus seems to have been in keeping with the beliefs of Edward Martyn, who had helped establish the family's neighbourhood Episcopalian church, St Chrysostom's, pledging the considerable sum of five hundred dollars towards the purchase of the church site.[27] Thereafter he devoted what free time he had to his duties as church vestryman.

Hazel was accepted as a pupil at Miss Masters in September 1896. There were fewer than a hundred girls enrolled and lessons were oriented towards the individual student. The teachers were university-educated women who encouraged their pupils to be independent free-thinkers. Students were offered tuition in English, French and Latin, with music and art as extras.[28] Hazel believed she should have been allowed to devote more time to music in her girlhood, later recalling, 'my family had other views and made me concentrate on drawing, and that was that'.[29]

Besides singing in the Glee Club (founded after the Yale Glee Club had cancelled a performance in 1829 and the pupils pacified the crowd by dressing as men and performing impromptu), Hazel showed marked ability as an actress in a number of school productions. She was selected as one of ten honorary members of the Players Club, and many believed that she could have made a career in drama.[30] Her talent was inherited from her father, who was known for his ability in parlour dramatics.[31]

In April 1897 Hazel had her first of several experiences of losing a loved one to a sudden death. Edward Martyn had taken some rime off work with a cold, assuring his colleagues that he would soon return. His cold developed into pneumonia and he died within a matter of days.* His sudden death, attributed by many to overwork, shocked the community. Philip Armour, who had been visiting Astor Street at the rime of Martyn's death, was reported to be devastated.

Hazel was summoned home when her father became seriously ill, but he was dead by the rime she arrived. The funeral had to be delayed for two days because Mrs Martyn was 'prostrate with grief'. The burial at Graceland cemetery was a quiet family affair. The Taggarts comforted their distraught daughter, with whom they had been living since Hazel's birth in 1880. Hazel promptly went back to Miss Masters.

The school sheltered its pupils from the outside world and yet trained them to move in society with ease. It was close to New York City, and there were frequent outings for afternoon tea, the opera, the theatre and lectures. Miss Masters girls attended dances at Yale University and in turn Yale men attended those held at Dobbs Ferry. Hazel attracted many suitors,[32] the most attentive being Edward Livingston Trudeau Jnr, eldest son of the eminent Dr Edward Livingston Trudeau Snr, founder of a tuberculosis sanatorium in the Adirondack Mountains in upstate New York. Ned had graduated from Yale Medical School in 1896 aged twenty-three, and was studying at the College of Physicians and Surgeons in New York when he met Hazel. He was tall and athletically built, with a sallow complexion and dark hair, perhaps due to his French lineage.** At Yale Ned pitched for the baseball

---

*According to his death certificate he also suffered from nephritis, or Bright's disease.

**The Trudeau family emigrated from France c.1838 and settled in New York.

6

team[33] and was a member of the Skull and Bones Society, a secret organization that accepted only the brightest and most talented of students. However, despite his attributes and great persistence in courting Hazel, Ned could not kindle her interest.

After graduation from Miss Masters in the summer of 1898, Hazel embarked on a visit to France. Little is known of this European sojourn but she must have been to Paris. The late 1800s saw the climax of '*la belle époque*' as new theories and practices in art developed around artists such as Edouard Manet, Claude Monet and later Paul Cezanne, Paul Gauguin and Vincent Van Gogh. Turning from traditional academic painting, some artists looked to contemporary life, and others depicted the landscapes surrounding them. Painting *en plein air,* they sought to capture the play of light and shadow using a greatly brightened palette. Artists exchanged ideas and gathered in the studios and cafés of Paris, and in the villages of Brittany, Normandy and the environs of Fontainebleau.

American artists flocked to Europe at the time. One of these, William Merritt Chase, claimed he would 'rather go to Europe than go to heaven'.[34] Wealthy female students, often denied a thorough artistic education at home because of their sex, sought private instruction in the studios of more liberal male painters and sculptors in Paris.[35] Hazel spent almost a year abroad and she later mentioned visiting Rome and the French Riviera. She loved Europe and there found an artistic atmosphere unlike anything she had known in America.[36]

Back home in Chicago, steel-framed skyscrapers were punctuating the skyline, and the elevated Loop transport was completed in 1897. Developers had no wish to preserve older buildings and Hazel, who loved the past, greeted these changes with little enthusiasm. She would later exclaim that the USA stood for 'the most hopeless modernity and vulgarity'.[37]

In the winter of 1899 Hazel came out in Chicago society. That season saw the largest number of debutantes ever, and society columnists enthused that it promised to be the gayest in years.[38] The social calendar was filled with dinners, luncheons, cotillions and opera parties. Hazel's debutante reception was held at the family home at Astor Street on the evening of Saturday 11 November, and several hundred callers came to inspect the young Miss Martyn in her gown of white organdie.[39] Ethel Hooper, Marie Truesdale and Rue Winterbotham were among the twenty-eight girls who assisted her. It was a modest affair compared with Marie's debut, which featured a reception at the Fine Arts Building for 500 guests and a ball for 200.[40]

Hazel's name soon began to appear regularly in the society columns. Contemporaries described her as an astonishing beauty, with immense presence despite her five-foot two-inch stature. Her small, rather pointed face was dominated by lustrous almond-shaped hazel eyes.[41] Despite these attractions, the educated, artistic and beautiful Miss Martyn did not have a steady beau, though Ned Trudeau continued 'to worship at the Martyn shrine'.[42]

The Martyns spent lavishly on clothing and entertainment, though the family fortune had dwindled since Edward Martyn's death. His estate had amounted to $100,000, with $75,000 invested in personal property.[43] The house on Astor Street proved too expensive to maintain and by the winter of 1900 it was necessary to sell. The Martyns moved into the luxurious Virginia Hotel, which rented suites to long-term guests. Alice Martyn, anxious to continue to provide for her daughters in the manner to which they had become accustomed, began to borrow money from Armour & Co.[44]

The family was now without a permanent residence in Chicago, and spent much of 1901 and 1902 in Europe. Hazel sought the company of artistic people wherever they travelled. During the summer of 1902, her mother and sister stayed in Chicago while she returned to Paris to study etching, an art-form that was undergoing a revival.[45] Hazel was tutored in the dry-point style, and by the end other stay had amassed a large portfolio. When she returned Hazel gained a reputation as one of the cleverest amateur artists in Chicago.[46] A realistic self-portrait in watercolour and gouache entitled 'Convalescence', with its subject propped up on pillows, wearing a lacy bed-jacket and cap, dates from this period (*see plate*).

In the spring of 1903 Hazel exhibited her European work and received notices from the critics; the *Chicago Daily News* reported, 'Men who know pictures are enthusiastic over her work.'[47] One journalist compared her etchings to those of the French artist Helleu.[48] That year the Arts Collectors' Club sponsored the publication of a book of six other sketches of women (*see plate*). Hazel announced that she intended to study art: 'I am so anxious to be taken seriously. My friends have known nothing of my aspirations.'[49] At a time when many female artists were exchanging marriage and domesticity for professional careers, Mrs Martyn accepted Hazel's artistic ambitions, at least until a suitable husband could be found.

II

'most great and wise and solemn John'
[1903]

EFORE HAZEL'S BOOK of sketches was published, she returned to France with her mother and sister, spending the summer of 1903 at an artists' colony in Brittany. Situated on a headland on the Breton coast between the villages of Concarneau and Pont-Aven, Beg-Meil had quiet shady beaches, rocky coves and dunes, and had been the haunt of Impressionists and Post-Impressionists over the previous forty years.[1] The destination was chosen by Hazel, who wanted to learn the techniques of Impressionism.

The Martyns' *entrée* to the artistic world of Beg-Meil was an Anglo-French-American artist, John Milner-Kite. Mrs Martyn had commissioned him to paint her daughters, and he had completed Dorothy's portrait and was struggling to depict Hazel when he enlisted the help of John Lavery.[2]

An established painter who had frequented Brittany since 1883, Lavery was born in Belfast in 1856,* the second son of Henry Lavery, a successful Catholic wine merchant. Three years later, the wine trade declined and Henry set sail for New York in search of new fortune, leaving his wife Mary and three young children

---

*The precise date of Lavery's birth is unknown. His baptismal certificate states that he was baptized on 26 March 1856.

10

behind. Disaster struck when his ship, the *Pomona,* was wrecked off the coast of Wexford and he was drowned. Three months later Mary Lavery, too, was dead.[3] The orphaned children were sent to live with relations. John Lavery was brought up by an aunt and uncle in Moira, Co. Antrim, and later by another relation in Ayrshire, Scotland. When he came of age, Lavery moved to Glasgow and worked in a photographer's studio retouching prints. This enabled him to attend art classes. He later acquired a studio of his own and struggled to establish himself as a painter. Ironically, it was only when his studio burned down that, using the insurance money, he could finally afford to study seriously – first in London and later in Paris.[4]

In 1885 Lavery returned from Paris and formed the 'Glasgow School' with James Guthrie, E.A. Walton and Joseph Crawhall, promoting modern French techniques in Britain.[5] His work began to earn critical praise and 'A Tennis Party' won him a bronze medal in the Paris Salon of 1888. Lavery then received a number of key commissions, the most important being to commemorate Queen Victoria's visit to Glasgow in August 1888 for the International Fine Arts Exhibition. The painting took two years to complete and involved 250 separate portrait sittings.[6] Though not a critical success, the studies helped develop his skill as a portraitist, and he became known for his flattering depictions of women.

At Beg-Meil Lavery was only too glad to show off his talent, 'especially before such loveliness'; he, too, was captivated by Hazel Martyn.[7] She now wore her red hair in a top knot, accentuating her small face and large brown eyes.

Hazel had first noticed Lavery from her seat on the hotel's veranda, as he struggled past with a six-foot canvas strapped to his back.[8] He was short in stature with a stocky build, and not particularly handsome. For Hazel, however, he was the embodiment of Beg-Meil's heady bohemianism and all that she was seeking in Brittany. She considered him a master painter, and to his delight treated him with the greatest respect and admiration,[9] despite the fact that her portrait, the combined effort of Lavery and Milner-Kite, was not a success. Perhaps to redress this failure, John made a cartoon sketch of himself with a turned-up nose while Hazel drew a self-portrait beside it (*see plate*).[10]

In the evenings Hazel joined Lavery and Milner-Kite in animated conversations on art, while Dorothy ignored them and read. Her introversion contrasted sharply with her sister's exuberance, and though there was a striking physical resemblance,[11] Dorothy's large brown eyes were marred by the sadness that would eventually consume her.

Milner-Kite described Hazel's mother as 'the old Chicago dame', referring more to her attitude than her age; at forty-six she was a year younger than Lavery. She was not favourably disposed to 'bohemians' and was upset to find her daughter engaged in such spirited conversations, particularly with Lavery. This Irishman with a teenage daughter was twenty-four years Hazel's senior; even worse, he travelled with an attractive young German, Mary Auras, the model for several of his well-known paintings.* Another young Irishman, P. Burrowes Shell, also accompanied Lavery to help amuse Mary and, as Lavery wrote in his autobiography, to 'share the scandal, if there should be one, of my taking a beautiful girl to the country for months at a time'.[12] Regardless of this precaution, Mrs Martyn was convinced Lavery was a wholly unsuitable companion for her daughter. These were not the sort of people whom the Martyns had travelled to Europe to meet.

Lavery was not Hazel's only admirer in Beg-Meil. Pompey Howard had followed her from Paris to advance (as Lavery smugly wrote later) 'his unsuccessful attentions'.[13] Hazel had never been in love and played romantic and emotional games with relish. She initially believed she was only 'sentimentally interested' in John,[14]

---

* Mary Auras was the model for 'Spring' (Musee d'Orsay, Paris) and 'Lady in a Green Coat' (Bradford Art Galleries and Museums).

but soon realized that he was different. On the third day of their acquaintance, John escorted Hazel to the nearby village of Pont-Aven, set in a romantic valley between two thickly wooded hills, where Gauguin had often painted, Here, Hazel first professed her feelings for John, and she would later write:

And you are *not* to mention the ever (to me) embarrassing fact that it was *I* who was the first to discover – Oh! well the fact that you wanted me to come into your garden.[15]

The 'garden' was to become the dominant motif of their love letters.

Mrs Martyn was unaware that her daughter had fallen in love. But Hazel admitted to John: 'You were not so clever to fall in love in three days after all. Why even *I* did that! and what is more did it much more completely and thoroughly than you.'[16]

The Martyns left Beg-Meil for Paris a few days after the Pont-Aven trip and John followed shortly after. He invited Mrs Martyn, Hazel and Dorothy to have lunch with himself and Sheil at their hotel on 24 September. The meal was a disastrous affair, and Mrs Martyn remained convinced of John's shortcomings as a suitor. He departed for London the following day with Hazel's promise to write. Her first surviving letter was written three days later to 'Dear dearer dearest and all sorts of other love names John':

... I am still in your garden still incorrigibly and unwarrantedly and unconcernedly sitting in the middle of your *best* flower bed just as though I had been properly invited! ... I have one eye on the gate of your garden John. You were foolish to leave it unlocked but perhaps you did that purposely.[17]

It had been many years since John Lavery had last been in love. Kathleen McDermott had been ill for most of their short romance. She suffered from tuberculosis and died only a few months after giving birth to their daughter Eileen.[18] Now, John was acutely conscious of the age difference. His reply expressed a fear that she would soon tire of him:

Well dear I am busily engaged in looking for the key and wondering how you would feel to be locked up in such an old garden with all the flowers to tend and the funny old paths to keep straight and if you wouldn't after a time get tired and want to climb the wall and get out one fine morning and leave it to ruin?[19]

The couple were anxious to be reunited. From London, John began making plans for Hazel to visit him, perhaps in October, 'usually a delightful month'. He busied himself, with enquiries about hotels and lessons for Hazel in dry-point etching.[20] He wished to paint Hazel again, this time in his South Kensington studio rather than in France, because he feared that 'working in a strange studio against time' might produce another failed portrait.[21]

When 'most dear decided Mamma' refused to go to London, Dorothy was 'popped' into boarding school, and Hazel enrolled with Edgar Chahine,[22] an etcher with a reputation for depicting the Parisian masses, though her interest in dry-point etching was fading. John urged Hazel to take advantage of her classes and suggested that she exhibit some well-known person's portrait at the new Society of Portrait Painters' gallery in London. The committee had asked Lavery to select a piece worthy of exhibit. John thought Hazel's self-portrait, 'Convalescence', 'really most charming' (*see plate*).[23] The suggestion was not welcome and Hazel protested that he was not attuned to her 'chaotic volcanic frame of mind'. Of her lessons, she declared she could not calmly draw flowing lines upon her beloved copper plates, but 'mutilated the dear things' in her agitation. She chided, 'I suppose that you will attribute all this to a becoming and seemly maiden hesitation.'[24]

The balance had been established, John the realist, Hazel the romantic. The steadfastness of the 'most great and wise and solemn John'[25] attracted her, calming and tempering her melodramatic nature. During their separation. Hazel's thoughts had returned to their customary 'wild, vivid, primitive intensity'.[26] On 11 October, two weeks after John left Paris, she wrote:

It has caught me now John Lavery, the storm and panic. All my fine recklessness and gay courage is gone. I am even no longer incorrigible! It is my turn
to beg 'Wait wait I must have time.' I am only a girl who is afraid to become
a woman. And I am alone. I belong to nothing or no-one in the world – I
could not *bear* to belong – and yet the very thought of giving myself is terrible and sweet. If I dared.[27]

John delighted in her reaction as 'right and proper and just as it
should be'.[28] He trusted that any difficulties could be overcome
and that Hazel would be his wife.

I believed that [you] alone of all those who had ever been in or near the garden knew and understood, and the mists cleared, and what was vague and
uncertain has become clear and defined. And behold here am I John knock-
ing at your gate Hazel dearest. And so the sovereign right of she whom I call
wife is asserted, and this tradition and principle remain undisturbed.[29]

There was extreme tension between mother and daughter by
the end of October. Mrs Martyn thought Hazel 'absolutely mad'
to want to travel to London, knowing so little of John Lavery.
Hazel continued to plead; she wrote to John that 'you may be
sure I begged to go ... it seemed the only way'. Mrs Martyn held
fast. Hazel worried that family strife would be worse in London,
bringing aggravation and stress to John, who asked of her only
peace.[30]

No Hazel! just the other way round, it would be madness and lunacy *not* to
come. Do please trust yourself. I know how difficult this is for one so young
and so impulsive but if you will just look through the proper end of the tele-
scope you will find me right in the foreground – not withstanding the charm
that distance may give – ready to take some small share of a responsibility
that the little Hazel thinks is all her own. It must be obvious to the mother
that vague and misty misgivings – if they cannot be removed by coming to
London, they can at least be made clear. It is not a question of knowing each
other – that we do know – no; it is of knowing ourselves, and as I have told
you my problem is solved and as far as human thought goes or my poor brain
can travel, the road seems clear. Of course it is easy for me after all these years
to know when I have reached my haven. It is not so easy for you, but we will
take all the time you desire and there shall be no undue haste.[31]

John awaited Hazel's telegram, but her mother sent one instead: 'Very sorry but impossible to go to London.'[32] She elaborated in a letter:

It was no idle decision that I sent by telegram this morning – Hazel is really a wreck and I am unnerved over the worry and anxiety this question has caused us – I alone am to blame for not going up to London and though the inducements in every way serious and otherwise are great I simply cannot let her go now – the situation is sudden and tremendous. I do not want to trust the added glamour of the atmosphere there would be in seeing you in your own attractive home. That Hazel cares a great deal for you there is no doubt but it is the question of her lifetime. She *must* go slowly. In every way she is disappointed in not going to London and I may be very very wrong – I have only the child's happiness at heart and I am doing what seems to me right – I will not try to say the conventional thing it seems too trite. I hope you will believe that I am doing what I feel will be best for the happiness of you both.[33]

Her authority undermined by the continued correspondence between Hazel and John, Mrs Martyn now resorted to more drastic measures. She cabled Ned Trudeau in the second week of October. The message was plain: 'Come quick or you'll lose Hazel.' Ned hastily packed for the journey, so anxious to make the first available sailing that he left without his overcoat.[34]

Unaware that Trudeau had been summoned by her mother, Hazel wrote to John: 'To complicate matters there arrives in Paris from America the one man in the world who the dear Mamma would not think me more than mildly insane to marry.' Hazel now confined herself to a 'darkened room – eau de cologne and tears'. She described herself as 'behaving quite like the languishing heroine of an early English novel when her love affairs grew too distressing'.[35]

Mrs Martyn and Ned Trudeau, determined to make Hazel forget Lavery, arranged to return to America immediately. Hazel, knowing her mother's determination, wrote pessimistically to John: 'I am very helpless more helpless indeed than you can know.' They planned to sail within the week: 'I cannot breathe when I think of crossing that dreary sad gray ocean.'[36]

John now rushed to Paris to claim Hazel's hand, arranging to see Mrs Martyn without her daughter. Indignant at her exclusion, Hazel warned John not to mention their intimacy at Pont-Aven: 'I shall *never* forgive you if you told Mamma how bold I have been.'[37]

Lavery's meeting was unsuccessful and he went back to London. The Martyns and Ned Trudeau set sail for New York on 1 November, on board the *Pennsylvania* from Boulogne. Hazel still hoped that she could convince her mother that her feelings for John were more than an infatuation bred by the romance of France. She shut herself in her cabin and refused to speak for the first week of the voyage.[38] By the time the ship reached New York fifteen days later, it had been decided that Hazel was to marry Trudeau without further delay. There was little to do but consent.

Ned Trudeau was now thirty and had devoted himself to his medical career. Having been president of his class in the College of Physicians and Surgeons, then house surgeon in the Presbyterian Hospital in New York,[39] Ned joined Dr Walter B. James' successful practice in New York City in the autumn of 1903.

Upon arrival. Hazel and Ned travelled to Saranac Lake, New York, a remote town in the Lake Placid region of the Adirondack Mountains, to meet Ned's parents. Ned's father recalled years later: 'It was love at first sight, and a violent love affair with Ned, and when she went abroad he left us suddenly, went to Europe, and must have carried the fortress by storm, for he soon returned in the same ship with Miss Martyn and her mother.'[40] Dr and Mrs Trudeau and Ned's younger brother Francis were staying at their hunting lodge deep in the woods.[41] Hunting, sailing and swimming, the activities of Saranac Lake, underscored Hazel's feeling that she had little in common with the Trudeaus. It was all so different from Beg-Meil. On her return journey to Chicago, Hazel wrote to John, enclosing a photograph of herself:

Goodbye John Lavery – As I came into your life suddenly and without warning so I go and there is silence once more. For I must go and you must not

17

cry out or lift your hand to bring me back – it is not to be – Let us forget – Before you read this I shall belong to Edward Trudeau utterly irrevocably. I may not tell you my reason and you shall not ask, this is at once a command and an entreaty. John Lavery believe in the truth of my every thought and word and deed toward you. There was no stain of falseness in there. Once you said it took a long long time to become young but one can grow old in a single hour. I am old and very tired. Please keep my letters. They are the real real Hazel you can remember her without bitterness – I have gone and again you are alone.[42]

John still harboured vague hopes that the wedding would not go ahead. He sent a forlorn telegram which arrived at the Virginia Hotel on 1 December: 'Any Hope.'[43] Two days later he cabled Mrs Martyn: 'Please delay proceedings serious consequences have written.'[44] Convinced that he must travel to America, the following day he sent a more frantic cable: 'Her future happiness possess undoubted proof. Delay can injure nobody. May prevent grave mistake. Do consider. Sailing shortly.'[45]

Lavery's appeals had no effect, and on 3 December Hazel released her wedding details. She would be unattended, save perhaps for her sister Dorothy; with no pre-nuptial entertainments, the wedding would be a simple one.[46] The next day the social column of *The Chicago Tribune* told of how this news had disappointed her friends.[47] Tales of a European romance were the subject of gossip in Chicago drawing-rooms and it was known that Hazel Martyn's suitor had cabled for postponement until he could make his plea.[48] John must have been convinced of the futility of sailing as the surviving correspondence gives no further indication as to why he never set to sea. He had always been thoroughly absorbed in his art, but as he wrote in his autobiography thirty-seven years later, 'I then realized that painting pictures was not everything.'[49]

The wedding, held at noon on 28 December in St Chrysostom's church, was not the planned quiet affair, but one of the most fashionable events of the season.[50] While the guests were seated, an organ played old-fashioned airs. The society columnist for the *Tribune wrote:*

It was not unlike the bride, who is noted not only for beauty and popularity but also for her artistic taste in all things, to select such time-honoured songs as 'Annie Laurie', 'How Can I Leave Thee' and 'Drink to Me Only with Thine Eyes' and instead of a modern love song as a setting for the holy words of matrimony a simple old German melody was softly played. With the coming of the bride, the wedding march from 'Lohengrin' was heard.[51]

Hazel entered the church alone. She wore a filmy gown of white tulle over shimmering white satin, with tiny white tassels on the sleeves and garlands of orange blossoms on the bodice and skirt; a coronet of buds held a long tulle veil. Instead of a bouquet, she carded a white prayer-book with a tiny sprig of orange blossoms held between the pages.[52] Father Snively, a well-known preacher who had confirmed Hazel eleven years before, conducted the ceremony.[53] Ned's father later wrote, 'I only repeat what I heard so many others say: that a handsomer couple than Ned and Hazel Martyn are not often seen.'[54]

The wedding, which had all the appearances of a perfect society match, represented for Hazel the loss of the man she loved and the life she craved. That morning, before the ceremony, she had written to John:

And this is my wedding day. I suffer. There is no such thing as joy or goodness or justice in this world and it is not true that hearts break they merely grow more keen with pain and ache ache through one's whole life. It is not true that duty should be a primary consideration. It is not true that I shall know in future the mercy of God and see that all is for the best – nothing is true save that there is no hope for me how terribly hideously well I know this to be true. I am yours the soul and the breath and brain and bleeding heart of me are yours – and my life will be lived for you whether you will or no – and you shall think and long despair with me – always – always – always. No law can hold my soul. No human creature can touch me. I am yours. I shall write to you my hearts dearest. Nothing shall be hidden from you. All that is mine is yours and and [*sic*] in an hour they will put on my bridal gown. And do you know what is the most bitter of all the great and little bitter thoughts that stab my heart? It is the silly frivolous wish that you are not to see my beauty in it ... I am a woman – once you told me that you loved me for it – and with a woman it is the little things that give most joy or pain. Your letter came this morning. God is indeed cruel to me. And I have nothing but bitterness in my heart. My love my best beloved do you suffer with me? or are you in your wisdom and greatness pitying me for my mad grief and unreasoning anguish. I am not a child. I am a woman and I have suffered as much as you have in your whole life – I know. Dear God I would go to you *now* proudly and gladly dear if I did not love you too well to hurt you and your love for me by such madness and folly. Dearest I wish my heart had stopped beating forever that night at Pont Aven. I remember how I trembled all the night through and prayed God to let me be happy and have my heart's desire. I knew then that I was to suffer ... I never dreamed how much. I *love* you supremely. I am not an ordinary woman and I do not love in an ordinary way.[55]

Edward Jenner Martyn, Hazel's father.

Alice Louise Martyn (*née* Taggart), Hazel's mother.

Hazel as a child.

Hazel at Miss Masters, Dobbs Ferry, her New York finishing school, aged sixteen.

Dorothea Hope Martyn, Hazel's sister.

ward ('Ned') Trudeau, Hazel's first husband.

Len Thomas, briefly betrothed to Hazel.

'Sketches', by Hazel Martyn. (Art Collectors' Club, Chicago, 1903)

'Convalescence', *c.*1903, an early self-portrait by Hazel.

Above: Letter from Hazel Trudeau to John Lavery, 1904.

Right: Sketches of Hazel and John executed at Beg-Meil, Brittany.

Hazel Martyn, *c.*1903.

John Lavery.

Hazel Trudeau with Alice, *c*.1905.
(Saranac Free Library, New York)

Alice Trudeau, *c*.1909.

Dar el Midfah, the Laverys' home in Tangier, Morocco, *Left to right*: Hazel on verandah, Eileen on Sunny Jim, John Lavery, Alice and Hadeshia, August 1911.

'Dame en Noir', 1906, by John Lavery. The first known portrait of Hazel, possibly as early as 1904, painted during her convalescence in Europe prior to her marriage to John, and dubbed 'The Widow' by their friend William Patrick Whyte. (Hugh Lane Municipal Gallery of Modern Art, Dublin)

'Japanese Switzerland', 1912/13, by John Lavery. This painting of Hazel and Alice was made during the Lavery's winter holiday at Wengen, Switzerland. (Hugh Lane Loan Collection, 1996)

'In Morocco', 1913/14, by John Lavery. *Left to right*: Alice on Lily Beau, Hazel, Moroccan boy and their greyhound Rodney Stone. (National Gallery of Victoria, Melbourne)

'The Artist's Studio', 1910-13, by John Lavery. A homage to Velasquez's 'Las Meninas', it depicts the Lavery household in the studio at 5 Cromwell Place, London. *Left to right*: Aïda, the Moorish maid, Hazel and Alice, Eileen (John's daughter) and Rodney Stone. (National Gallery of Ireland)

III

'the siren calls'
[1904-8]

Your wit is inclined to many conversations, and you will do great mischief against your will, dangerous to others, therefore you will have bad luck.
– Fortune-teller's prediction for Hazel, July 1905

THE TRUDEAUS moved to 772 Park Avenue, an apartment house furnished by Ned's parents as a wedding present with a small studio built for Hazel. Rather than the customary gift of diamonds or pearls. Hazel had asked for an etching press, which she described as the most precious gift she could have received. Ned and Hazel included visiting cards with their wedding invitations, opening their new home to guests after 1 February 1904.[1] Hazel missed life in Chicago, and returned in mid-March to celebrate her twenty-fourth birthday with her family. Small affairs were held in her honour and she went several times to the opera.[2]

Ned was a surgeon at the Vanderbilt Clinic and the Bellevue Hospital in addition to his private practice.[3] Bellevue, a municipal hospital, served the poor and destitute of New York City. Built to accommodate 933 patients, it was chronically over-crowded in 1904, partially due to a pneumonia epidemic.[4] In April, four months after the wedding, Ned contracted pneumonia, but recovered after a short stay in hospital and returned

21

home by early May. On the afternoon of his release, Ned was sitting beside Hazel when, without warning, he fell to the floor.[5] By the time the doctor arrived, Ned was pronounced dead from a pulmonary embolism. Dr James contacted Ned's parents and cabled Mrs Martyn. She and Dorothy immediately travelled to be with Hazel.[6]

The day of the funeral, 6 May, was gloriously sunny. The service was held at the tiny wooden church under the pines in the village of Paul Smiths, a few miles from the Trudeaus' home. In keeping with the tradition of the Skull and Bones Society, those who had ushered at Ned's wedding now carried his coffin to his grave. There was no place in the Trudeaus' grief for Hazel, whom they knew had not truly loved their son. Four months pregnant, she returned to Chicago shortly after the funeral, and reverted unofficially to her maiden name.

On 10 October 1904, in the Martyns' new home at 566 Division Street East, Hazel gave birth to a baby girl. She had a difficult confinement and almost died during the birth, having contracted nephritis, a post-natal condition with symptoms including headaches, swelling of the face and ankles, dimness of vision and neuralgic pains. For several weeks Hazel's condition was critical and she needed full-time nursing. Recurrences of nephritis were to plague Hazel for the rest other life.

She had wished for a boy and was disappointed with her baby girl.[7] She wrote of baby Alice, named after Hazel's mother, 'she is very wee and ugly and queer but her ears and hands are beautiful and her mouth and chin go so \/'.[8]

A month after Alice's birth, Hazel urged her mother to send news to John Lavery. Mrs Martyn's concise cable read: 'Hazel barely lived – improving – daughter.'[9] Lavery apparently knew of Trudeau's death and Hazel's pregnancy but there is no surviving correspondence between December 1903 and November 1904. It is evident from the first surviving letter from Hazel to Lavery after Alice's birth that she had never stopped loving him:

How good you are John Lavery and how beautiful your garden is. I have been so very far away and my suffering and my need have been very great. I am groping my way slowly back to the world and life although it may be weeks and months before I am strong again.[10]

By early 1905 Hazel's health was improving. She wrote to John that she wished to recuperate in Europe where she would be reunited with him." By June she was able to travel, accompanied by her mother, sister and nine-month-old Alice.

The family stayed initially at Malvern Wells in Worcestershire, a popular health spa. Hazel passed the time there walking in the Malvern Hills and painting.[12] She enthused:

Today has been such a wonderful day John for I painted all morning and walked on the hills all afternoon. If you could have been near me I should have asked nothing more of the *very* Bon Dieu. But I am so wildly excited about painting! It surely is fairyland and the brushes are fairy wands that have the power to make everything change and become beautiful![13]

With her health restored, Hazel chose a subject close at hand, her baby daughter. The painting, entitled 'The Brown Baby', depicts Alice in her pram sheltered from the sun by a bush. The tide refers to Alice's sallow skin, which contrasted with her white bonnet and the lace pram covers. John sent Hazel an umbrella to protect her from 'Father Sol' and a box to carry her canvasses,[14] and advised her to keep her brushes clean and her feet dry.[15] He visited Malvern on several occasions, painting a portrait of Hazel wearing black. This is now known as 'Dame en Noir' (*see plate*).

Hazel and John were now conducting a formal courtship, but Mrs Martyn still opposed Lavery as keenly as ever. She was 'agitated' by the frequent exchange of letters, feeling that a respectable amount of time had not elapsed since Ned's death, and deemed her daughter's behaviour 'quite deplorable under the circumstances'. Hazel assured her 'with great vehemence and a holy expression' that they were 'only interested in each other's art', but Mrs Martyn remained unconvinced. Hazel complained to John: 'I seem *never* to be alone and she has the most wonderful way of knowing all about everything I do or say or think.

It is quite uncanny. ... I get *so* nervous when Mamma fixes me with her large blue eye and says: "Are you writing to Mr Lavery *again?*"[16]

Few things pleased Hazel more than John's visits. 'It is wonderful how much you have improved the garden Johnnie! there are magic corners everywhere now', she wrote.[17] But Mrs Martyn's persistent opposition to the relationship took its toll on Hazel's health. Almost two years had elapsed since she and John had first met and they were still no closer to becoming husband and wife. At Malvern Wells they conspired to marry, to elope if necessary, before the year was out.[18] To placate Mrs Martyn, they decided to correspond less frequently.

As the Martyns left for France at the end of July, Hazel wrote, 'Mother and Dorothy both want France, and I really cannot be selfish (I mean more than usual).'[9] They journeyed to Etretat, a 'little fisherman's village turned into a gay parterre; its shingly beach is lined with chairs and its shores smoothed and levelled for delicate feet'.[20] Finding that the 'villas were not attractive and none were to be had near the sea', they checked into the Hotel des Roches Blanches,[21] situated next to the cliffs where Claude Monet painted. Hazel described the view of the beach from her window: 'all very gay and merry so much scarlet and white and the blue ocean and white cliffs. I am sure you must think it paintable, even though the French woman singular does not inspire you collectively they are charming.'[22]

With fewer letters from John, Hazel was miserable, though she knew the arrangement was 'so much wiser and more sane', for her mother was now 'bland and smiling'.[23] During John's visit in late August, Hazel confessed to her mother that they had been conducting an illicit courtship. Mrs Martyn was affronted to have been so long deceived. Hazel wrote: 'She is suffering most deeply it all breaks my heart and I blame myself entirely. I have been very stupid selfish and cruel.'[24]

The following day Mrs Martyn wrote to John:

... revelations of yesterday were a terrible blow to me but it is far better to be out and understood. We will be at home between three and four if you will come then we will endeavour to adjust matters – I certainly shall not stand in the way of Hazel's health and happiness.[25]

They agreed to a six-month separation, after which, if Hazel was still determined, Mrs Martyn would not stop their marriage; in the meantime there would be no contact. John asked Hazel to write should she become seriously ill and promised to send her his address if he left London.

Hazel secretly sent John a note just before their departure from Etretat, in late October, to say that they would be at Hotel Foyot in Paris for 'the next month or more'.[26] A few days later John was in Paris, en route to Italy; he was unable to resist going to the Foyot for lunch but did not see Hazel. He then wrote from Venice, to arrange a rendezvous on his return.

As the letter was in Italian, Hazel asked Dorothy to translate it. Dorothy thought it 'a tribute from a rapturous admirer'; Mrs Martyn knew it was from John. Afraid that John would call to their hotel. Hazel scribbled a brief note: 'Do *not* do *anything* until you get a letter.'[27] She then wrote frantically: 'I *know* she will never forgive you for writing an *anonymous* letter in a *disguised hand*. Her remarks were very scornful as to the kind of person who would do such a thing ...'[28]

Diplomacy had failed and John now was determined to speak frankly. He wrote to Mrs Martyn:

If you remember when I came to Paris to see you two years ago I said nothing because she [Hazel] thought it hopeless at that time, that if she went home she might manage our point better. You know the result. The knowledge to such an exalted mind as hers that this fire which was consuming her was not a normal one, lent force to the arguments against it and thinking to escape in some way she married and found then that she had made a terrible mistake and now after two years of the most appalling anguish she feels her mind going ...[29]

Mrs Martyn staunchly believed that Hazel's health made it impossible for her to marry for at least a year. Nephritis troubled

Hazel throughout their stay in Paris and she complained to John of 'blinding headaches' and 'neuralgic pains'. She endured bed-rest and an all-milk diet, the commonly recommended cures. Hazel's frailness, aggravated by emotional stress, made John fear a nervous breakdown. He warned Mrs Martyn that 'doctors can attend to the body but the mind can only be reached by others',[30] and that 'unless she is subjected to a different kind of mental food to that which has been provided during the last two years she will not live.'[31]

John believed the key to Hazel's peace of mind lay in reconciliation between himself and her mother; he wished them to be 'good and true friends with one common object her happiness'.[32] But Mrs Martyn blamed John: 'The relationship between Hazel and myself until you came into our lives has been one of great devotion and sympathy. I have almost made an idol of her and she has always been in every way worthy of all our devotion ...'[33]

Life for the two former intimates, confined together in hotel suites and unfamiliar locales, must have been unpleasant. Hazel wrote:

Mamma ... is so terribly unhappy about everything and sometimes we have dreadful hours – such struggles and consequent fatigue and despair ... sometime I will tell you everything all the hidden underside of things and you are sure to understand my heart's dearest.[34]

Mrs Martyn had never accepted that a man old enough to be Hazel's father could make her daughter happy. Her feelings of animosity had become entrenched with the passage of time. She wrote to John: 'Pardon my being quite frank but I have been told things about you that makes it seem perfectly *impossible* that a sweet sensitive woman like Hazel would find lasting happiness with you.'[35]

While Mrs Martyn never substantiated these rumours, John admitted having been cruel to his sister Jane in his autobiography, written when he was in his eighties. He had forced his sister to marry the man by whom she had become pregnant, and refused to help when the marriage proved disastrous. When Jane subsequently took her life, Lavery denied kinship lest it taint his reputation.[36]

John had also been neglectful of the young woman who had given birth to his child. He had met her in 1889 in London, where she was selling flowers, and asked her to sit for him. A teenager who had run away from home, Kathleen persuaded John to let her live with him. He thought she was an Irish girl, but it later transpired she was Welsh. She was suffering from tuberculosis, and she became seriously ill. Lavery was preoccupied at the time with the painting of Queen Victoria's visit to Glasgow. William Patrick Whyte, a fellow artist who was apparently in love with Kathleen, took her to numerous health resorts; when she proved terminally ill, he rented a furnished house at Kilmalcolm where Lavery could visit her daily. After Kathleen's death, it was Whyte who cared for John's young daughter Eileen, living with her and her nurse in the country throughout her infancy.[37] Lavery was ruthlessly ambitious and, as he candidly attested in his autobiography, he was not willing to let his wife's illness or his new-born daughter interfere with his work.

Lavery was anxious to know the source of the allegations made in Alice's letter. He responded promptly, asking to be informed of 'every tittle of scandal or shadow of an objection'.[38] Mrs Martyn did not reply; for her the matter was closed. She had at last convinced Hazel of the perils of a hasty marriage. 'Driven and hurried' over the previous two years. Hazel now decided 'to stand quite still and not step quickly in any direction'.[39] Although Hazel accepted a postponement of their marriage, she was worried about the future. 'John my dear John there are no barriers or even mists between us? assure me of that ... I fear perhaps you will gradually care less and I cannot be with you to *make* you love me and find me charming!'[40] John's reply assured her that never since the evening on the bridge at Pont-Aven had she been absent from his mind: 'My own my dearest nothing under heaven shall ever part us and I shall pray that even heaven shall not come between you and me.'[41]

Hazel was recommended to a doctor in Rome and the Martyns moved there in December 1905. Delighted, she wrote to John: 'The sun warm and yellow and comforting is streaming into my room. The air is delicious and I can *smell* Rome through the open window a kind of exquisite compound perfume of pine and violets and ... antiquity that is full of memories and promises.'[42]

Her joy was short lived. In early December she fell ill with tonsillitis and a chill contracted while attending a Mass said by Pope Pius X in a cold and draughty church. Her kidneys were affected and she feared she would not live to see John again.[43]

I've got no strength ... and there were complications. I don't dare think how far this puts me back. It gives me a sort of baffled feeling. Some hand like the great Rodin 'Hand of Fate'seems to pluck me from the rocks I cling to and drops me to the foot of the mountain again. However I am so small and unimportant I shall scramble up again unobserved this time to a more secure foothold. As for my mind it is as agile and futile as ever. You are so dear to understand how I storm and fret in my soul while my bundle of nerves and bones and my 'hank of hair' are chained to a pillow.[44]

Her condition improved within a week thanks to a 'sweet' English nurse, and by Christmas Day she was allowed to sit up once more. To create a festive atmosphere for young Alice they bought a Christmas tree. Alice, now a year old and saying 'Look at that', 'Who is it' and 'I want it',[45] refused to acknowledge Hazel as her mother; only months later did she address her as 'Muffle'. Hazel was not close to her daughter, perhaps due to her illness after Alice's birth and the difficulties of the previous year. As Alice developed a personality very different from her mother's this distance became more evident.

Hazel, trapped in bed, longed to revisit her favourite haunts, such as the Spanish steps, the house where Keats had lived and the Protestant graveyard where he was buried. Instead she drew, completing a pastel sketch of Keats, as she loved 'that poor young dead John so well'. She studied Italian and Roman history to escape her unhappy reality.[46] The historical characters became more real than John Lavery, who by now was merely her lover by correspondence.

John Lavery is no more *real* to me than Napoleon or Whistler or Emma! You are just a hero that I adore and admire and dream of and love of course, as much as I dare – of course on the other hand nothing is so real as the unreal and I understand you and appreciate you far more than I do the tangible people of my daily life. You see I can't believe in our personal relation to each other. I suppose it is because really I know you so little. It has nearly been all letters and dreams. Now please you are not to read alarming things into this ...[47]

Letters were infrequent over Christmas, and to the 'Only One' she complained of neglect. 'I am a spoiled child Johnnie but please do go on spoiling me for whereas when others do it I feel it is quite usual and my due with you it becomes the sweetest most desirable thing in the world and I cannot live without it.'[48] His weekly letter apologized for being '*en retard*' due to 'artistic and social complications',[49] and they arranged to meet in Italy before Hazel returned to America.

Her health regained by the end of December, Hazel began to mix with other Americans in Rome. 'I thought I should go quite mad if I stopped at home another hour. ... However I am going to be temperate it is so frightfully easy to be drawn into all sorts of frivolity here in Rome and as I belong to you now I must be very careful of your valuable possession!'[50]

Despite her bouts of illness. Hazel at twenty-six was as attractive as ever, and a much sought-after escort. Her life in Rome was soon enlivened by a twenty-eight-year-old American named Leonard Moorhead Thomas, the second secretary in the U.S. Embassy. Len's background was strikingly similar to Ned Trudeau's; both were educated at St Paul's and Yale, where Len, who excelled in sport and composed a light opera, was voted 'the most versatile man in his class'.[51] He had spent five years in Rome by the time he met Hazel in February 1906.[52]

By mid-February, Hazel hinted to John that something had changed: 'Lately I have been beset by all sorts of doubts and fears and panics but I will not give them being and identity by writing them in black and white. You will drive them all away dearest when you come. My true heart for you Hazel.'[53] She knew that she was falling in love with Len Thomas and wrote deceptively a few days later: 'There are no real "mysteries" dear do not feel anxious about anything and keep me fast and close in your heart. I need an anchor so.'[54] But by the end of February Hazel could no longer hide her secret:

O! If l could die before writing this to you ... John there is something terrible that I must tell you – it is like being killed or killing you to say it. I am such a worthless coward so poor a thing. I have prayed something would happen, that I would be released from this madness that has hold of me. Listen I have been thinking for weeks of another man. I have fought every way I know how. My mind is full of him and he is the wrong man. There is no joy or good in it at all and I have been unfaithful to you only in thought but I cannot go to you now. I love him. John Lavery neither you or the God who made us can curse me too heavily for this there can be no forgiveness for me but my dear great generous man thank that same God that you are done with me. There can be no bitterness or loss when you see what I am. I've no right to ask anything but John I have not lied to you ever nor been untrue and I cannot explain what devil has grasped my mind and heart and soul that I should turn Oh! my God from *you*. I would have better died and I could never have deemed this madness a possible thing or to be dreamed of- and so throw me away. A worthless thing, untrue to you to myself and my vows. I've wrecked everything and my shame is so great I long to hear you tell me just what I am to my face. Lash me with your scorn John Lavery and turn on your heel – Hazel Martyn.[55]

John's reply indicates he suspected Mrs Martyn might be forcing Hazel to marry:

Poor Dear what a time the Bon Dieu gives you. Being in love is just a worry and a sweat and a wishing you were dead most of the time, and I have given it up for good and instead of being bowled over completely there is just a dull numb feeling through which the warmth of the sun perqulates [*sic*] and life is not an enure blank. You may remember my having remarked that this might be the result if I were again thrown up upon the bank. You dear have done nothing that a woman should have any reason to blush for. When love comes in everything goes out. But Hazel Dear you say 'the wrong man' I do not know what this means, but I would like to know. Because Dear I am not going to stand aside for anything of that kind. You must make this dear to me and right or wrong you must not do anything in haste. I want you to let me into your confidence and not treat me as one who has been outraged and upon whom your back is turned because the conventions that you have broken down mean nothing to me in the presence of nature. So come to me Dear now or at any-time for I am also your friend.[56]

John wrote from Florence of his imminent departure for Rome. She replied by telegram: 'Beg you – not to come or try to see me – await letter – H.'[57] The following day she wrote:

Your letter has just reached me. ... John I will not see you. I can't have the added torture (my great selfishness again). There is nothing to be done I tell you. It would only be useless and agonizing to talk together. He cares. I did not dream of it when I wrote at first that is why I said it was 'wrong' – Dear dear John *don't* be generous it breaks my heart – and there is no use in trying to convince me of anything now. I have forgotten everything except that I am happy! *Now* do you see my utter worthlessness. Do you understand what I am? Surely you do ... I'm not hiding anything dear John Lavery always I shall kneel to you. You are the noblest and best and greatest of men. I bless you and thank you but I cannot stay – the other call has come something I have never known or heard before something I must answer. Cost what it may to you or me – Goodbye and forget everything. Hazel Martyn.

She did, however, inform him that the Martyns' bankers, Brown Shipley of London, would know of their whereabouts.[58]

The romance between Hazel and Len Thomas progressed and by the summer they had made plans to be married. At the end of August the Martyns returned to Chicago to await Len's arrival. Hazel was anxious to be married immediately, but on the eve of the wedding Len disappeared. The events surrounding his departure were never publicized, but in society circles it was con-cluded that Hazel had been jilted. Margaret Canover, a friend of Dorothy's who was nineteen at the time, heard rumours that Len had illegitimate children – and that Hazel was spreading the story out of spite.[59]* Hazel was humiliated and agonized by the

---

* Thomas left the diplomatic service in 1906 and became a successful businessman. He was later declared a millionaire. Thomas was first married in January 1910 to Blanche Oelrichs, who was considered by

knowledge that she had lost John Lavery, a man who truly loved her. In November she finally contacted him:

I know that you will not care to read this or any letter from me John Lavery and I am only writing because you should know that I am 'paying'. There is no escape is there? One is forced to it if one is unwilling. Briefly it amounts to this he *was* the 'wrong man' as I wrote you and I knew it always really, but I *chose* to believe in him and to be happy at any cost. I didn't care enfin. *You* know what the fever is when at its height. But I listened to nothing but the siren calls and you know all about that too – they are so sweet so loud one hears nothing else. Then he came to me to marry me as he begged 'at once' – also came following him a woman – with tales so black that the pretty colours were smirched *forever* and ever and that is all – this was eight weeks so since then I have been very ill so near death and so longing for it but it seems one is not permitted to 'pay' as easily and sweetly as that. I've come back from the shadows again. I am getting better indeed I am 'almost quite well' thank you. Please you will never speak of this – I have told no one, no one knows the truth of the breaking with him on the very eve of the wedding. Today I read the last letter you wrote me and the wonderfulness of you John Lavery came about me like a great cloak. After all you have lived through so much *are* living through so much now and you seem to look with kind wise eyes on the world on poor struggling passionate exhausted me but I've no right to talk like this. I only can't help saying that although I have put great distances between us so vast they can never be bridged – still I have always from you things you told me a year, two years, three years ago. I remember and understand anew. Perhaps for the first time ... This letter were perhaps better unwritten but it is of small moment and no importance as such I value it and so will you. I bless you that is permitted.[60]

John's reply left little doubt that he still loved Hazel and was willing to forgive her.

Yes Hazel dear where you are there is danger I know still I believe one would get accustomed to it in time. True the training is somewhat stiff and may appear easy when one is not in it. Anyway let us talk it over. ... No I don't see Hazel dear, that anything has been spoiled either finally or utterly or that the situation is anymore changed than is customary with the hand of time.

Helleu to be the most beautiful woman in America *(The New Tork Times,* 30 May 1942). They divorced in 1919 and she married the actor John Barrymore. Thomas remarried in 1921 to a divorcee, Marie Sackett *(N.T.T.,* 3 March 1921). Len Thomas died in 1937.

She was forgiven but he concluded his letter 'Yours sometimes generally always.'[61]

Another trip to Europe was to have taken place early in 1907, but was postponed by the declining health of Hazel's maternal grandparents, the Taggarts. Hazel wrote to John that 'poor mother has actually had a nervous collapse in consequence I am more bound than ever'.[62] Forced to remain in Chicago, Hazel regained her place in Chicago society, becoming a member of John McCutheon's select but unpretentious Social and Pleasure Club, held in his studio in the Fine Arts Building.[63] Between March and June of 1908 Hazel was enrolled in the Chicago Art Institute for lessons in drawing and painting, and her work received an honorary mention.[64]

Dorothy had come out in Chicago, her debut being 'quiet without ostentation'.[65] She showed talent as a writer, and her play *Grove Eden* was presented by students at the Anna Morgan Studios, a school of dramatic expression. The play mirrored her life, featuring an overbearing society mother and a young heroine who cannot choose between her two suitors.* Dorothy, like Hazel, had gained a reputation as a beauty and when Hazel posed in a *tableau vivant* as Romney's 'Lady Hamilton', many remarked that it was Dorothy who looked like 'a replica of Romney's portrait'.[66]

But Dorothy's beauty masked an emotional instability. Hazel had claimed centre stage and her letters bear little more than passing remarks to her younger sister. To emulate Hazel, Dorothy followed the craze of fasting 'for the sake of health and comeliness'. In August 1906, at the time other sister's engagement to Len Thomas, Dorothy entered the care of doctors.[67] Hazel, feeling obliged to remain in Chicago to look after her sister, mother and ailing grandparents, inevitably grew distant from

---

* This one-act farce was not considered Dorothy's best work, but it is her only surviving manuscript, as she destroyed everything else. *Grove Eden* was accidentally retained by the Chicago writer Harriet Monroe, and published posthumously in 1912.

John. No correspondence between the two survives from 1907 through the summer of 1909, when the death of Mrs Martyn was to remove the most redoubtable obstacle to their marriage.

IV

'all wife'
[1909]

I N THE SPRING of 1909 the Martyns – and Mrs Taggart, who had been widowed the previous winter* – crossed the Atlantic to spend a few months in Paris. Their stay was dogged by illness as Dorothy was still obsessively fasting; for weeks she was in critical condition.[1] By May she was able to travel again and the party left for London. En route, Mrs Martyn fell ill with appendicitis and never fully recovered. She died on 20 June 1909 at the age of fifty-one.[2]

It appears that Hazel and John were not in contact at the time of Mrs Martyn's death. Hazel later recounted that it was Dorothy who persuaded her to get in touch with John,[3] who promptly found them rooms at the Hotel Van Dyke on Cromwell Road. Hazel wrote to thank him: 'This hotel is so clean and comfy and the food is so heavenly I could weep from sheer pleasure in the decency and daintiness of it all.'[4]

The hotel was close to John's home and he visited frequently. One night he wrote: 'From early morning till this moment I have been in the hands of others and even now I have had to explain

---

* John P. Taggart died on 16 September 1908, aged eighty-nine.

35

that I have an important note to write and I so wanted to write and tell you that I also grow in grace and realize more and more how wonderful my Dear One is.'[5] After six years Hazel was at last free from her mother, and she and John arranged to be married on 22 July.

The bereaved Dorothy became completely uncooperative, exasperating the ever-patient John, who wrote to Hazel: 'I really can't understand why Dorothy – after the fatal experience – can go on making life a burden for those she loves – seriously she cannot surely be responsible.'[6] In a conciliatory mood, Dorothy wrote the night before the wedding:

Dear Brother
I am very near tears tonight ... because you are taking Hazel away ... I am letting you take her without a word because I know that she will be *safer* and *happier* with you, and that you will make *her well, sooner* than any one else. You are the only man who could possibly make her happy! Mother knew this before she died Thank God – and I know it tonight and have known it a long long time ... I send you lots and lots of love and I am wishing *all the* good wishes for *you two* tonight. Loving oh so lovingly yours and sister's.[7]

She then telegrammed the Armours: 'Hazel will be married tomorrow to John Lavery.'[8] Friends in Chicago were surprised, as many had been unaware of the couple's lengthy courtship.

The wedding ceremony was held at noon at the Brompton Oratory, the second largest Catholic church in London. The pair married at St Patrick's altar, in tribute to their Irish ancestry, with Dorothy and young Alice as bridesmaids.[9] Two artists, Robert Cunninghame-Graham and Alexander Jamieson, attended for John at the small ceremony with only a few other intimate friends.[10]

The Laverys spent their short honeymoon at Southend-on-Sea in Essex, because Hazel had been told that the town had a romantic setting. It rained for their entire visit, and Hazel later wrote, 'English sea-side is horrible.'[11]

On their return to London, John was extremely busy and Hazel was again unwell. The staff carried notes between bedroom and studio:

This is a love letter from your wife most beloved John please you are to come and see me soon and not bother with visitors! *I* am your most distinguished guest today. I love you and I am yours. I started to arise but I feel a bit painy so I shall only get up in time for luncheon *and*, I love you.[12]

Eileen Lavery, John's eighteen-year-old daughter, had not been in London for the wedding though she did not oppose the union. It is not clear whether she had ever met her new stepmother when Hazel wrote to her shortly after the wedding: 'I love you my darling and I always shall. I am going to be a happy girl* ... and you have helped to make me so'[13] Eileen, an independent-minded girl, was tall and dark-haired, resembling her late mother. She had been sent to board at the Sacred Heart Convent at Roehampton as a young girl and spent much of her childhood apart from her father. Her real father-figure was William Patrick Whyte, who after taking care of Eileen as an infant moved with her to Cromwell Place, where he remained until John married Hazel.[14] Whyte became a recluse, though he continued to eat regularly at the Laverys'; guests recalled him 'in the background like a grey ghost, oblivious of them and his surroundings'.[15] Eileen and her father never experienced the closeness that Lavery enjoyed in later life with his stepdaughter Alice.

A week after the wedding, Hazel and her family returned to Chicago to bury Mrs Martyn's ashes and to settle the estate. John stayed behind to complete his numerous commissions. During Hazel's absence he busied himself in London, eating at the Chelsea Arts Club and revisiting places where he and Hazel had been together. He sat at 'their' table in a restaurant in Earls Court. In the Rose Room at Cromwell Place, a painting of Hazel, perhaps 'Dame en Noir' (1906, *see plate*) looked down from its frame 'with sad eyes and makes John feel that he ought not to have let his darling wife out of his sight'.[16] Hazel was also lonely and wrote from the ship:

---

* Despite Hazel's reference to herself as 'a happy girl' she was by no means a child-bride. Her marriage certificate stated that she was twenty-seven; she was in fact twenty-nine. By the 1920s she was lying about her age by seven years.

I have always particularly scorned the loving spouse who merged her personality into that of her Lord! maintaining that she could have had a meagre personality to start with! However I [have] become all wife it seems to me the most wonderful and glorious career in all the world. Just to be John Lavery's wife Hazel. ... I have longed for you – each night I turn my head to kiss you goodnight but only Alice is there and dear and loved as she is it is you that my heart seeks and cries for. ... I sleep with your two dear letters under my pillow and they crackle cheerfully when I turn in the night and say 'John loves you, loves you, loves you.' Are you *miserable* without me? don't say '*Yes, of course* in that horrid husband way you have which means 'don't be silly my dear girl' but kiss me instead with a hungry kiss and say 'I shall *die* if you go away again my darling.' You must learn this by heart and say it to me directly we meet.[17]

On the ship, the party's various names created a focus of curiosity – Lavery, Trudeau, Martyn and Taggart. One inquisitive lady questioned five-year-old Alice, who was overheard to reply, 'But I tell you she *is* my mother that prettiest one and she has been for a *long* time but I have a dear new father just a week old!' Alice, who already loved her stepfather with an intensity that would never diminish, frequently remarked: 'Poor John how lonely he must be without *me*.' [18]

During the passage there were blue skies and a calm sea; Hazel wrote to John that 'Neptune was a smiling friendly creature'. Despite the smooth voyage Dorothy was petulant and still refused to eat. Hazel wrote: 'It is too heartbreaking to see her growing weaker and weaker everyday ... perhaps she will be better and more sensible when she sees people in Chicago.'[19] John had already recognized the gravity of Dorothy's condition:

I am so sorry about Dorothy and hope she ... is not adding to the difficulties of your task .... You see Hazel darling she only plays upon your good nature and it is injurious to both. I think that if she is still playing the fool you might put her in the charge of a brain specialist because I expect as time goes on she deteriorates and her lucid intervals become briefer.[20]

They were met in New York by friends from Chicago, and though Hazel had hoped to travel incognito,[21] the press awaited her. She told *The Chicago Tribune:*

Indeed my marriage to Mr Lavery and the settlement of my mother's estate does not mean severing of the Chicago ties. We couldn't have that you know. Mr Lavery could not come with us on this short trip but next Spring we expect to come over for a good visit. I must bring him over to know Chicago and my friends.[22]

To Hazel's delight, Ethel Hooper travelled hundreds of miles to visit them for two days. Charles Hodges, a former friend of Hazel's father, came from Detroit with his wife.[23] Hazel commented: 'It is people, people, people, flowers, flowers, flowers, reporters, telephones, telegrams and under it all this sordid worry about money.'[24]

A year before her death, Mrs Martyn had been anxious about the family finances, and visiting the lawyers, Hazel and Dorothy learned that their inheritance had been greatly depleted. Mrs Martyn had spent excessively and borrowed $12,000 from Armour & Co. Worse, she had re-written her will in 1905, when Hazel was seriously ill, to prevent the Trudeaus (whom she disliked) from obtaining any of the Martyn estate. However, the wording of the will also prevented her own children from obtaining 'the principal', a reduced sum of $65,000, which was held on trust with an annuity payment to begin after one year.

Dorothy was 'perfectly crushed and dumbfounded'; the sole consolation was that the remainder of the family possessions would be made over to herself and Hazel as part of a Children's Award. The Armours generously offered to pay over a thousand dollars towards Mrs Martyn's medical bills.[25] Hazel wrote to John: 'I cannot see for tears and my mind is quite gone – I can only remember a few great facts the most important is that I am your wife, your beloved wife am I not John? even if I am dismantled and impoverished and a beggar child?'[26] John replied that perhaps financial loss would help Dorothy to 'wake up and live a healthier life', and suggested that Dorothy take Hazel's share of the income until she married.[27]

At Mrs Martyn's burial at Graceland cemetery, Dorothy, who had eaten no solid food since London, fainted several times. Dr Favill, a family friend, examined her and pronounced that it was not 'a question of what it is best to do but what *must* be done at once'.[28] It became imperative to move Dorothy away from family pressures to recuperate and she was sent to the Hodges for two or three months. Meanwhile, Mrs Taggart, who had tuberculosis, was admitted to a sanatorium.[29] Hazel explained to John: 'I have had a rather bad time of it even in comparison to the other dark times I have been through this seems rather blacker and more dreadful.'[30]

Dr Favill urged Hazel to return to her new husband.[31] Before this was possible Hazel arranged for the sale of family effects to raise money for Dorothy's care. In one day Hazel organized the unpacking and repacking of twenty-nine barrels of china and glass.[32] 'I shall not try to take anything but my silver and linen because everything that comes from the sale must go to her. Things look very beautiful to me now they are no longer mine!'[33]

Their affairs settled, Hazel and Alice departed from New York on the *Oceanic* on 1 September 1909, disembarking at Southampton on the 8th. Hazel now turned her back on her life in America, and found solace in her role as John's wife.

V

'a society star'
[1909-18]

THE LAVERYS lived at 5 Cromwell Place, a Regency house in fashionable South Kensington, opposite the Victoria and Albert and the Natural History Museums. John had moved in 1898. He and John Singer Sargent, who had also been looking for a studio at the time, admired the house's first-floor studio with its Venetian window and glass roof. Sargent found the lease too expensive,[1] but John, 'in a fit of Irish recklessness', bought the lease from the painter Sir Coutts Lindsay.[2] He wrote in his autobiography, 'nowhere I have lived has had the appeal of London nor its freedom. Cromwell Place has been my home for forty years without my knowing my next-door neighbour, and it has a call for me that no other corner of the globe has been able to give.'[3]

This was Hazel's first real home since Astor Street, and after her extended travels she longed to put down roots. When she moved to London in 1909, the Edwardian era was at an end. The Liberals, with H.H. Asquith as Prime Minister, had a comfortable majority in the House of Commons and society was changing to embrace artists, entertainers and other temporary celebrities.[4] Hazel was eager to enter the London arena, and soon became 'a society star' who lent 'radiance to the Asquith set'.[5] John, as a successful artist and a Liberal, was already in the Prime Minister's circle. Number 10 Downing Street and the Asquith summer home at The Wharf, Sutton Courtenay, in Berkshire were centres of lively entertainment. Asquith's second wife Margot was a noted hostess and wit, known for her *outré* comments. Later in the relationship she rankled Hazel with 'Why do you neglect your boys so? I *never* see you with them!' and 'Why are you losing your looks so soon: you aren't forty yet, are you?'[6] Hazel disliked being teased but routinely accepted invitations to The Wharf. Asquith admitted to 'a slight weakness for the companionship of clever and attractive women',[7] and Hazel would often accompany him to Oxford to meet the dons while John painted. In 1910 Asquith often recited a popular song to her:

> Fair as a lily joyous and free
> Light of that prairie home was she
> Everyone who saw her felt
> The gentle power of Rosalie
> The prairie flower.[8]

Lady Diana Manners, later Cooper, first noticed Hazel in 1911 when she appeared at a 'fancy dress orgy at Shannon's* studio' in a velvet dress and hat after Dürer.[9] Fancy-dress balls were in vogue, and Hazel was ingenious with costume. Appearing as 'Flora', she was photographed with Somerset Maugham. 'The boldest thing she was ever persuaded to do was to impersonate Botticelli's figure of Spring. Even that – the impossible – was a success.'[10] (*see plates*).

Her talent for costume translated into her everyday attire. In her youth she had worn Paris couture but, as her reputation for style grew, she employed a seamstress, Miss Hodge of Pimlico. This might have been an economic as well as a creative measure. When the London fashion house of Reville and Rossiter, dress-makers for Queen Mary, offered to dress her, she refused,

---

* Either Charles Haslewood Shannon (1863-1937) or Sir James Jebusa
  Shannon; (1862-1923), both of whom were London society painters.

preferring to wear clothes of her own creation.[11] A contemporary recalled:

Her clothes were generally concocted by herself and her maid. She would appear in public faultlessly wearing organdie frills and a picture hat she had pinned together. The result was in the best picturesque style ... Often she met with failure in these home-made efforts. Once she became so irritated that she burnt a fur muff.[12]

She rarely got up before noon and, when in bed, would spend the day sewing a hat or doll-clothes for Alice, who christened one of her dolls 'Pink-Purple', Hazel's favourite colours.[13] Her industry was not wasted, as over the following decade ladies' magazines noticed her creations:

Mrs John Lavery, who started some pretty fashions ... now affects a sort of nun head-dress, under a wide brimmed hat. She has also been seen with floating lapels of clear fine lawn under a country hat, and amazingly becoming they were.[14]

While Hazel was being feted in London, her new friends seem to have remained unaware of her protracted courtship, the loss of her family fortune, or the existence of a sister in America. After Hazel's marriage to John, Dorothy complained that she had no part in her sister's life,[15] but since Dorothy refused to live in England, it was arranged she would remain in Chicago with her grandmother. Dorothy needed family and security, but Mrs Taggart was seventy-two and in poor health. A few months later, on 14 November 1909, she died of a heart attack.

During the next year Dorothy lived with family friends and although she was now twenty-one there seemed no prospect of marriage. She aspired to a literary career and worked briefly as a private secretary for the novelist Kellogg Fairbank. Hampered by continued ill-health she was unable to continue.[16] Concern for Dorothy was exacerbated by slow trans-Atlantic communications, so John and Hazel decided to make a visit in the spring of 1911.

In Chicago for the first time, John was impressed by the hospitality. The Laverys were greeted at the station by a number of professional painters, and during their stay John was given a tour of the Chicago Art Institute.[17] Lavery's autobiography makes no reference to the real reason for the trip to Chicago. Dorothy was increasingly anti-social as a result of her failing mental health. Hazel persuaded her to return with them to Europe, but she remained unhappy. Hazel approached writers with her sister's literary work, but Dorothy was uninterested in efforts on her behalf,[18] and later destroyed her manuscripts.[19] She refused to remain in England and in the summer of 1911 went back to America.

She was frail and emaciated, described as broken in health and spirit. Friends found her 'lying in a big four poster as white as the pillows she rested upon. Death was written on her features in unmistakable letters.'[20] In mid-September Dorothy was admitted to St Luke's Hospital. Hazel only received a telegram with this news on 9 October and the Laverys set sail immediately. Ten days later. Grace Honore Palmer met them in New York with the news that Dorothy had died on 13 October, while they were at sea.[21] The cause of death was acute enteritis exacerbated by years of fasting. The death certificate cited acute mania as a contributory factor.

A headline in *The Inter-Ocean* read, 'Deserted by sister. Miss Dorothy Martin [*sic*] passes away alone at St Luke's Hospital'. Chicago society was shocked that the daughter of a once-prominent family should die in a public hospital. The newspaper criticized Hazel, reporting that Dorothy had died 'without a relative by her side' and 'under circumstances unusually pathetic', and that 'It was known that she suffered largely from neglect and a lack of those things in life to which she had been accustomed in her earlier years.' The paper speculated that her relationship with Hazel had been difficult, 'for no-one can understand, if it were otherwise, why they should be so widely separated'.[22]

The Laverys' arrival in Chicago was quiet. They booked into a small hotel and made arrangements for the funeral, to be held at the chapel in Graceland cemetery.[23] Five hundred dollars worth of flowers were sent to the cemetery,[24] marking the passing of a young woman who ended her life in self-imposed isolation. After Dorothy's death, Hazel never returned to America until the late 1920s, when John received several lucrative commissions. There is no record of her ever revisiting Chicago.

Hazel became plagued by the fear that she would lose John too, asking Alice: 'What will we do if he dies?'[25] She had always been looked after, first by her mother, later by John. Although physically mismatched – John once likened his wife and himself to Juno and the Worm[26] – John supplied Hazel with the security and devotion she required. Hazel once told a reporter:

Woman has much the best out of life. She has only to know how to be helpless and some man will most certainly come along and look after her. She need not assume any responsibility: he will enjoy doing it. So she has the advantage of being spoiled and of giving pleasure at the same time.[27]

It was quite common for society spouses to spend long periods of time apart; Hazel and John at this time were an exception, 'the most devoted couple who seem to do everything together'.[28] John willingly escorted Hazel to formal occasions although he found it trying to make polite conversation after a day amusing his sitters. At the Asquiths' he found a companion who disliked these occasions as much as he did. Countess de Benckendorff, the Russian Ambassador's wife. When the men joined the ladies after dinner, she would make her way over to John, link arms and say, 'Now, Mr Lavery, we shall sleep togezzer on the sofa!'[29] Hazel, by contrast, was happiest playing to the crowd, keeping the entire company enthralled with a shamelessly exaggerated story. Her popularity was well recognized: 'Any woman who wants to make a dinner-party "go" invites Hazel Lavery to be her guest; but she is difficult to track to her lair, for all the world runs after her, and it would have been just the same if she had not married the great painter John Lavery.'[30] Victorian standards still held sway and dictated that a wife was 'to act as a hostess, to create an impressive domestic facade, to mix readily with those who were useful to her husband'.[31] Hazel

45

was John's keenest supporter and his principal critic; she had admired his work ever since the days in Beg-Meil. During their early courtship she had teased him, 'I love your *work* almost as much as I love *you*.'[32] She gave up her own ambitions of becoming a professional artist, claiming she was too lazy. She could not bear to be tired or dirty and gave up as soon as her hands were smudged. An observer remarked, 'She drew expertly but never concentrated long enough on her work.'[33] Hazel declared that One artist was enough in any family, and probably irked the more liberal members other sex when she said:

I don't think that we women can ever do anything as well as the best men, with the possible exception of acting. Take painting, for example. No woman has ever been a great painter, for the simple reason that she has not the requisite amount of physical and nervous strength.[34]

In spite of these sentiments, she never abandoned her artwork completely. Signing her work 'Hazell Lavery', she painted, sketched, and made etchings, which she exhibited with John at the Chenil Gallery and Alpine Club in later years.

Lavery had had a well-established clientele even before his second marriage, including the Irish Parliamentary Party member T.P. O'Connor, the historian William Edward Hartpole Lecky and numerous society ladies. But he gained popularity after his marriage to Hazel, becoming one of the best-known society portraitists in London, The women he painted at this time included Gwendoline Churchill, wife of Jack Churchill, and Elizabeth Asquith, the Prime Minister's youngest daughter.

In 1913 he was given a commission to paint a group portrait of the Royal family, which brought King George V and Queen Mary to his studio.[35] The oil sketch of the Queen is visible in the background of John's painting, 'The Artist's Studio' (1910-13), a work that contrives to show the affluence of the artist's family (*see plate*). The figures are arranged informally on a huge canvas. Hazel dominates the foreground, seated on a small couch in a flamboyant pink and purple ensemble, with an arm cradled around Alice. Eileen is behind them, in profile and leaning across the grand piano, and seems secondary. Rodney Stone, the dog named after the Conan Doyle hero,[36] lies at Alice's feet. The dog, the arrangement of the figures and the inclusion of the artist's own work all pay tribute to Velasquez's 'Las Meninas'.

'The Artist's Studio' also depicts a Moroccan servant named Aïda, whom the Laverys employed during their several winter holidays in Morocco and then smuggled back to London with the connivance of John's diplomat friend Reginald Lister. John had fallen in love with Morocco in the 1890s during an expedition with his friend Robert Cunninghame-Graham. The two men crossed the interior on horseback, visiting Arzila, Alcazar el Kebir and Fez, accompanied by Walter Harris, correspondent for *The Times*. 'In steady sunshine our horses waded girth-deep through the amazing verdure of wild hyacinth, anemones and narcissi stretching away to a ringed horizon,' Lavery reminisced in his autobiography.[37] They ended their journey in Tangier, the diplomatic capital of Morocco, where every language was spoken and every currency accepted.[38]

Lavery loved the cosmopolitanism and the bright sunshine, which inspired his painting, and at the time of his marriage to Hazel he was spending part of each year in a small house outside Tangier, at the summit of a steep hill known as Mount Washington. Named Dar el Midfah (the House of the Cannon) after a cannon half-buried in the front garden,[39] the house was ringed by a verandah covered with purple bougainvillaea. John had built on a spacious studio with a large flat roof, an ideal place to view the city and the sea. A nearby eucalyptus wood sent a rich scent wafting into the house.[40]

Hazel made her first journey to Morocco with John in 1909, the first winter of their marriage. Word spread quickly that John Lavery had a new wife, and many came to see this American beauty for themselves.[41] The English-speaking community was of old colonial stock; their main sporting activities were polo and pig-sticking. Hazel thought them odd, describing one individual as nice but suffering from 'a slight softening of the brain'.[42] The path to the beach ran over the land of an eccentric neighbour named Levison, who kept an armed guard with orders to shoot trespassers.[43]

Hazel tried to make Dar el Midfah as European as possible, laying a tennis court and crowding the house with possessions from London. She made no effort to communicate with her Arab servants and wrote contemptuously that she longed to go home 'to speak to human beings again'.[44] Ill-made for solitude, she gradually made friends and entered the social life surrounding the legations. The Laverys' friends included Sir Reginald Lister, Minister Plenipotentiary at the British Legation, who was particularly fond of Hazel, and Sir Mennebhi, a local character, who often invited them to dine. Hazel loved the local custom of using her fingers to eat, but did not appreciate the traditional burp or hiccup.[45]

Alice's happiness compensated John for Hazel's dislike of Morocco. She developed a passion for animals and outdoor life and became an avid collector of insects and butterflies, which she kept in cigar-boxes.[46] Quickly learning more Arabic than John, she imitated the grooms and was heard telling her donkey, Moses, 'go on, thou son of an adulteress'.[47]

As there were no paved roads around Mount Washington it was necessary to ride, and John bought Hazel a silver-maned Arab stallion named Lily Beau. It was said that the battle-scarred old horse had served the Sultan and had even saved his life.[48] Hazel was not used to temperamental Arab horses who fought each other and screeched, and told John to return Lily Beau. But Alice wanted the stallion and went on hunger-strike, refusing to leave the stable until her parents agreed to keep him. Hazel, terrified that Alice would be hurt while riding, insisted that their groom Absalom walk in front of the horse. Eventually, Alice begged Absalom to ride alone and she seized the opportunity to show off her equestrian skills, riding into town to meet her parents. On seeing Alice, Hazel screamed, 'John, tell her to get off!' but John, recognizing Alice's prowess, calmed Hazel down.[49]

In exchange for Lily Beau, Alice's donkey was given to Hazel. She felt safer on his back as she was closer to the ground, although according to Alice, Moses was 'far naughtier than any horse' and had to be led by the groom.[50] Hazel was an unusual sight when she arrived at functions wearing gowns and furs and riding a pack saddle. Although this typified the discomforts of Morocco for Hazel, a London society magazine made it sound more exotic:

In Tangier, where the Laverys have a charming villa, life is a combination of ul-tra civilization and primitive conditions rather difficult to reconcile. For instance, when going out to late dinners where full dress is "de rigueur" Mrs Lavery found it, to say the least, trying to have the London taxicab or brougham replaced by a donkey and a saddle. To ride this lowly beast through streets so narrow that your feet scrape the walls on one side while your shoulders brush the opposite masonry is especially trying when you have on a low-necked gown of frail and diaphanous texture and white satin slippers. But this is the sole means of transport through the steep, dimly lit, thoroughly mysterious highways and byways of this picturesque and semi-barbarous African city. And as, wherever two or more English people are gathered together, dining is the principal manner of entertaining, this mode of communication must be accepted.[51]

Eileen accompanied her father and stepmother to Tangier for the first few winters, but she also spent time with Mary Auras, John's former model, who was married and living in Casablanca.[52] In April 1912 Eileen married James Dickinson, in the studio at Dar el Midfah. Alice was bridesmaid.[53] The ceremony was attended by the Laverys' friends in Tangier, among whom were Baroness de Seckendoroff, wife of the German Plenipotentiary, Walter Harris, Sir Mennebhi and Reginald Lister.[54]

Eileen's marriage and the sudden death of Reginald Lister from malaria later that year marked the end of an era. When the Laverys returned to Morocco for the winter of 1913-14, Hazel found Tangier 'full of sadness'. Before they went back to Lon-don, she wrote:

... I think we shall not come back again. John says he is 'painted out' and the whole place is changed, all the wild, primitive charm almost destroyed and in its place there is a sort of tawdry pitiful attempt at civilization which makes everything more sordid and uncomfortable.[55]

It was the last time that John and Hazel wintered in Tangier, although they toured the interior of Morocco in 1920.

❧◦❧

Hazel, now Mrs Lavery, was the first true mistress of Cromwell Place. Over the years Hazel transformed the house, her individual style evident on arrival at the scarlet-painted front door. The house was filled with the exotic and unusual, and Hazel's flair did not go unnoticed. *Vogue* photographed the interior for 'Notable Women at Home', as did *Lady's Pictorial* which observed that 'As in all artist's houses, there is nothing fixed and prim; the furniture seems inevitable, and not brought from another place.'[56] The drawing-room walls were covered in a gold cloth which was crinkled to produce a crepe-like surface that caught the light. Butterfly specimens with matching hues (perhaps caught by Alice in Morocco) were mounted on the mantel.[57] The dining-room, in yellow accented with black, boasted one of Hazel's prized possessions – a glass cabinet, lined with mirrors, made from pieces of King George IV's state coach.[58]

Hazel received visitors in what became known as 'her ladyship's sitting-room'. Positioning her desk by the window so she could see callers approaching the house, she spent a part of each day writing letters. Hazel visited the studio whenever John had sitters, and Lord Northcliffe enjoyed Hazel's company so much that he claimed she had revolutionized sittings and presented both John and Hazel with cheques.[59] Lord Beatty, whose portrait was not a success, wrote to John: 'I am afraid it is my fault being a restless individual. However when I have really accomplished something you can have another shot, but Mrs Lavery must be there and I will promise to be still.'[60] Cromwell Place was known as Hazel Lavery's house, not John Lavery's studio, as John recorded later:

My life has been largely a question of painting in my various studios .... Yet Cromwell Place, for many years, achieved another status: it was the meeting ground of a large number of famous people holding all sorts of views and engaged in many different activities. These people did not come to see me. They came to see Hazel.[61]

Hazel gave most of her at-homes in her husband's lofty studio. The studio's usual function was obscured by Chinese screens concealing unfinished canvasses. Around the glass roof were small gold stars against blue paint, giving the room a nocturnal feel.[62] As the Laverys' income was unreliable, they frequently held luncheon rather than dinner parties. Hazel's bohemian mode of dining in the studio was noticed by envious contemporaries, who claimed she was 'one of those Londonised Americans who are adept hostesses'.[63] *The Anglo-American Year Book* of 1916 listed John among seventy-six 'distinguished Englishmen with American wives'.[64] Free from restrictions imposed by family connections and political animosities, many American women in London created salons independent of established English hostesses. Emerald Cunard, a flamboyant Californian, delighted in mixing her guests 'like cocktails with unexpected ingredients'.[65] Hazel loved to befriend those who excelled, whether rulers or writers, soldiers or artists, and was almost childishly anxious to win their esteem and affection.[66]

Women of the period, particularly attractive ones, often gathered a coterie of adoring men. Hazel was no exception. Admirers who came to Cromwell Place included Lord Basil Blackwood, Lord Alexander Thynne, Duff Cooper, Sir Shane Leslie, Charles Beresford and George Bernard Shaw. Thynne and Blackwood both complained that they could never meet Hazel alone, for the other was always there. One night at a dinner party the two were giving vent to their woes when Asquith remarked that he found the Diploma Gallery at Burlington House the perfect place for an assignation. Thynne duly arranged his next rendezvous with Hazel in the nearby Victoria and Albert Museum, a more secluded setting.[67]

Society women were highly competitive in the pursuit of men as husbands or lovers. As Edith, wife of the 7th Marquess of Londonderry, wrote: 'Up till the war the great bulk of women acquiesced in the generally accepted idea that women did not and never would be friendly with other women, and that they always quarrelled together over some man, sooner or later.'[68] Hazel's coquettish nature caused some ill-feeling. Lady Cynthia Asquith, wife of Asquith's son Beb, indignantly recorded in her diary after a dinner with the Laverys at the Café Royal: 'I find Hazel Lavery a bore at a small party – at any rate a non-conductor to me – she never listens and entirely checks my flow.'[69]

Love affairs were accepted, provided they did not bring public scandal. A wife could behave as she wished once she had produced an heir and performed the duties of a loyal and devoted spouse. The sarcastic Margot Asquith often told Hazel that she saw no future for her: 'Hazel dear, I despair of you! I'm told you're virtuous, you aren't intelligent and you seem devoted to your husband.'[70] Speculation as to whether Hazel's admirers were also her lovers fuelled society gossip. John wrote:

... she came to have a host, a regiment of friends and admirers – and they numbered as many women as men. Not so many women at first; but as the years passed and no scandal could be fastened on her in any way at any time, her women admirers – especially the married ones – increased and became more and more amicably disposed towards her.[71]

She was a calculatingly whimsical hostess, sometimes inviting husbands without their wives or hosting exclusively male parties. In response Lady Beatty and Lady Leslie were said to have established a Husband Protection Society.[72] Even as late as the 1920s, when Hazel wished to paint Beatty's portrait. Lady Beatty refused to allow it.[73] Lady Leslie, too, was infuriated by her husband's undisguised adoration of Hazel. Sir Shane Leslie composed love poetry to Hazel lamenting the fact that she had spurned him:

Farewell beautiful and dearest: I left some red roses under cover of night to float in your bath. No eyes have they and it cannot be said that they smell not. They

The Laverys at Tangier. *Left to right*: Hazel, John, Alice, Eileen and Hadeshia.

John painting Hazel in Tangier.

John and Alice riding in Tangier.

Hazel and Alice at 5 Cromwell Place, 1911. 'Dame en Noir' can be seen in the background.

Hazel and Somerset Maugham in fancy dress.

Hazel as Flora from Botticelli's 'Primavera', at the London Picture Ball in 1914.

Left: 'Madonna of the Lakes', 1917, by John Lavery, formerly in St Patrick's Church, Belfast, now in the Ulster Museum, Belfast, with Alice as Boy Patrick, Hazel as the Madonna and Eileen as St Brigid. Lavery presented this triptych in honour of his mother to the church where he was baptised.

A page from *Lady's Pictorial*, 13 December 1919, showing 'The Silver Turban', 1911 (now in a private collection in the USA), and Cromwell Place interiors.

A page from *Vogue*, 1930, showing a variety of *tableaux vivants*.

Portrait-card of H.H. Asquith, British
Prime Minister, 1917.

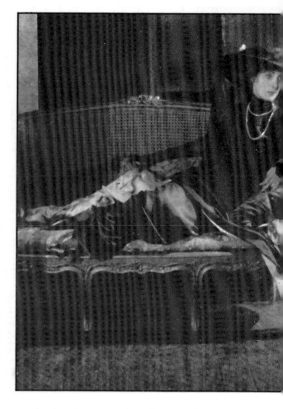

Updated studio portrait of Hazel by Baron de Meyer,
photographer for American *Vogue*.

Photograph by
Hoppé of John and
Hazel Lavery, used as
frontispiece for the
Laverys' joint exhibition
catalogue, introduced
by Winston Churchill,
in the Alpine Club
Gallery, October 1921.

'The Court of Criminal Appeal, London', 1916, by John Lavery. Casement can be seen in the dock. John was commissioned to paint the passing of the death sentence. Hazel's frequent attendance at the trial marked the beginning of her passionate involvement in the Irish cause. (Hugh Lane Municipal Gallery of Modern Art, Dublin)

Hazel's painting of George Bernard Shaw, *left*, was later reworked by John, *right*, in 1930.

Correspondence from William Orpen to John Lavery.

will make blind exquisite companions accordingly of your splashes. Tomorrow I shall mention you in church – at the altar and in the confessional.[74]

Leslie would leave his poems scattered around Cromwell Place, and although John was amused, it irritated him if the servants found them. Anita Leslie, Shane's daughter, noted: 'John Lavery was very tolerant but under the surface he was upset by all the admiration she received. She was proud of that.'[75]

Charles Stewart Henry Vane Tempest-Stewart, 7th Marquess of Londonderry, noticed Hazel at the first ball she attended in London and sent her the Londonderry pearls as a token of his admiration, but Hazel soon returned them at John's suggestion.[76] Londonderry remained one of Hazel's key admirers. There is no suggestion of impropriety in their relationship at this stage; their friendship intensified in later years as they sparred over Irish politics.

Sir Patrick Ford, a Scottish lawyer, was another attentive admirer who became one of John's greatest patrons. By 1929 he had accumulated fifty-eight works by Lavery, mainly portraits of the enormous Ford clan.[77] He sent Hazel scores of love poems over a period of twenty years. Under the pseudonyms of A. (O.E.) and O.E.A., he may have been the author of *The Hazel Wand*, a book of poetry written about and dedicated to Hazel, published by Grant Richards of London in 1925, and was possibly the secret admirer who sent her a purple orchid each morning, which she wore on her lapel, wrist or collar. Sir Patrick's adoration of Hazel seems to have been accepted without rancour by both families, as each September the Laverys spent two weeks with the Fords in North Berwick, Scotland.

❧⊙❧

By 1911 Hazel had become one of the best-known women in society, numbering among her friends the prominent artists, writers and politicians of her day. As letters from her admirers grew, she began assembling memorabilia. Her earliest known scrapbook dates from that year, although much of the material is from an earlier period, including a cheque signed by Aubrey Beardsley, Rodin's signature, an invitation to an early Lavery exhibition in Glasgow, her own sketches of Alice as a baby and family photographs. The scrapbooks became a life-long preoccupation; later books were bound in red leather with pages edged in gold leaf and 'Hazel' incised on the covers.*

The cult of the Laverys was well established and newspapers recorded their presence at every major social event. Hazel's image was familiar not least because she was so frequently painted by her husband. 'In the case of Lavery's portraits of Hazel, it was not just the projection of a life style but the manufacture of a mystique,' writes John's biographer Kenneth McConkey.[78] John immortalized his wife in 'The Mother and Child' (1909), 'Mrs Lavery' (1909) and 'The Silver Turban' (1911).

'The Mother and Child', painted shortly after Hazel's arrival in London, depicts Lavery's new wife and five-year-old Alice. Although the canvas consists mainly of muted tones of brown, Lavery delights in their winter attire, paying particular attention to their hats and muffs. In 'Mrs Lavery', Hazel sits in a chair, her hand under her chin and her head turned as if to observe the viewer. John records her ring and her flamboyant hat, the accessories that had become her trademark. 'The Silver Turban' is a formal portrait of Hazel. Her regal pose is accentuated by the fashionable titular turban.

Hazel undoubtedly influenced the nature of John's artistic output. Apart from his preoccupation with her as a portrait subject, the lifestyle that Hazel desired dictated that he have the steady income he could earn only through portraiture. Lavery had been at the peak of his career in the 1880s and 1890s. Like many artists of the day, he chose to continue working in the Impressionist idiom in which he had had so much success,

---

* Lady Lavery's scrapbook collection is now divided between two of her descendants and a private collector in America. There are seven scrapbooks accounted for to date.

rather than experiment with new styles. When he married Hazel he began a life of weekend parties and society events that often restricted his creativity. Lavery's work can be seen as an illustrated diary of his life. Later, when Hazel became interested in Ireland, she encouraged her husband to devote himself – when free from commissions – to creating an 'Irish Collection' documenting the political events and figures of Ireland's tumultuous bid for independence. Many of these works, particularly his portraits, are dull and uninspired, but the Irish Collection as a whole comprises a breadth of subject-matter that hints at what he might have achieved had he not married Hazel.

Hazel denied that she was John's muse. She told a reporter: 'I have certainly posed a lot for him, and I suppose that saved him a considerable amount of trouble, but as for inspiring him – well he was painting long before he married me.'[79] She often quipped that John used her because he didn't have to pay her,[80] and wrote, 'All artists take liberties with wives and daughters and we all have had amputations of arms, legs and hands which are attached to other bodies in John's pictures.' He often demanded her presence in the studio: 'John does not hesitate to say off with her head and on with yours if it suits his mood.'[81] Hazel illustrated the life of a painter's wife in verse:

> Popes, Kings and Queens he paints
> Wives, daughters, dealers, saints
> Heedless of their complaints
> and lamentations.
>
> His wretched wife at home
> starving and all alone,
> gets scarce a single bone
> save of contention!
>
> Yet glories in his name
> and wallows in his fame
> and tries in vain to claim
> public attention.[82]

John received numerous commissions from ladies wishing to be painted *à la* Hazel, as portraits of her became more numerous. 'Circumstance ... has dealt unkindly with the Provosts, Professors and Politicians in giving Mr Lavery a wife who offers a perpetual invitation to portraiture that is not masculine', wrote one newspaper. 'This lady has, in consequence, become one of the most familiar figures in contemporary painting.'[83]

Hazel also sat for portraits by Ambrose McEvoy, Oswald Birley and the miniaturist Alfred Praga, while Sargent sketched her and Clare Sheridan made a bust. The Irish artist William Orpen, however, never chose to use her as a model despite Hazel's habitual visits to his studio in elaborate, eye-catching dresses. One day when Hazel arrived wearing a pretty orange organdie ensemble, Orpen decided to end the charade and asked his daughter Kit to show her the sticklebacks in the garden pond. As she did, he stepped back and switched on the fountain. Hazel was soaked and humiliated.[84]

The German photographer E.O. Hoppe moved into 7 Cromwell Place in 1913, and Hazel was often seen running across the road in various costumes to pose in his studio. In 1914 Hoppe's photographs of Hazel in furs and a richly patterned wrap, with her young Moroccan servant in ornate ethnic garb, were featured in *The Tatler*.* Hoppe considered Hazel among the most beautiful women he had ever photographed[85] and in 1922 he challenged Americans to produce five women equal in beauty to those in his *Book of Fair Women*. When it was discovered that one of Hoppe's English beauties was an American, however, the photographer claimed she belonged to 'a distinctly British type'.[86]

⁂

The Laverys were in Dublin when war was declared on 4 August 1914. They returned to London to find St James's Park converted into an army camp. A letter awaited Hazel from the young Duff Cooper, sent from the Foreign Office in Whitehall.

---

* The son of their Moroccan cook, Ben Ali, only stayed with the Laverys for two years. He hated the British climate and was bitterly unhappy in London.

I hope you aren't stranded in Ireland with no ships to take you back. ... It was rather exciting here last night – huge cheering crowds of wild people. I drove about in them ... and I wished you were there because I thought it would amuse you. The afternoon was still more exciting when *I* with my own hands sent off the ultimatum to Germany. I will tell you about it when you come back. Come soon.[87]

John began to record the war as it unfolded. Before August was over the first casualties had returned to London and became the subject of a painting entitled 'The First Wounded in London Hospital'. Despite his pacifist stance, John was determined to go to the front and joined the Artists Rifles, a group of sculptors, painters, hairdressers and musicians who formed their own battalion.

His enthusiasm notwithstanding, Lavery was fifty-eight years old and unable to complete the intensive training, although at the start he believed himself 'equal to, if not more fit than, some of the youths'. After the third march he had to seek medical attention. The doctor advised John to go back to his paint-pots, as he could do more for his country with his brush than with his rifle.

The status of women changed radically during the war as they entered the work-force to replace the enlisted men. The Laverys' maid Aïda ran away to work in a munitions factory, eventually marrying one of the managers. Like many others in domestic service, she did not return to her former employers in 1918.[88]

Lady Edith Londonderry founded the Women's Legion and orchestrated exclusive but informal 'Ark' parties, with guests each assigned the name of a beast or a bird.[89] Hazel was 'Hazel Hen', while John was 'John Dory'. Winston 'the Warlock' Churchill and Edward 'the Eagle' Carson.[90] The parties were conceived as a relaxing distraction from the war, but the 'Ark' became an important political meeting-place and survived into the 1930s. Hazel continued to hold her own dinner parties throughout the war years, feeding her guests nettles and champ when rations were enforced.[91]

Eileen's husband, John Dickinson, enlisted in 1915 and she was left alone with their baby daughter Diana, During his absence, Eileen fell in love with Colonel William Francis Forbes-Sempill. After the war Dickinson divorced Eileen, citing her adultery. In 1919 Eileen married Forbes-Sempill, and they had two daughters – Ann, born in 1920, and June, born in 1922.

The Laverys became friendly during the war years with Winston and Clementine Churchill, who lived nearby at 41 Cromwell Road. Winston had been removed from his position as First Lord of the Admiralty in May 1915, following the disastrous Dardanelles campaign. While at Hoe Farm in Surrey, he painted during his unwanted leisure time. One day he ran out of turpentine, and his wife Clemmie telephoned the Laverys to enquire about alternatives. Hazel responded by taking a taxi to Surrey to deliver the turpentine. Seeing Winston struggle with a small brush, she pushed a large one into his hand, dipped it in the paint and so began the first of several informal lessons she and John would give him over the years.[92] 'Women with achievements in their own right seldom crossed Churchill's path or impressed him when they did', writes John Colville. 'There were I exceptions. [Hazel] Lavery spent hours teaching him to paint, and he was grateful for that.'[93] Neither the Laverys nor the Churchills could have known that this friendship would one day prove to be of crucial importance in Anglo-Irish relations.

John still wanted to go to the front, if not as a foot-soldier then as a war artist. He approached the head of propaganda and was offered a commission. His preparations for departure were made in secret, as Hazel would have objected had she known of his plans: 'As it was, I could never be out of her sight a minute, so I decided that when everything was ready I would say nothing and wire when I was safely on board the transport.' William Orpen had written: 'Do come out, Lavery, I think you would like it – but it's so vast and overpowering it is difficult to grasp anything.'[94]

But on the night of 14 July 1915, John and Hazel were travelling home in a cab which crashed into a lamp-post in Park Lane, killing the driver. John escaped with only slight bruises but Hazel had head injuries and was taken to St George's Hospital. Although she had a severe concussion, she refused to stay and was nursed at home instead. Newspaper reports monitored Hazel's condition, expressing fears that the lacerations about her face would mar her famed beauty.[95]

Hazel's physical wounds soon healed but the accident was to have a more profound effect. The shock, coupled with tragedies of the previous decade, culminated in a nervous breakdown.[96] Hazel's doctor believed that John's departure to the front would have a negative effect on her fragile health.[97] Her fear that something would happen to her family became obsessive, and John was only able to leave her side while she slept. When she was well enough to travel, John took her to Brighton to recuperate. From there he wrote to Eileen:

Hazel is not so well as yesterday. She gets so nervous that I never know what to do. You have no idea how sensitive she has become. I used to flatter myself that I was as tactful as most people. I now feel as delicate as a bull in a china shop. The progress is very slow and disappointing. Yesterday I thought she would be better in a few days. Today, I feel it will take weeks.[98]

John celebrated his wife's recovery with a full-length portrait entitled 'Hazel in Black and Gold' (*see detail, cover*). It depicts Hazel in a black and gold dress, standing sideways, left hand resting on her hip, left foot advanced and turning towards the viewer. Her hat, touched with red, reflecting the red of her lips and her heels, caused one commentator to call it 'The Crimson Heels'." At the private viewing at the Royal Academy, Hazel ensured she would be noticed by the press by wearing a dramatic black satin cloak and a small hat with sweeping feathers.[100]

Hazel now took on an active role as a fund-raiser for the war effort, although she had helped organize the American Peace Ball in June 1914. By 1916 she was arranging matinées and luncheons where society women took the part of performers, ushers, and ticket- and programme-sellers.[101] *Tableaux vivants* were another popular form of fund-raising, and Hazel repeated her Chicago performance as Romney's 'Lady Hamilton' to great acclaim in London. Before one performance Hazel made up Cynthia Asquith, whose diary entry read, 'My tender make-up was soon cancelled and Mrs Lavery made me into a real deader – corpse-white, with eyebrows done with red pencil, so close they were just gashes.'[102] Hazel took her roles seriously; she would study the selected portrait and adopt the pose with the ease of an accomplished model.[103] She posed as the Madonna in a *tableau* performed at Mrs Leeds' in Grosvenor Square, based on Bouguereau's painting 'La Vierge Consolatrice'. Hazel sat with her hands in prayer, while across her knees lay Violet de Trafford as the 'fallen woman', a role declined by Lady Nancy Cunard, Emerald's daughter, and Lady Diana Manners.[104] One critic wrote, 'it really was one of the most perfect *tableaux* I have ever seen, so restrained and so true to the spirit of the picture'.[105] But Hazel's pious expression masked a feeling of impatience; she later admitted that Violet was a rather heavy girl.[106]

During the war Hazel joined a private theatrical group, The Plough, based in Hoppe's house. Their aim was to produce plays that were 'new and original in conception which had not previously been performed in England'. Members included Alvin Langdon Coburn, Clifford and Arnold Bax, Jacob Epstein, Glyn Philpot, Charles Rennie Mackintosh and George Sheringham. Between 1917 and 1919 they produced several plays, including Clifford Bax's *The Sneezing Charm*, with music by Gustav Holst, but despite ambitions to make a film, the group disbanded.[107]

The deprivation of the war did not prevent the Laverys from travelling abroad. In 1917 they went to the Duke of Westminster's hunting lodge at Mimizan, sixty miles from Bordeaux.* They were unprepared for the devastation of France. Whereas in London business continued as usual despite food shortages and disturbances, life in Paris had changed profoundly: 'Dirty streets,

---

* The Duke dated this visit as late 1915 but the photographs in the Lady Lavery Collection are dated March 1917; it is possible that they visited twice

shutters up, miserable people ... everyone looked sad.' All of the Laverys' Parisian haunts were deserted, and Hazel's and Alice's bright dresses were out of place. John asked his friend Jacques Emile Blanche about the Salon and was told, 'Ah, you English do not know what we French are going through. It is hell. There is no Salon. No one paints.'[108]

As a war artist on the home front John visited military camps in the London area, and was one of the first to work from an airship.[109] In 1916 the Royal Navy commissioned him to record activities at the naval bases. Even at home, he never missed an opportunity to capture history: during London's second aerial bomb raid on 7 July 1917, John painted Hazel observing the Zeppelins from the studio window.[110] The picturesque composition belies the terror Hazel felt while posing. Seen from the immense studio window, Lavery's Zeppelins resemble birds more than the massive airships of an enemy power.

In January 1918 Lavery was included in the Honours List and knighted for his work as a war artist. The American Ambassador Walter Hines Page congratulated him: 'Fighting men, I am sure deservedly, now hold the centre of the stage; and it is for that reason the more gratifying that work like yours is not forgotten in the bestowal of honours.'[111]

Orpen, who was also knighted, sent a note with a cheeky drawing of himself kneeling in homage to John, with his pyjama bottoms down around his ankles (*see plate*):

Somewhere in France – New Year's Day
Let not a moment be lost my dear Sir John in writing you my congratulations also to her Ladyship, Queen of Beauty. It was with great joy I read my Paris *Daily Mail* this morning. I immediately arose and did due homage to you on the cold floor. My best wishes to you and all you love for 1918.
Yours ever Orpen
(I am sorry my pyjamas fell down.)[112]

Lady Lavery was naturally delighted with their titles and often referred to her husband in a pretty, mock-prim way as 'Sir

John'.[113] There was, however, one drawback: an unfortunate similarity between her new name and 'ladies' lavatory'. At one function the master of ceremonies misheard her name and proceeded to give the appropriate directions.[114]

One of John's final war assignments was to portray the dictating of terms between Admirals B catty and Meurer on the *Queen Elizabeth* in November 1918, in a painting entitled 'The End'. John was disguised in a post-captain's discarded uniform, hiding his palette and paints behind flowers on a side-table. Despite such efforts, when he later viewed Orpen's war paintings in the Agnew Gallery, he felt his own work 'totally uninspired and dull as dishwater' by comparison. 'Instead of the grim harshness and horror of the scenes I had given charming colour versions, as if painting a bank holiday on Hampstead Heath.'[115]

At the end of the war, Hazel helped organize the Victory Ball at the Albert Hall and Lavery depicted a euphoric crowd in Grosvenor Square on Victory Day. War losses had marked everyone's lives. The Laverys had lost their close friends Lord Basil Blackwood and Lord Alexander Thynne. Hazel preserved their photographs, and Blackwood's richly decorated letters, in her scrapbooks.

VI

'a simple Irish girl'
[1916-21]

HAZEL HAD A 'dreamy romantic view' of Ireland, the ancestral home of her Martyn forefathers. John felt that her Ireland was as 'unreal as a mirage in the desert', conjured from the pages of literature – 'the Ireland of Yeats, James Stephens, AE, Lennox Robinson, Synge and the rest'. In London Hazel discovered that it was 'positively chic' to be Irish.[1] She deplored 'that awful thing an Irish-American', referring to herself as 'a simple Irish girl' and even cultivating an Irish accent.[2] She also began to celebrate her birthday on the 17th of March, St Patrick's Day, rather than the 14th. Her voice was described as 'low and attractive without a trace of an American accent but a whisper of an Irish one'.[3] She proudly proclaimed herself a Martyn from Galway to the Irish dramatist Edward Martyn, insisting they were cousins, which he denied, saying there were never any beautiful women in his family.[4] Amidst this posturing it was easy to forget that John – though he had made his name in Glasgow and London – was an Irish Catholic. The Laverys' first recorded visit to Ireland together was to Killarney House, the residence of Lord and Lady Kenmare, in 1913. They were enchanted, and returned the following year for a motoring tour that had to be curtailed when Britain entered the First World War.

At the time of the Laverys' second visit, the passage of the Home Rule Bill was imminent. The Laverys' political ideas at. this time are undocumented but their support for Home Rule may have originated through the influence of their friend T.P. O'Connor, the Irish Parliamentary Party member for Liverpool. The majority of the Irish people welcomed Home Rule legisiation, though a sizeable minority wished to remain in the Union. In Ulster, Edward Carson rallied the Unionists to resist Home Rule, by force if necessary, forming the Ulster Volunteer Force (UVF). Andrew Bonar Law, the British Conservative leader, pledged unconditional commitment to the Unionist cause and made veiled references to physical resistance. In response to the formation of the UVF, Eoin MacNeill, a university lecturer and Gaelic revivalist, called for a counter-resistance movement in the South, and the Irish Volunteers were formed. The outbreak of the First World War came almost as a relief to Prime Minister Asquith and his Liberal government, allowing them to shelve the troublesome Home Rule Bill until the end of the war. The Laverys would have been familiar with Asquith's Irish difficulties. In his company John was known to read aloud from the nationalist *Freeman's Journal* and Asquith would teasingly call Hazel the 'Queen of Ireland'.[5]

In 1916 John invited the Unionist leader Carson and the' Nationalist leader John Redmond to sit for him – on condition that they allow their portraits to be hung side by side in a Dublin gallery. Hazel believed her idea of an 'Irish Collection' of paintings could help reconcile the opposing sides.[6]

While John was busy painting Irish political figures, a group of advanced nationalists who had repudiated Redmond's support for Britain in the war were engaged in very different plans. This 'minority within a minority, within a minority'* was committed to

---

* A reference to the numerous sub-divisions that existed within the nationalist ranks – the National Volunteers, the Irish Republican Brotherhood and the secret Military Council that orchestrated the Easter Rising. This council was made up of men who later signed the Proclamation of the Irish Republic.

an uprising. They had obtained assistance from Germany but were thwarted when arms being smuggled in by Sir Roger Casement were intercepted by a British patrol boat off the Kerry coast.

Nevertheless, the uprising went ahead on Easter Monday, 24 April 1916, and the Republic was proclaimed. There were only a few hundred insurrectionists because of a countermanding order from MacNeill, the commander-in-chief of the anti-Redmondite Volunteers, and the action was largely confined to Dublin where key buildings in the centre of the city were occupied. The small Irish force held out for six days. The extensive damage to Dublin's city centre, and the fact that large numbers of Irishmen were fighting in British battalions on the western front, caused many Dubliners to echo the outrage of the British administration, and to ridicule the insurgents as they surrendered. Irish public opinion began to shift, however, when the British arrested large numbers of civilians, many of whom were not involved in the Rising, and shipped them to internment camps. When the leaders were subsequently executed, they were viewed as martyrs.

Within three weeks of the executions, John had pledged his support for the interned, offering to paint a canvas for a sale (held by the National Aid Society in the Mansion House, Dublin) to help their families.[7] In July he became further involved when he accepted a commission by Mr Justice Darling to record passing of a death sentence. One of the prosecutors. Lord Birkenhead (F.E. Smith), said John's picture (*see plate*) 'was in the worst possible taste'.[8] The trial was that of Roger Casement, a former member of the British consular service. He was regarded as a traitor and his conviction was a foregone conclusion. The *Weekly Dispatch* reported:

Much astonishment has been caused in artistic circles by the statement, *so far un-contradicted*, that Mr John Lavery is engaged in painting the final scene in the Casement trial. ... Mr Lavery ought not to paint his picture without knowing the contents of the two diaries* found on Casement. ... From all of which it follows that

---

* The so-called Black Diaries attested to Casement's homosexuality. They were circulated to various influential people to counteract sympathy for Casement.

the forthcoming picture is sure to attract immense attention,, but scarcely the kind of notice that so popular an artist is seeking.[9]

In the Central Criminal Court in London, John sat in the jury-box and tried to keep his paintbox hidden. Casement wrote' to his cousin Gertrude Parry asking:

Who was the painter in the jury-box painting a picture of the court? I should think that he came dangerously near 'aiding and comforting' if not indeed 'compassing' from the way he eyed Mr Justice Darling delivering judgement Surely it is treason to take a Judge's head off on the Bench![10]

Hazel also attended the trial, with the former commander-m-chief of the British army, Charles Beresford, and John painted her seated in the gallery. Casement noticed her:

Who was the lady who sat near the painter in the jury-box? She was there yesterday too – to-day she came in late – I thought I knew her face. It was very sad – and I keep on trying to remember. She had a wonderful face. I saw it all the time today. I wonder if she came in with Beresford. I hope not.[11]

Casement was convicted of High Treason and hanged on 3 August 1916. From subsequent sittings with the members of the courtroom, those in the dock and the gallery, Lavery made contacts with political activists.[12] Hazel herself was profoundly affected and became passionately concerned with Ireland's welfare.

The Lane paintings controversy later in 1916 was to bring the Laverys into closer contact with Irish affairs. Hugh Lane, an art dealer who had drowned on the *Lusitania* in May 1915, left his collection of paintings to the Irish people in an unwitnessed codicil to his will. Lane had wished to establish a modern art gallery in Ireland as early as 1903,[13] and provided a number of paintings to form the nucleus of the collection. He also loaned his French collection to Dublin on the condition that a permanent home be built for the works there. In 1908 a temporary gallery had been established at Clonmell House in Harcourt Street, with the help of the Dublin Corporation, but as a permanent gallery was the essential prerequisite of the donation, Lane removed the French paintings from Dublin, and in October 1913 bequeathed them to a collection of modern continental art in London.[14] In February 1914, when Lane was appointed Director of the National Gallery of Ireland, he once again circulated his plan for a modern art gallery in Dublin. Before travelling to America in 1915 – he was justifiably apprehensive about sailing in wartime – he wrote the codicil to his will returning the paintings to Dublin. After Lane's death his aunt, Lady Gregory, had the codicil published and gathered statements to testify to his change of mind. In addition, she organized a petition by thirty-two artists – including Lavery, who was represented in the collection – to the trustees of the National Gallery, London.

When in Dublin, Hazel and John managed to combine nationalist sympathies with an unapologetic involvement in the social round of a still-loyalist city, visiting the Viceregal Lodge in the Phoenix Park as guests of Ivor, Lord Wimborne, the Lord-Lieutenant, in September 1917. Hazel was impressed with the eighteenth-century elegance of the building, which reminded her of the White House in Washington D.C. John later wrote that 'from that moment there was no other Ireland for her'.[15]

❧❧

In December 1916 the remaining prisoners who had been held in internment camps since the Rising were released in a general amnesty. The camps had become the 'Universities of Revolution'. New activists grouped themselves under the collective banner of Sinn Féin, an advanced nationalist party that had been founded in 1905 by Arthur Griffith. Sinn Féin elected as its new leader Eamon de Valera, one of the 1916 leaders,[16] and aimed to establish an alternative Republican parliament in Dublin. The party won a number of seats in by-elections in 1917; and in the general election of November 1918, aided by a successful anti-conscription platform, Sinn Féin swept to victory over their Irish Parliamentary Party rivals. On 21 January 1919 Sinn Féin's alternative Irish parliament, Dáil Éireann, assembled for the first time.

On the same day, a group of Volunteers killed two policemen at Soloheadbeg, Co. Tipperary, and what came to be known as the Irish War of Independence had begun.

The Laverys, unaware of how much this war and its aftermath would affect their lives, took advantage of the end of the First World War and resumed their travels, departing in February 1919 for North Tunis to stay with Baron Rudolph and Baroness (Baba) d'Erlanger in Sidi-bou-Said. The next year, with Alice, they returned to Morocco and toured the interior with Mary Auras and Nora Kerr Clarke, a sister of the British Consul. They travelled in two tin lizzies (Model T Fords), with drivers who doubled as cooks. Sir Mennebhi lent them his two palaces at Fez and Marrakech, where they were attended by slaves and visited a harem. Over the following weeks they travelled to Rabat and Casablanca before returning to Tangier, where they stayed until May 1920.[17]

During their time in Morocco the fighting in Ireland had grown increasingly fierce. The Volunteers, now known as the Irish Republican Army, had adopted guerrilla tactics. The flying columns, as their ambushing units were called, aimed to intimidate the police force and undermine the administration. Britain responded by drafting in extra manpower to support the police: a rank-and-file detachment called the Black and Tans because of their makeshift uniforms, and an officer force known as the Auxiliaries. These units retaliated against those supporting the flying columns by burning houses and creameries and shooting civilians. Moderate elements in England, who had supported Irish Home Rule by parliamentary methods, were disenchanted by the events unfolding in Ireland. Hazel was horrified by the violence and became an outspoken opponent of British policy.

Asquith had been replaced by David Lloyd George in 1916 as leader of an uneasy coalition of Liberals and Conservatives. & Shortly after the Laverys' return from Morocco, Hazel secured an invitation to meet the new Prime Minister at the home of the well-known political host Sir Philip Sassoon. Charmed by the

'Welsh Wizard', she felt he would be sympathetic to Ireland, and was therefore dismayed to read in *The Times* that 'some thousand Black and Tans had landed and were driving all before them ...'.[18] Thereafter her suspicions of Lloyd George outweighed any feelings of friendship.

By 1920 Irish politics had become Hazel's principal interest. One evening she argued with Charley Londonderry, who as a wealthy Unionist landowner with an estate in Co. Down was acutely aware of the importance of Irish economic links with Britain. Hazel's views enraged him and he retorted, 'You've been listening to that [Shane] Leslie', grabbing her arm and bruising it. Leslie challenged Londonderry to a duel, which Hazel promptly forbade, saying that it would do no good for Ireland.[19] Leslie recalled, 'I can see her amusement tearing up the challenge. How excited London would have been if we had met with rapiers after dark in Grosvenor Sq.![20]

Sinn Féin's popular support was confirmed by local elections in 1920. By this time, the organization had established law courts and departments of Defence, Trade and Commerce, Agriculture, Home Affairs, Local Government, Labour, and Propaganda. Revenue came from interest-bearing bonds, and de Valera raised $6,000,000 in America. A powerful spy network, founded and directed by Michael Collins, infiltrated the British administration. Collins had risen to prominence while interned at Frongoch and was now Minister for Finance, President of the Irish Republican Brotherhood and Director of Intelligence.

The Laverys visited Ireland in October 1920, while the War of Independence was at its height. John had come to paint the portraits of Catholic and Protestant religious leaders. Hazel deemed the Carson and Redmond portraits of 1916 'a good beginning' for John's Irish Collection and was anxious for him to continue.[21] Keen to make friends on both sides, the Laverys lunched with the Unionist Lord Mayor of Belfast, attended a Royal reception 'with leading lights of the Orange World' and travelled on to Armagh where they both completed portraits of Cardinal

Logue.[22] They also visited Mount Stewart for sittings with the Protestant Archbishop. An anonymous letter was sent to John warning that 'parasites' like him should be exterminated but Hazel dismissed the threat with: 'Never mind, carry on,'[23]

From Mount Stewart a letter signed by John and Hazel was sent to Winston Churchill, then Minister of War. Its tone suggests that it was written by John at Hazel's prompting.

> You asked me the other day what I thought of my country's state, and I had not the courage to tell you. But if one artist may speak to another I will give you my beliefs. The Prime Minister has said that he is prepared for a million casualties and a five years' war. I believe that ten million and a fifty years' war would not bring about the result he desires. I believe that Ireland will never be governed by Westminster, the Vatican, or Ulster without continuous bloodshed. I also believe that the removal of the 'Castle' and all its works, leaving Irishmen to settle their own affairs, is the only solution left. I am convinced with the knowledge I possess of my countrymen that such a situation would make her one of your staunchest allies instead of an avowed enemy for all time. Love is stronger than hate.[24]

After their appointments in the north, Hazel and John toured the country, visiting Larne, Bundoran, Westport, Ballina, Athlone and Maynooth.[25] In Connemara Hazel believed that she had found the Martyn ancestral homestead. John wrote to his daughter Eileen: 'Hazel wants to buy the old farm and set up in Ireland. It looks as if in no time the farm and the rest of Ireland are going to be wiped out. Tangier may be the one peaceful spot.'[26]

Hazel had hoped to meet Michael Collins, the thirty-year-old Cork Republican whose exploits and evasion of arrest had attracted so much press attention.[27] As soon as they returned to London Hazel wished to go back to locate Collins for a portrait, despite Winston Churchill's friendly warning that this might put the artist in jeopardy: 'Be careful, my dear John, our men are not all good shots.'[28]

John continued to document events in Irish politics. 'Southwark Cathedral, London' depicts the Requiem Mass held in October 1920 in London for Terence MacSwiney, Lord

Mayor of Cork, who had died on hunger-strike in Brixton Prison after seventy-four days protesting his status as a prisoner of war. Thousands attended the memorial service, which generated strong sympathy for Irish independence.

It was during this period that Hazel converted to Catholicism. Hazel's family background had been strongly Episcopalian and one of the few possessions she kept from her life in America, apart from family photographs, was her Episcopalian Bible from Miss Masters.[29] In 1914, at the age of ten, Alice had surprised the family by announcing her decision to become a Catholic. Hazel had been amused by her decision but John, although not a devout Catholic, supported her. Alice thenceforth received religious instruction and was sent to the Assumption Convent in Kensington Square. When Alice heard of her mother's decision to convert she asked: 'Why do you want to become a Catholic? You are such a bad Protestant.'[30] Alice did not record her mother's reply.

Father Joseph Leonard, a Vincentian based at St Mary's training college at Strawberry Hill in Twickenham, was Hazel's confidant and spiritual advisor during the 1920s and was most likely her religious instructor during her conversion. When in the 1950s Lady Audrey Morris wanted to interview Father Leonard for her proposed biography of Hazel he refused to talk to her, and no material relating to Hazel's conversion has been preserved. Throughout her life Hazel searched for an identity; perhaps her conversion, like that of Sligo aristocrat turned Irish revolutionary Countess Constance Markievicz, was linked to an increasing desire to define that identity in Irish terms.[31]

By December 1920 the Government of Ireland Act had passed into law. Adapted from the pre-war Home Rule Bill, it provided for two parliaments in Ireland – one in Belfast and one in Dublin. Nationalists promptly boycotted the workings of the British administration in Dublin. Northern Ireland, governed by the King, Senate and House of Commons, came into existence on 22 June 1921. The speech of King George V at the inauguration of the Northern parliament in Stormont was conciliatory, formally opening the way for negotiations to end the war. Lloyd George invited a delegation from the Dáil to London to discuss plans for a settlement, and a truce was agreed on 11 July 1921.

The Laverys now saw an opportunity to bring the leaders together by offering the use of their home as 'neutral ground where both sides might meet'.[32] Whereas the Irish Parliamentary Party had been welcomed in London society. Irishmen who had won the right to negotiate independence by means of guerrilla warfare were shunned. Hazel's unconventionality and freedom from political allegiances made her home an ideal location to entertain the visiting Irish. She persuaded John to extend an invitation to the Irish delegates to have their portraits painted at Cromwell Place. The day after the truce, Eamon de Valera, Arthur Griffith, Robert Barton, Austin Stack and Erskine Childers arrived in London; the Laverys cancelled all their summer plans.[33] The Irish nationalists initially questioned Hazel's true sympathies. However, her furious reaction to rumours that she was a British spy persuaded Michael Collins – in Ireland monitoring intelligence reports – that she was an ally.[34] As Oliver St John Gogarty, surgeon and poet, wrote subsequently:

Anyone from outside who becomes interested in Irish affairs is apt to find that interest more an object of suspicion than of gratitude. For a while Lady Lavery's association with the cause of Ireland was unwelcome until her unshakeable sincerity, unswerving devotion and solid help during the negotiations that followed, gained the confidence and the gratitude even of Arthur Griffith ... As a medium of this kind she was invaluable; and the fact that this role did not add to her social popularity did much to remove any lingering doubts as to her unselfishness and sincerity.[35]

De Valera met Lloyd George four times in July but the two made little progress towards a permanent settlement of Ireland's political status.[36] De Valera, committed to the ideal of a Republic, refused to accept Dominion status involving allegiance to the Crown. The negotiations left little time for de Valera's portrait and in later years all John could remember of the visit was de Valera's statement 'to the effect that the mass of the people were like sheep in that they run after each other'.[37] On 16 July Shane Leslie described in his diary how, when Hazel entertained at home that day, the delegates were 'nervous and reticent as though gunmen were watching them'.[38] By the end of the talks, John had managed to complete only preliminary studies of de Valera and Griffith. The delegation returned to Dublin with the proposals, but received no support from the Dáil or Cabinet. The terms were officially rejected on 10 August.

The stalemate ended on 30 September when de Valera accepted an invitation for a new delegation to visit London to determine 'how the association of Ireland with the Community of Nations known as the British Empire may best be reconciled with Irish national aspirations'.[39] De Valera opted to remain in Ireland as the 'symbol of the Republic', and Griffith was chosen to head the delegation. Michael Collins, much against his will, was included in this second delegation. He considered himself a soldier, not a politician, and was reluctant to reveal his identity lest the war resumed. Austin Stack and Cathal Brugha refused to join the delegation, so even before the negotiators left for London, an intransigent Republican faction in opposition to the negotiations was forming.

Griffith, Collins, Childers, Barton, Eamon Duggan and George Gavan Duffy arrived in London between 8 and 9 October to feelings of animosity even among the Irish community in the city. The words 'Collins the Murderer' were whitewashed on the footpath outside 22 Hans Place, the house where the delegates stayed.[40] Staff were brought over from Ireland. Collins chose to live separately at 15 Cadogan Gardens, protected by 'The Squad', his bodyguards used for special missions during the War of Independence.

On 11 October, the Irish political representatives met the British delegation, consisting of Lloyd George, Austen Chamberlain, Lord Birkenhead, Winston Churchill, Sir Worthington Evans, Sir Gordon Hewart and Sir Hamar Greenwood. Lloyd George, who had been the principal British delegate at the Paris

Peace Conference of 1918, led the team. On the first day of the conference there was awkwardness even over how to deal with official handshakes. Lloyd George dispensed with this formality altogether; he alone shook the hands of the delegates as they came into the conference room and waved them to their seats.

Lavery believed a painting documenting the signing of the Treaty might be as important to posterity as his Casement study.[41] This proved difficult to arrange, so he decided instead to do individual studies of the delegates. He wrote requesting three hours from each of his prospective sitters: 'I expect every minute of your time is taken up, but merely telephone the day before and I shall be at the disposition of the sitter.'[42] Of all the delegates, the charismatic Collins seems to have attracted the most interest. Augustus John had also wanted to paint Collins' portrait,[43] and Orpen, according to Hazel, was dreadfully jealous, openly abusing John for siding with murderers and asking why a 'Scotchman' dared to interfere in Irish affairs.[44] Lavery received several anonymous threatening letters, one of which claimed that his painting of 'the murderer' Collins would no doubt be 'hung at No. 10 Downing Street by his friend and fellow Republican Lloyd George'.[45]

The day before the conference opened. Hazel brought Shane Leslie (upon whose less-than-authoritative political views she still largely relied) to Sir Philip Sassoon's in Park Lane. There Leslie met Lloyd George, 'who listened to me for half an hour on the Irish Conference pending. The points he talked of were Michael Collins; a possible Tory revolt ... what was real Irish Independence? all vital queries ...'.[46]

Like other hostesses in London, Hazel wished to entertain Collins; unlike most others, however, she had a genuine interest in Irish politics. Shortly after Collins' arrival Hazel managed to discover his older sister Hannie's* address and wrote to him there but received no reply. When he came to Cromwell Place for his portrait sitting on 16 November, he arrived unannounced.[47] This

---

* Hannie Collins had lived in London for many years. Michael lived with

characteristic gesture appealed to Hazel's sense of drama. John recalled:

Hazel got in touch with Collins's sister, and one morning he walked into my studio, a tall young Hercules with a pasty face, sparkling eyes, and a fascinating smile. I helped him off with a heavy overcoat to which he clung, excusing himself by saying casually, 'There is a gun in the pocket.'[48]

There is no record of Hazel's first impressions, though John remembered Collins's alertness and desire to sit facing the door. That night Collins wrote to Kitty Kiernan** – to whom he had become engaged the day before he left for London – in Granard, Co. Longford: 'By the way I sat today for my portrait[49] – my interesting life! Absolute torture as I was expected to keep still, and this, as you know, is a thing I cannot do. ... Sir John Lavery is painting me. Will probably get photograph of the painting, so I'll send you one.'[50] Collins did not mention the painter's wife.

During the conference John painted portraits of Collins, Duffy, Barton and Duggan from the Irish team; he later painted Lloyd George, Birkenhead and Chamberlain of the British delegation (*see plates*). Hazel and John developed a rapport with the Irish delegates, who were dining frequently at Cromwell Place by mid-November. Hazel also entertained influential British friends including Eddie Marsh, Churchill's private secretary. Churchill was initially annoyed to see his aide mixing socially at Hazel's table with avowed enemies of the Crown. In his memoirs Marsh wrote that Churchill, who espoused a policy of '"not shaking hands with murder", was cross with me at first for being thus beguiled; but in daily contact he came to recognize Collins's quality'.[51]

---

her in West Kensington after emigrating from west Cork as a teenager. They both worked for the post office, though Michael later moved to a stockbrokers' firm, the Board of Trade, and the Guaranty Trust Company (Coogan, *Michael Collins*, pp. 15-17).

** Kiernan had been the sweetheart of Collins's close friend Harry Boland, who intended to marry her, but it was Collins who eventually won her affection. They met in 1919 but the romance began in earnest in mid-summer 1921.

The informality at the Laverys' was crucial for Collins, whose language was 'more suited to the docks than the drawing-room'.[52] According to his biographer Frank O'Connor,

Collins did not like the London trip. It involved a certain number of social contacts, and four years of secret life had been bad preparation for that. He had always been shy and rather self-conscious, hating formalities. ... His companions noticed that he tried to dodge functions, and when it was necessary for him to attend any he was ill at ease.[53]

O'Connor may have overstated the case. Hazel was adept at making people from different backgrounds feel comfortable, mixing literary figures with those in politics. Collins befriended the writer J.M. Barrie – who had links with the Bloomsbury group – at Cromwell Place, and John was surprised to discover they spent 'odd moments' of leisure together at the British Museum, Brompton Oratory and Cromwell Place.[54] According to Hazel, Barrie was '*such* a help' and defended them to 'people like the Londonderrys and other mutual friends'.[55] Barrie, the author *of Peter Pan*, admired Collins's 'boyishness' and intelligence.

An unlikely friendship also developed between Collins and the Unionist Lord Birkenhead, without which Chamberlain believed agreement with the Irish would never have been reached.[56] But relations were not always harmonious. At a luncheon during the Treaty negotiations, Hazel's small Peke began to paw at Birkenhead. Hazel apologized for the dog's show of affection, whereupon Birkenhead replied mischievously, 'Oh, I am sorry. I thought you were making advances.' Collins rose to his feet and said, 'D'ye mean to insult her?' When Hazel remarked that Birkenhead was only joking, he replied, 'I don't understand such jokes.'[57]

In 1921 Hazel was forty-one – although claiming to be thirty-six – and still very attractive. She tinted her hair red-purple and used more make-up. One admirer quipped that she was 'youthful to a sinister degree'.[58] Collins and Hazel were immediately attracted to each other and throughout the negotiations they were close companions. It was said they would meet each morning for eight o'clock Mass in Brompton Oratory, a few minutes' walk from both Cromwell Place and Cadogan Gardens.[59]

Collins was a welcome guest at the Laverys' and would often stay late into the night reading books from their shelves.[60] Hazel wrote to him: 'I found this portion of a wonderful book in an old shop. I am trying hard to get an intact copy to send you as you would delight in it I know, and be interested in all the facts about the French Revolution.'[61] Collins gave her a Kerry Blue, and she named the dog Mick.* Shane Leslie alleged that the dog was intended to frighten away everyone except Collins.[62]

The nature of Hazel's relationship with Collins cannot be established with certainty, as Hazel's own comments on such matters are notoriously unreliable and all other existing 'evidence' is hearsay. In Hazel's social world, where extra-marital affairs were commonplace, it was believed that Hazel and Collins were lovers. Lady Diana Cooper said, 'I think they, Michael Collins and Hazel, did have a love affair but I am talking out of guesswork. I suppose the story has grown ... but there was an excitement at the time.'[63] Anita Leslie was not convinced: 'They were soul mates rather than bed mates.'[64] John, aware of Hazel's flirtatious nature, accepted their intimacy and welcomed Collins to his house. For the first time Hazel seemed to view her life as having purpose,[65] and her happiness was John's primary concern.

⚓

By November, after a month of Anglo-Irish negotiations, progress was being made. The talks had opened with seven plenary sessions, then divided into sub-conferences for direct negotiations with Griffith and Collins.[66] Lord Longford writes that the two 'had the same conception of an Ireland free from British occupation, British penetration and British laws; the same concern for practical construction',[67] which distanced them from Barton, Duffy and Duggan as the sub-conferences continued. The British remained

---

* This was a common nickname for Collins himself, but Hazel always called him Michael.

unwilling to consider Irish independence from the Empire, and de Valera was still adamantly against Dominion status. On 24 October he wrote to Griffith of the impossibility of subjecting the Irish people to the Crown. His concept – 'external association' – stipulated that Ireland should be a republic without allegiance to the Crown; that Irishmen should not be British subjects; and that the two countries should have reciprocal citizenship. De Valera warned: 'If war is the alternative we can only face it, and I think that the sooner the other side is made to recognize it, the better.'[68]

The Irish delegates were agreed that Ireland should be a republic, and that breakdown in the talks could only be forced over Ulster. The latter view was rooted in a belief that international opinion would not condone Britain's resumption of hostilities if Northern Unionism proved the sole barrier to an agreement. Lloyd George, who was as anxious as the Irish to avoid a permanent partition of Ireland, tried to persuade Sir James Craig, the new Northern Prime Minister, to come to London for negotiations, and told the Irish representatives that he was prepared to resign if Unionists rejected an all-Ireland parliament. He was anxious to have assurance from the Irish delegates that they would not oppose him over Ulster when the Unionist Party gathered in Liverpool on 17 November.

On 8 November, Tom Jones, Lloyd George's Welsh secretary, met Griffith and Collins privately to inform them that Craig had rejected an all-Ireland parliament. Lloyd George was preparing to meet the Northern Parliament to urge their acceptance. If they refused, he would resign and retire from public life. Jones reminded the Irish that if Lloyd George quit they would be faced with the threat of Bonar Law, the militaristic Conservative leader, becoming Prime Minister. Griffith agreed to the creation of a Boundary Commission as a tactical measure to prevent Lloyd George's resignation.

Divisions within the Irish side were now acute. Childers, Barton and Duffy repeatedly asserted that all the concessions were being made by the Irish delegates. Barton and Duffy, though unaware of how close Collins and Griffith had already come to accepting Dominion status, more than once considered resigning. After years as a covert military leader, Collins's associations with the Laverys and their set and his exposure to the British at the conference table now contributed to his growing conviction that independence would have to be attained gradually.[69]

Childers alone staunchly refused the Laverys' invitations, and wrote to his wife Molly in early November: 'I have a reputation for overwork because I don't go junketing, theatre-going etc. Couldn't stand it and work would suffer anyway if I did ... I hate the very idea of merry making in this city at this time there is too much of it, entre nous.'[70] There are no references to the Laverys in his letters, but Childers noted in his diary, 'Sir J. Lavery asked to do my portrait. Refused.'[71]

On 1 December the British handed over their final proposals, which included an assurance that Ireland's Dominion status would be similar to Canada's and concessions over the use of the designation 'Irish Free State' and the oath of allegiance. The Irish delegation travelled that weekend to Dublin to meet the Cabinet.* At the meeting Griffith and Duggan stated that they believed this to be the final offer from the British. Barton and Duffy disagreed. Stack later recalled that Collins 'did not speak strongly in favour of the document at all'.[72] The Cabinet decided that if it was not amended they would reject it and prepare to meet the consequences. Alternatively, they could bring the Treaty before the Dáil and if necessary submit it to the people.

The delegates returned to London with the Irish Cabinet's amendments. Griffith, Collins and Duggan refused to present the changed document to the British, assigning Barton and Duffy to the task. Duggan later recounted: 'We put up the proposals that the Cabinet said we should put up. They were turned down, and had been, two or three times previously.'[73] Although

---

* The seven members of the Cabinet were de Valera, Griffith, Brugha, Stack, Collins, Barton and W.T. Cosgrave. Kevin O'Higgins, Assistant Minister for Local Government, was accustomed to attending Cabinet meetings, though he did not vote.

Griffith disapproved of the amendments, he still argued in favour of them, determined that when the break came it would not be over allegiance to the Crown.

Duffy, however, undermined negotiations when he stated: 'We should be as closely associated with you in all large matters as the Dominions, and in the matter of Defence still more so; but our difficulty is coming into the Empire.'[74] Talks now broke down, but Lloyd George, aware of Griffith's willingness to compromise, moved to win Collins. On the night of Sunday 4 December, Jones urged Griffith to arrange for Collins to meet Lloyd George alone.[75]

The Laverys' friends believed Hazel played a central diplomatic role during the Treaty negotiations, particularly as an influence on Collins. A frequent guest of the Laverys', Daisy, Countess of Pingall, wrote later (albeit naively) that 'it might be said truly that the Irish Treaty was framed and almost signed at 5 Cromwell Place.'[76] In his autobiography John claimed that Hazel persuaded Collins to accept the Treaty at this critical juncture, and that it was generally felt that 'had it not been for Hazel there would have been no Treaty – certainly not at the time it was signed'.[77] On that fateful evening – probably 4 December – Collins visited the Laverys at Cromwell Place. John recalled:

[Hazel] had given up Erskine Childers as impossible to move, but she had overcome Arthur Griffith's objections. Michael Collins stood firm to the last minute. He seemed to have lost his temper. Even I, whose head was never really out of the paint-pot, could see that he who loses his temper in argument is lost, and told him so, but I failed to convince him. Eventually., after hours of persuasion. Hazel prevailed. She took him to Downing Street in her car that last evening, and he gave in.[78]

John's autobiography, written almost twenty years after the event, is obviously not the most reliable of sources, particularly in his naive estimation of Hazel's powers of persuasion over Griffith. Even so, Hazel clearly had an influence on Collins. That December evening, presumably informed by Eddie Marsh and others that this was the final British offer. Hazel reportedly counselled Collins, 'Take what you can get now and get the rest later,'[79] According to Clemmie Churchill, it was widely known that Hazel, dressed in her favourite opera cloak, brought Collins to Downing Street.[80] Lloyd George convinced Collins that the Boundary Commission would preserve the 'essential unity' of Ireland, using Collins's own theory that economic considerations would force the North to join the South.[81]

When the delegates convened at 10 Downing Street on 5 December, Lloyd George opened discussion with reference to the North. Relying on Griffith's assurance that he would not break over Ulster, he asked Griffith if he conceded that the Boundary Commission would ultimately preserve essential unity. Griffith agreed to sign, though he refused to speak for the rest of the delegation. Lloyd George then produced two letters and held them up, one in either hand. He told the group:

I have to communicate with Sir James Craig tonight. Here are the alternative letters which I have prepared, one enclosing Articles of Agreement reached by His Majesty's Government and yourselves, and the other saying that Sinn Fein representatives refuse to come into the Empire. If I send this letter it is war, and war within three days. Which letter am I to send? Whichever letter you choose travels by special train to Holyhead, and by destroyer to Belfast. The train is waiting with steam up at Euston. Mr Shakespeare [the messenger] is ready. If he is to reach Sir James Craig in time we must know your answer by 10 p.m. tonight. You can have until then, but no longer, to decide whether you will give peace or war to your country.[82]

Lloyd George impressed upon the delegates their personal responsibility should war break out. They retired for a discussion at Hans Place in preparation for the decision at 10 p.m. Almost immediately, Collins announced his intention to sign, and Duggan joined Griffith and Collins. Barton, reminded by Duggan of the horrors of the recent fighting, yielded and Duffy finally gave his consent. As Childers wrote on 6 December: 'Everything changed at the last moment ... This placed the minority in a frightful position – a cruel position. Nevertheless B. [Barton] held out till the last moment. Then he weakened, overcome by M.C. I think.'[83]

At 2.20 a.m. on Tuesday 6 December the Treaty was signed. Later that day Collins went to the Laverys'[84] where he recounted the night's events. He told of his reply to Birkenhead's remark that he, Birkenhead, was signing his political death warrant: 'I may have signed my actual death warrant.'[85] The next day Collins again visited Cromwell Place, signing and dating Hazel's scrapbook. He left for Ireland that night.

VII

'guiding the splendid studs'
[1921-3]

WHILE THE TREATY was being debated in Dublin, Hazel began a busy social round, which she described to Michael Collins in her frequent letters. On 10 December 1921 she alluded to a Commons speech by Churchill on the Treaty: 'It was very long *but excellent...* and generally well received, excepting *of course* by the Tories who still rage, albeit more and more powerlessly.'[1] She lunched with the wife of the Lord-Lieutenant of Ireland and the Chamberlains and visited the House of Lords, hearing Birkenhead, the Lord Chancellor, respond 'with his usual devastating urbanity to the bitter but rather futile sarcasm of Carson'.[2]

Hazel also discussed with Churchill the shooting of six members of the Crown forces on 11 December, and reported to Collins:

[Winston] is much concerned over the two shootings ... and he asked if I would please write to you and say how difficult the incident has made matters here. The old Die Hards have taken a vigorous new lease of life on it. Of course he *knows you* are doing everything you possibly can, and *I* hate to write to you and add a further weight of anxiety to your many cares. Please, please forgive me.[3]

Anxious that the Treaty should be accepted, she continued: 'All our thoughts and prayers are with you Michael. I purchased a most expensive and gigantic candle on Sunday at early Mass and burnt it for your victory.'[4]

Shane Leslie, who saw the entire collection of the correspondence before most of it was destroyed, stated: 'Collins's own letters to Hazel were of a type – full of half educated half romantic stuff but ending up with vital messages to the English Cabinet which were shown to Winston, Londonderry and others.'[5] The only complete letters from Hazel to Collins that survive date from December 1921.*

When the Treaty was brought back to Dublin for debate and ratification, its terms caused a split in the Dail, the issues of the new state's constitutional status and the oath of allegiance to the King being central. The opposition were committed to the Republic, accusing the plenipotentiaries of failing to adhere to President Eamon de Valera's instructions. Those in favour feared that rejection would bring renewed hostilities. Collins asserted that the terms gave 'freedom, not the ultimate freedom that all nations desire and develop to, but the freedom to achieve it'.[6]

In the Dail on 7 January 1922, sixty-four voted in favour and fifty-seven against ratification. De Valera resigned on 9 January along with others opposing the Treaty. A provisional government – consisting of Collins, Arthur Griffith, W.T. Cosgrave, Kevin O'Higgins, Eamon Duggan, Joseph McGrath, Fionan Lynch and Patrick Hogan – was formed a week later. O'Higgins characterized them as 'simply eight young men in the City Hall standing amidst the ruins of one administration, with the foundations of another not yet laid, and with wild men screaming through the keyhole'.[7] Collins was elected as Chairman, responsible for upholding and implementing the Treaty. Griffith was appointed President of the Dáil, which was still

---

* Letters from Michael Collins to Hazel Lavery were destroyed by Hazel herself or by her daughter Alice. A number of them passed into the possession of Kitty Kiernan. Leon O'Broin, who published a book of the correspondence between Collins and Kiernan, thought that they might have been sent selectively to Kitty to offset rumours of a liaison between Collins and Hazel.

recognized by the anti-Treatyites but was now largely symbolic and unacknowledged by the British.

Opposition intensified early in 1922 as the and-Treatyites (also known as the Irregulars) were arming and preparing to use force. Collins assisted British ministers in implementing the Treaty, while unofficially sympathizing with the Republican ideals of his former colleagues.

On 23 January Hazel held a dinner party for Collins, Duggan and O'Higgins to introduce them to her English friends. Lady Juliet Duff later remarked that 'three nicer men she'd never met', particularly Collins, who was 'quite irresistible' and 'a real "play boy", with a tremendous twinkle and sudden quick impulsive gestures'. That day Collins had met Craig to discuss the implications of the Treaty and the lifting of the boycott of goods from Belfast, which had been imposed in 1920 in response to anti-Catholic rioting there. Lady Duff recalled:

It was a dramatic evening and they were all as pleased as punch at having agreed so far with Craig. They were *so* interesting about everything, no bitterness nor boasting nor crowing, just talking things over quietly and dispassionately.[8]

The Churchills were among the guests. Winston, as British Colonial Secretary, was a vital ally, though during Treaty negotiations he had been thought to be a typical imperialist, not a friend to Ireland.[9] During the critical months of 1922, as he oversaw the terms of the Treaty, Irish opinion of him was to change.

Throughout the spring and early summer, Collins and other ministers made numerous visits to London. Hazel's Irish scrapbook records numerous dinner parties at Cromwell Place for Irish and English political figures, including Collins.[10] Shane Leslie noted in his diary that 'the people who were not asked said with some jealousy that those who went were consorting with murderers!'[11] Hazel had long since overcome any fear of disapproval, and enjoyed the notoriety other guests.

Collins saw these trips to London as an escape from pressures in Ireland. 'The negotiations had opened a new world to him',

Frank O'Connor wrote in his biography of Collins. 'It had been the Childers, the Bartons, the Davies. Now it was Cope, Churchill, Birkenhead, the Laverys.'[12] Unlike Collins, Kevin O'Higgins felt ill at ease in such company and wrote to his new wife that the Laverys were 'fine folks', but that he could only take so much of 'boiled shirts and painted ladies' and wanted 'to goho-am!'[13]

Hazel also kept in contact with Charley Londonderry, now Minister for Education in the Northern Ireland government, who had refused to meet Collins during Treaty negotiations, claiming there was 'a very unhealthy curiosity to meet this celebrity'. He deemed Collins an assassin, and did not wish to socialize with someone who had been party to the murders of 'brother officers of my own and many friends who lived in Ireland'.[14] He did, however, agree to meet Collins in the conference chamber. The conference, held in Churchill's room at the Colonial Office on 30 March 1922, was called in response to sectarian violence that had erupted in Northern Ireland. Londonderry agreed to the reorganization of the police force in the North to provide equal protection for Catholics and Protestants. Churchill suggested a further meeting between the two the next day.[15] Londonderry later stated:

I can say at once that I spent three of the most delightful hours that I ever spent in *my* life and I formed a conclusion of the character of Michael Collins which was quite different from the one which I would have formed if I had only known him as I had read of him before this particular interview.

Hazel, who had few qualms about sharing her personal correspondence, gave Londonderry a letter she received from Collins after this encounter:

Forgive me. I bitterly regret my outburst about L[ondonderry]. You were very kind to arrange the meeting, and I am well aware that I was very miserably minded to listen to W[inston]. It is all very well to tell me as you do that he has no 'interest' in you. But how can you expect me to believe that, feeling as you know well how I feel? So you must forgive my bitterness, and try to imagine what it means to be a man like myself, entirely self-made, self-educated, without background and trying to cope with a man like Lord L., a man who has every advantage I lack. This is not self-disparagement, a mean quality that I think I do not possess; but I cannot help recognizing the fact that you and he speak the same language, an alien one to me, and he understands to perfection all the little superficial things that matter in your particular world – unimportant things maybe – but oh! my God, not to be underestimated with a woman like you. I know that instinctively. I feel savage and unhappy, and so I blame you for a situation for which I alone am to blame, but I contrast myself with him, my uncouthness with his distinction, my rough speech with his unconscious breeding and the worst of it is I *like* him and admire him, and feel that he is brave and honest... [16]*

Londonderry kept the original and wrote a copy in his own hand. The Lady L. to whom the letter was written was later mistaken for Londonderry's wife, although it was written on Cromwell Place notepaper and there is no evidence of a relationship between Collins and Edith Londonderry. Furthermore, Robin Londonderry, Charley's eldest son, was later to attest to a romance between his father and Hazel:

My father had an affair with her. He was having several others at the same time. Whether she dropped him for Mick Collins or he her for political reasons, I do not know. However, I found letters suggesting that they might resume where they left off. I do not think anything happened.[17]

Shane Leslie thought Collins had replaced both himself and Londonderry in Hazel's affections.[18] Though Leslie never had an affair with her, he wrote:

... nobody has changed my soul more than you. Some have presumed to say you have made love to it. But you have taught me to be a lover and you have given me the wonderful experience of intellectual love and I go out into the world as it were with another sense – a different soul and a spirit of aching fire ... I meant to ask John last night to forgive me on the day of Judgement for having loved you but I saw he understood.[19]

---

* This letter was written in pencil. One of Collins's biographers, Tim Pat Co-ogan, questions its authenticity, as it carries neither date nor signature and Collins disliked writing in pencil (Coogan, *Michael Collins*, pp. 291-2).

Hazel enjoyed Leslie's 'undoubted charm' although she was aware that it was artificial and that he exaggerated everything for effect. Collins found him maddening and could not understand 'what in heaven's name' she saw in him.[20] Of Lord Londonderry Leslie observed, 'She was taken deeply with him and that is why old John was jealous of Londonderry and not of the others. He had also the Belfast street boy's hate of the aristocrat.'[21] As this is the only account of John's response to his wife's many admirers, it would seem that he had adopted the role – common to the times – of complaisant husband.

Hazel never considered leaving John. In an interview she once stated: 'I do not believe in divorce. I am, of course, a Catholic, and Catholics cannot be divorced.'[22] She and John still loved each other and a contemporary of theirs wrote in retrospect: 'We always saw him in the aura (half humorous, half venerating, wholly devoted) which was cast around him by his wonderful wife.'[23] What is clear is that Hazel was not an easy person to live with and both John and Alice treated her like a spoilt child. Often they couldn't give her the attention she demanded. Hazel complained that John was the most silent man she had ever known, going 'about night and day with his head in a paint box',[24] and her admirers filled the void created by his preoccupations.

In these early months of 1922, Michael Collins was still very much in love with his fiancée Kitty Kiernan. In February he wrote: 'All of a sudden I am called away to London ... I wish you were coming to London with me tonight ...'.[25] He craved her companionship and they exchanged letters constantly. When Kitty was not as prompt with her replies, Michael wrote ruefully, 'more keen than you now'.[26] As the months passed, however, Collins became immersed in London politics. His trips were fraught and it was to Hazel he turned for support, rather than the politically naive Kitty. In April he wrote to Hazel: 'I know I shall never again meet anyone so beautiful, so gay, and so sad as you.'[27] At times their closeness was evident in public; the papers reported that Collins 'had driven with his sweetheart' when the Laverys took Collins to Downing Street on 27 May. He wrote to Kitty:

You ought to have seen some of the papers here yesterday – M. Collins in Downing St. with his sweetheart. I can have all sorts of lovely libel actions. The Laverys took me there in their car. Some of the correspondents recognized my friend but the story was too good! I must bring you back some of the papers to show you.[28]

Kitty was quite insecure, but never having met Hazel she was unaware of her charisma and made no reference to any jealousy of her in correspondence. Kitty did, of course, have cause for concern. As Oliver St John Gogarty later wrote, Hazel wanted to share in Collins's 'dangers and responsibilities. She was willing to be identified with him in every way.'[29]

Collins visited the Grosvenor Gallery in early June where his portrait was hanging beside Lavery's latest picture of Hazel, 'Rose and Grey'. Leslie wrote of 'Rose and Grey' to John: 'It is certainly a very celestial picture. ... I have never seen a more haunting picture. ... Surely men have said their prayers and burnt waxen tapers before less beautiful Eikons and such a face has loosed a thousand pens and pencils even if it has not launched a thousand ships!'[30] Collins asked if he could keep Leslie's letter, which he then carried in his wallet. On 22 June he wrote in Hazel's scrapbook under a photograph of the painting: 'A 1000 ships launched Helen, Poets relate – Yet Hazel is content with ships of state.'[31]

The surviving fragments of letters and poetry from Collins to Hazel were preserved in Hazel's scrapbook. From West Kensington Collins wrote a verse to 'Hazel Darling':

> Oh! Hazel, Hazel Lavery:
> What is your charm Oh! say?
> Like subtle Scottish Mary
> You take my heart away.
> Not by your wit and beauty

Nor your delicate sad grace
Nor the golden eyes of wonder
In the flower that is your face.

On the reverse side he wrote: 'I did love the play and it was so
sweet of you to take me and bring me home. I hope you were not
too miserable after I left.'[32]

Hazel continued to communicate with the British Cabinet and
colonial officials on Collins's behalf. In June she wrote to Lord
Cavan to query the government's stance on the *Upnor* incident.
In May 1922, the anti-treaty IRA had intercepted the *Upnor*, a
naval vessel carrying arms, in Strangford Lough. Collins believed
there was collusion between the British and anti-Treaty forces.
Lord Cavan's reply read: 'Mr Churchill asked me to have an
interview with Mr Collins, which I did tonight. Of course you
will understand that I am the servant of the Government and
could only try to show Mr Collins that the Army stood for fair
play all round.'[33]

Collins continued working on a pact with dc Valera, proposing
that after the June 1922 election pro- and anti-Treatyites should
form a coalition government. On 11 June he sent Hazel an article from the *Irish Times* in support of the plan, underneath which
he wrote: '*The Irish Times* is our most conservative old Unionist
paper, sort of [like the] *Daily Telegraph*. If any of them find fault
with my Friday night's speech show this to them.'[34] The British
Cabinet would not approve the pact; meanwhile, Collins's lack of
partisanship was alienating him from his colleagues. Still, he was
determined to explore every option. The provisional government
hoped for a constitution that would appeal to all sides, but Collins's
draft, released on the eve of the election, undermined the original
terms of Treaty. Churchill wrote to Hazel: 'I ought, I think, to let
you know *confidentially* that my colleagues take a most grave view
of the Constitution ...'.[35] Collins wrote to Kitty from London on
30 May: 'Things are bad beyond words, and I am almost without
hope of being able to do anything of permanent use. It's really

awful – to think of what I have to endure here owing to the way things are done by the opponents at home.'[36]

In London between 1 and 13 June, Hazel recorded that she had arranged a round of meetings for Collins, although only one is documented. Years later, Hazel told a friend how they visited Churchill at Philip Sassoon's in Port Lympne:

Like most Irishwomen,* I saw the necessity for Irish Independence. Matters were looking desperate in the Irish troubles, so I arranged for a special meeting ofCollins with Winston Churchill. ... At first Churchill was hesitant about coming to the meeting. But I impressed upon him the urgency of the situation, and he finally agreed ... this meeting, arranged when Michael Collins was on a 48 hours visit to England, really saved Ireland, and brought about the creation of the Irish Free State.[37]

Though Hazel was exaggerating her self-appointed role as an *éminence grise*, communication through her was undoubtedly vital for the British and their understanding of Collins's intentions.

Despite the theft of ballot boxes by Republicans, the pro-Treatyites returned with a majority after the elections of 16 June. Within days of the election Sir Henry Wilson, the Unionists' military advisor, was assassinated in London. Hazel wrote to the Irish Attorney-General, Hugh Kennedy:

As you may imagine the death of Sir Henry Wilson has thrown us here into a tumult at first it seemed too cruelly disastrous, but today things are steadying. I think and hope. Poor Winston and in fact all of us including poor Lady Lavery have been called 'conspirators' 'murderers' and other ... terms of approbation by our dearest friends. I have faith however that this will pass and reason prevail even if *truth* alas! does not.[38]

Hazel's disquiet was well-founded. Her alliance with Collins, who was widely suspected of having ordered Wilson's assassination, was now objected to in London. Fearing for Hazel's safety,

---

* Hazel saw herself as Irish. She wrote to Hugh Kennedy, 'I am an Irish subject now, aren't I Mr Kennedy? Being married to a Free Stater so I can say what I like about Americans and it is a delicious relief to me.' (8 August 1922, Kennedy Papers in UCDAp4/1432[2]).

Collins appointed a special guard for her. Leslie noted in his diary: 'Nobody feels safe, but Society ladies are thrilled and are going over to Sinn Féin.'[39]

In the wake of the assassination, the British put pressure on the provisional government to attack the anti-Treaty forces who had been occupying the Four Courts in Dublin since April. The attack on the Four Courts on 28 June launched the Civil War. Collins's predicament was illustrated in this prayer written for him by Hazel during June:

> Dear God make strong and bold my hand,
>
> Oh! let my eye see far and clear,
>
> To serve my well beloved land,
>
> Give me high hope to conquer fear.
>
> Free thou my country from the thrall
>
> Unbind at last her fettered feet
>
> Uphold her lest she faint and fall
>
> And help her broken heart to beat
>
> Let me fight on to set her free
>
> Fight on for her 'til life is fled,
>
> And if her voice cry out to me,
>
> Oh! Let me hear tho' I be dead.[40]

Hazel wrote to a friend that Michael 'always said it, and thought it safe-guarded him'.[41] As military action began, Collins gave up his ministerial position and on 12 July 1922 became commander-in-chief of the army.

Hazel continued to entertain members of all political groupings, and she used the rounds of exhibitions, opening nights and weekend parries to promote the Irish cause. At the Chamberlains' weekend party in Polesden Lacey, Dorking, she described 'a distinguished house party of super "die hards"'. She had to endure 'a five mile walk across wet fields' in order to 'gain a friend for Ireland'.[42]

As the centre of Irish political gravity shifted from London to Dublin, some members of the Irish government wished to distance Hazel from politics, feeling she was a distraction to Collins. Hugh Kennedy wrote to Hazel in early June:

As we have come to the end of a chapter, and a new chapter opens whose scene will hardly be laid in London and whose cast may be varied, may I take this opportunity ... of confessing my share of the general indebtedness to you and Sir J.L. Your insight and sympathetic understanding so often translated into happy action and your charming hospitality had already woven a bright thread through the earlier chapters of the story before my unromantic role of the black and prosy robe opened, but even I have been admitted to share in the glamour which you have shed upon events as they moved. I am full of appreciation of the help and the hospitality and all the diverse kindness of Sir John and yourself.[43]

Hazel replied:

It gave me a real pang of sadness when you spoke of 'the end of the chapter!' for you have all made my life much more worth while and interesting to me and it will seem flat and dull if I am not even to *play* at helping any more! You must just indulgently let me hold the ends of the reins as you would a child so that I may imagine I am guiding the splendid studs that you will control and handle so well ...[44]

The Civil War escalated rapidly, and within days of the government attack on the Four Courts there was fighting on the streets of Dublin. By 30 June the Four Courts were in flames and the insurgents had surrendered. In the first days of July government troops bombarded the anti-Treaty headquarters at the Gresham Hotel and its surroundings, leaving Dublin's main thoroughfare, O'Connell Street, in ruins. John wanted to paint history in the making and cabled to British official Andy Cope: 'Would it be poss. to paint things in Dublin. Would cross Sat. night if you approve. Please reply.'[45] Cope passed the request on to Kennedy, who replied: 'Your wire received. Courts quite burned out nothing spectacular now street fighting and sniping with considerable danger to civilians.'[46] The Laverys, isolated from the chaos in Ireland, found the fighting difficult to envisage.

Meanwhile, Kitty Kiernan was feeling neglected and all but accused Collins of having 'somebody else':

The first and best goes to Ireland, I am only a good second, at least at the present time. Almost a year ago you would have written a more affectionate letter under the circumstances ... if I was sure you really missed *me,* and had not somebody else. Knowing a little about you that, if you really wanted me badly, you would wire or write as you often did to have me near you. ...[47]

Collins, caught in a battle as bad 'as Easter week', replied: 'And who's the somebody else? ... And if I'm in places where I can't even wire to you or where you don't hear at all of me or from me, I'll think of you. ... And, fondest love, no matter what. ...'[48]

But a few days later Collins did find time to write a poem to Hazel, leaving little doubt that she was the 'somebody else'.

> Cucugan I call thee,
>
> Cucugan the dove,
>
> Because of thine eyes and the voice that I love.
>
> Cucugan I call thee.
>
> Hast thou no fear, little bird, little love,
>
> I am an eagle and thou art a dove
>
> Hast thou no fear of me?
>
> Wild is my nest in the mountain above,
>
> Wilt thou fly there with me lovely white dove,
>
> Shall my wings carry thee.[49]

Collins's views on events in Ireland influenced Hazel deeply. Londonderry's letters of this period complained that Hazel's opinions were dictated by the 'Sinn Féiners':

I was sorry to hear from *you* the fantastic story of the origin of the trouble being a pogrom against the Catholics in Ulster. I am well aware that amongst the lowest classes this doctrine is held ... when you tell me that the whole of the movement in the South is the direct corollary of a concerted plan of extermination of the Catholics in the North, I can only gaze at you in astonishment and feel that either you are so prejudiced as to be unable to see any justice, or that you are enunciating phrases which you are passionately anxious to compel yourself to believe.[50]

Londonderry also saw the stumbles of the Free State ministers as evidence of Ireland's unsuitedness for independence.[51]

I do not see Ireland deriving all the Imperial advantages and yet not being in the Empire ... I cannot subscribe to the littleness of thought which envisages a tiny little island, speaking a language which no one understands, self-centred, proud, and unduly sensitive ...

Hazel may have agreed on the language issue, but her loyalty lay with Collins. Londonderry was unwavering:

You suggested that I personally had a great power, and that Mr Collins felt that if only I had helped him, that we should have changed everything between us. That is a complete fallacy and the wish is obviously the father to the thought. I disagree profoundly with Mr Collins' theory of Government.[52]

✿⊃⊂✿

The Laverys remained eager to visit Ireland. The Earl of Dunraven had offered them his fishing lodge on Garnish Island in Bantry Bay for August and September. It was also suggested that they stay at the vacant Viceregal Lodge in the Phoenix Park. Nothing would have appealed to Hazel more, but she wrote to Hugh Kennedy: 'They want us to go to the Vice Regal but I wouldn't *dream* of it and John wants to be quite free to go off painting at a moment's notice.'[53] The Laverys arrived at Kingstown Pier on 13 August. They were met by a government car and driven to the nearby Royal Marine hotel. Hazel had no wish to stay in the city:

I would much rather not be in Dublin. One runs across all the people who have very kindly invited us to visit them, their one idea is to save you from "Hotel Life" and I *adore* it as I never have a chance of staying in hotels and I *loathe* visiting.[54]

Arthur Griffith had died suddenly of a brain haemorrhage on the previous day. His death profoundly affected Collins. Bishop Fogarty commented: 'Michael, you should be prepared – you might be next.' Collins joked, 'I hope nobody takes it into his head to die for another twelve months.'[55]

By August 1922 the few tantalizing scraps of poetry and letters that survive find Hazel and Collins addressing each other lovingly. Hazel later told Collins's close friend Emmet Dalton, in terms suggesting intimacy, that she and Michael had spent a weekend together, although there is no proof of this. Dalton was with Collins when he left on Saturday night, 19 August, for his tour of duty in Cork. Dalton was later to allege that they had had a physical relationship.[56]

One story was to gain currency. While at Ardogon House in Co. Waterford, Collins supposedly warned Hazel of a curse condemning anyone who stayed there to a terrible end. He consoled her by saying that they were safe, with 'the sea on one side, and his forces on the other in a turret keeping watch'.[57] Hazel, anxious to demonstrate Collins's love for her, repeated such tales after his death. She told Lord Longford that Collins was so disillusioned and in love that he wanted her to run off to America with him.[58] Hazel informed others that Collins had stopped his car outside the window of her room at the Royal Marine. She looked down at him, then at John asleep. Conscience-stricken, she remained at the window, and the car eventually drove away.[59]

Their contemporaries could only speculate about their relationship. Leslie compared Hazel to Madame Recamier,[60] a salon hostess with a coterie of admirers, who had remained a virgin. Hazel's daughter Alice stated:

My mother was always believed to have had an affair with Michael Collins. She never believed in affairs. She said, 'Affairs are such shabby things; all that sneaking about by the back stairs.' She was almost undersexed if you know what I mean, she had no interest. She liked things to be beautiful. Michael Collins was a very gallant hero.[61]

Many people noted that Michael and Hazel were inseparable that August. Collins dined with the Laverys twice at their hotel that week and spent his last two nights in Dublin, before his tour of Cork, in Hazel's company. On 19 August they travelled together to Kilteragh, Foxrock, the home of the co-operative leader. Sir Horace Plunkett. Hazel had been anxious for Collins to meet Plunkett, and had written to him on 17 August. Plunkett replied:

I have now received your kind letter as well as the verbal message – General Collins will be a welcome and honoured guest whenever he can come ... If he is able to take pot-luck with us all on Sunday for any or all of the meals, perhaps you can let him know that there will be no one here he would rather not meet.[62]

The dinner at Plunkett's ninety-acre estate is well documented. Lady Gregory received a letter from Lennox Robinson describing the event and noted in her diary: 'Collins is safe ... and dined at Kilteragh on Saturday, he came in Lady Lavery's train, or rather she in his for she is his abject admirer.'[63] Hazel asked some of the guests, including George Bernard Shaw, to sign her scrapbook. Daisy Fingall and Charlotte Shaw also attended. John, who was not there, wrote in his autobiography: '[Hazel] was anxious that [Collins] should meet Horace Plunkett and took him there ... alone. I was a little anxious, but for some reason did not go.'[64]

During the course of the evening, Hazel wrote to Eddie Marsh: 'I am trying to write this with a babel of conversation which I dare not miss, going on around me. G.B.S. is reading aloud to Michael Collins his article for *The Irish Times* on Ireland, it is very funny but quite futile ...'.[65] Daisy Fingall found the evening quiet, almost dull, and later wrote, 'Collins was not at all an eloquent man.' The guests left early, as Collins was leaving for Cork the next day.[66]

In his diary Horace Plunkett noted the risk that Collins took in coming to Kilteragh without an escort: 'I fear he is too careless of his life. His car was bombed only yesterday when, luckily, he was not in it.'[67] The evening after Griffith's funeral, Collins had been dining at the Royal Marine with the Laverys. John later learned from the night porter that a sniper lurking in the hotel grounds had been blocked from his target by Hazel seated at the window and unwittingly shielding Collins.[68] Later, returning from the hotel, Collins's car was attacked, as Hazel recounted in a letter to Eddie Marsh:

I'm enclosing a cutting to show you that I am in the thick of the fight! The car that was ambushed had just been left by Michael as something had gone wrong with the clutch and he had jumped into a Ford car standing near, so his lucky life was spared again. He had been dining with us at an hotel near Dublin and it happened on the way home – he rang us up from H.Q. at three in the morning to assure us of his safety because we had heard the ambush which wasn't far from the hotel.[69]

Three days later, the car carrying Hazel and Collins from the dinner at Kilteragh was ambushed. The official report stated: 'The C.-in-C.'s car ambushed today at 1pm* about one mile the Dublin side of Stillorgan on its way from Greystones.'[70] Hazel's version appeared in Shane Leslie's diary:

I asked her if the rumour was true that they had shared an ambush. It was! While they drove through Wicklow [*sic*] the bullets passed through the glass. Collins took her by the neck and pushed her into the well of the car. The newspaper account was less romantic.[71]

When Collins departed for Cork, his home county and a Republican stronghold, Hazel was naturally apprehensive for his safety, as John remembered:

Hazel was pale with excitement and woke up screaming once or twice that night. Next day she was strange and silent. I could not get her to talk. She had fearful premonitions. ... Now she said at last, looking away from me, 'All day I have been seeing them carrying Michael covered in blood. Wherever I go I cannot get rid of the sight.' I got her to bed and sat with her until well on into the night, and at last she went to sleep.[72]

On the evening of 22 August, Collins and his convoy were travelling along the valley of Beal na mBláth in Cork, when they were ambushed. Collins made a fatal mistake by countermanding Emmet Dalton's order to 'Drive like hell!' and choosing to stay and fight. The battle lasted for forty to fifty minutes until Collins shouted an order, giving away his position. A bullet hit him in the head behind the right ear. Sean O'Connell, realizing that Collins

---

* In the newspaper cutting in her scrapbook. Hazel corrected the time from 1 p.m. to 1 a.m. and wrote, 'I was in the car when this happened' (*see plate*).

had been fatally wounded, knelt beside him and whispered an Act of Contrition. He was rewarded by a slight pressure of the hand.[73] Moments later, Michael Collins, aged thirty-two, was dead.

Hazel was awoken the next morning by her maid, to be informed, 'They have shot Mr Collins, my lady.'[74] The grief-stricken Hazel went to Kilteragh, where Daisy Fingall and Charlotte Shaw were sitting in front of the drawing-room fire. She told them, 'I knew it before I saw the papers. I had seen him in a dream, his face covered with blood.'[75] As soon as possible Hazel and Daisy went to the mortuary chapel of the Sisters of Charity at St Vincent's Hospital, Dublin. Hazel wanted to wear widow's weeds, but Daisy restrained her.[76] Gogarty commented: 'We had Lady Lavery ... full of confidences of Collins. Lady Fingall made her go home and leave the arena to Kitty Kiernan.'[77] To preserve the reputation of Collins the dead hero, who in the tradition of Irish patriots was to be more revered in death than in life, Hazel's grief had to be concealed. As usual, John took refuge in his work, and painted Collins lying in state. The small canvas, of Collins in uniform draped with the tri-colour, was entitled 'For Love of Ireland' (*see plate*). He later wrote:

I was allowed to paint him in death. Any grossness in his features, even the peculiar little dent near the point of his nose, had disappeared. He might have been Napoleon in marble as he lay in his uniform, covered by the Free State flag, with a crucifix on his breast. Four soldiers stood around the bier.[78]

John painted quickly, returning to the hotel at midnight when the body was moved to City Hall to lie in state. On Monday 28 August, at the funeral Mass in the Pro-Cathedral in Dublin, John painted the requiem from the gallery. Hazel wrote to Eddie Marsh a few days later: 'At the Memorial Mass the Cathedral was crowded right out into the street, people kneeling on the steps.'[79] Collins was buried at Glasnevin cemetery, on the north side of the city, where Parnell, O'Connell and other Irish patriots were interred. John's granddaughter, Lady Sempill, recalled being told:

As the crowd moved away. Hazel took her rosary beads and threw them on the grave. Sir John bent down and retrieved them, and handed them back to her. Once again, she threw them on the grave. Once more, Sir John picked them up and gave them back to her. 'Listen,' he said, 'don't you know the first person to come along will pick them up and go off with them?' She put them back in her handbag. The reason for John's concern was that they were made out of real pearls.[80]

Hazel revisited the grave over the next few days, and described 'a constant and daily pilgrimage to his grave at Glasnevin, and so many wreaths you cannot get within twenty feet of it'.[81] When the grave was deserted and the flowers were gone John painted the scene. Some months later. Sean O'Connell, a soldier who had been at Beal na mBláth with Collins, fulfilled a promise to Hazel:

You will probably remember the wreath which stands at the head of Michael's grave. I placed the beads under the glass frame and attached it with a fine wire at the points suggested in your letter the *only* difference being that it is now placed under the glass instead of over it as heretofore so that there isn't much chance of its being removed.[82]

The Laverys returned to England in the first week of September, earlier than planned, after deciding not to visit Garnish Island. They did not go back to Cromwell Place but took a houseboat on the Thames. At the end of September they travelled to North Berwick for their annual visit to the Fords. On the surface, it was life as usual, but Hazel was still in deep mourning. On 14 September she wrote from there:

I saw him the very last hour when he started for Cork on that Sunday early morning. He came back two days later dead on the same ship which had carried him living and so vigorously confident in his 'Star'. ... Never was there more strange and romantic and fatal a story. It could only take place in Ireland. I have been very sick in soul and body since, but this sane, healthy, normal place and the great content of Alice and John with this sporting life here makes me less miserable, and the soft, strong air is a great healer. I dread going back to London ... I have been very idle, only walking and reading and alas! thinking more than is good for me of that tragic Ireland, and what it has cost us all.[83]

She wrote a poem entitled 'To a Dead Lover' in tribute to Collins. In the final verse she wrote:

> I will forgive you both,
> Wild Michael,
> Forgive her living,
> forgive you dead.
> Your passion and beauty
> are day – Cold Michael,
> And lie alone in your
> deep dark bed.[84]

She also began a scrapbook with photographs, press-cuttings and other memorabilia relating to Collins's life and death. Included was his name card, mortuary card and a shamrock from Beal na mBláth, given to her by his sister Hannie and kept in an envelope labelled 'where Michael fell'. She made copies of the letters that Collins had written to Hannie from the internment camp at Frongoch.[85] Some personal effects were returned to her by Collins's secretary, Gearóid McGann, who wrote:

Enclosed little note in Michael's writing* I came across the other day in one of my private files and I am sure you would like to have it. I don't know that he ever meant me to file such things, but he was so extraordinarily exact and methodical in all his work I considered it well to keep accurate records of everything.[86]

Hannie Collins and Hazel remained in contact and were friends for the rest of their lives. Hannie later recalled: 'She was an exceptional character in every way – in addition to her beauty, kindness and charm of manner she was extremely well endowed mentally – a thing she generally managed to conceal.'[87] After her brother's burial, Hannie returned all the material relating to Hazel that was found with Michael when he was shot.** Only fragments of letters survive, but enough to confirm Hazel's

---

* The note is not in the Lady Lavery Collection, unless it is one of the poems already mentioned.
** These documents were donated to Kilmainham Gaol by Shane Leslie's

emotional attachment, including part of a letter Collins wrote to Hazel the day he was killed, a section of a letter from Hazel, the Leslie letter on 'Rose and Grey', a lock of Hazel's hair and a ruby brooch which he kept in his scapular case. The only complete document was a short letter written on a scrap of paper ripped from his notebook (*see illustration*), addressed to:

> Hazel, Dearest
> Hazel, *My* dear dear Hazel
> I too wish it was 'tomorrow'
> With *all* my love
> *Yours* M.[88]

Hazel felt no need to conceal her grief in letters to friends including Philip Sassoon, Winston Churchill, J.M. Barrie, and George Bernard Shaw. Sassoon replied sympathetically, 'You were his star.'[89] Eddie Marsh wrote:

I felt that with opportunity we might be real friends – so it was a personal loss even to me – But to you, who cared for him because you had helped and fended for him so much, and because you were so necessary to him, which is one of the best reasons for loving a person, it is too grievous for word or thought.[90]

Shaw was the only one of Hazel's correspondents who referred to their intimacy: 'I had no right to assume – though I knew – that Michael was what I call your Sunday husband ...'.[91] Many of Hazel's friends soon became bored by stories about Michael Collins. As Collins had affectionately called Hazel 'macushla', now Lady Cunard and Lady Colefax teasingly called her 'macushla' and 'Darling' with a mock-Irish accent.[92]

Hazel found solace in supporting implementation of the Treaty and keeping in contact with Collins's friends, including Emmet Dalton, Gearóid McGann, Kevin O'Higgins and Joe O'Reilly. O'Higgins wrote:

---

widow in the 1960s. The section in Hazel's scrapbook relating to the death of Collins is damaged; it is possible that the donated items had been removed from the book.

I can well imagine how greatly shocked you must have been at the tragic news. There are times when the only safety valve is work, things so terrible that one dare not stop to think on them. There is work enough to our hands. God knows and there is the clear duty to carry on and endeavour to save Michael's achievements for the country from destruction ... One thing you may be sure of – there will be no quitting, and no trifling with the bond of the two [Collins and Griffith] who are gone. We will "get on with the work" – and *you*, who Michael loved so well, will pray for our success and help when you can in the way that only *you* can. I wish you could realize how much all here appreciate your help and sympathy.[93]

In Dublin, wrangling over the Treaty continued. The Dáil assembled on 9 September and elected W.T. Cosgrave as President of the Executive Council of the Free State. De Valera refused to recognize the Dáil, and on 26 October he joined the Irregulars' executive to form a Republican government, of which he was made President. A concerned Hazel wrote to Churchill in October: 'Everyone assures me nothing *can* go wrong with the Treaty, but one always trembles for the tragic fate that pursues Ireland, there seems no end to it.'[94]

By late October 1922 Lloyd George's coalition had lost the support of right-wing Conservatives over a perceived leniency towards Ireland. When Lloyd George was suspected of crusading for the Greeks against the Turks in Asia Minor, Bonar Law spoke out and forced him to resign. Bonar Law became leader of the Conservative Party and won the election of November 1922.

Southern Ireland was now riven with hostilities. The new police force and judicial system were not yet fully functioning. Many big houses around the country, including Horace Plunkett's Kilteragh, were burned to the ground by the Irregulars. Dáil deputies were forced to live in government buildings for their own safety. On 7 December a member of the Dáil, Sean Hales, was shot dead in Dublin, and in retaliation four anti-Treaty prisoners were executed the following morning. As the Minister for Home Affairs, Kevin O'Higgins was obliged to defend this action in the Dáil, although he was firmly opposed to it and had argued against the decision in the Cabinet. One of the executed,

Rory O'Connor, had been best man at his wedding the year before, and from this point on O'Higgins was held in particular contempt by the Irregulars.[95]

Hazel's perceived influence in Collins's support for the Treaty appears to have put her in danger. Leslie wrote to her: 'You were always watched when you were with him in London or Ireland and a word is enough to set fire to a field in Ireland. I am glad you were not killed together as they doubtless planned in their myriad scheming minds.'[96] An anonymous letter was sent to Cromwell Place:

Sir — Are you aware that you and your wife are watched especially Lady L. – as it is well known in Irish Republican Circles that she caused Collins to go against his friends and principles entirely. They have letters of hers which the late Harry Boland (RI.P) secured. ... All know that Lady Lavery obtained complete control of Collins and his unlucky death could have been avoided but for his infatuation causing him to listen to her policy which was dictated by Churchill *against* Collins' former *friends* who he was forced to attack and murder and who were forced to retaliate on him RI.P. This is to warn you not to allow Lady L. to see strangers *alone* or to go to any place of meeting. They will endeavour to get her to call for her letters which will only be used against her. I am against violence although never never will we forsake freedom and the Republic + how can you an Irish man side with England the blood stained murders of our beloved Race. I am ashamed to warn you an enemy but your wife was once *very* kind to a brother of mine killed last year in Ireland like Collins shot through the head RI.P. But do not think that otherwise I would have tried to save a woman, who what ever her reasons ruined Collins as sure as Parnell* was ruined and is an enemy to Ireland. + [97]

The week Collins was shot, Hazel had written to Emmet Dalton of Collins's concern that anti-Treaty forces followed his movements through her letters. As Dalton's correspondence with her in November makes clear, Hazel's letters were still considered by Republicans as a source of confidential information on government activities:

---

* Parnell, Charles Stewart (1846-91), was leader of the Irish Parliamentary Party and might have succeeded in achieving Home Rule for Ireland in the 1890s but fell from power following the revelation of his affair with a married woman, Katherine O'Shea.

I sincerely hope that the news I now have to give you will not disturb you, but I feel it is best to let you know the romantic, if not tragic, interlude your letter passed through before it reached me. About a week or so ago a prominent irregular was captured in a house in Dublin ... My brother, who is our Chief Intelligence Officer in Dublin, discovered your letter amongst the many other valuable documents found amongst Ernest O'Malley's personal belongings and he handed it to me. It is fairly clear that some of the irregulars captured it in a raid on the mails in Dublin. I cannot see what use it could be to them, but they retained it and evidently placed some importance upon it as they marked it 'valuable document'.[98]

A cease-fire was finally announced on 24 May 1923. Kevin O'Higgins believed it was 'the calm of exhaustion, not of peace'. He introduced the Public Safety Act of 1923, imprisoning those considered to pose a danger, and wrote:

... the twelve thousand prisoners – the vast majority of them harmless 'poor divils' (as 'M' would say) the victims of circumstances, but with a very nasty and dangerous sediment ... The national hysteria is almost gone – a few ladies drumming their heels on the ground, but the acoustics for that kind of thing are not as good as they used to be.[99]

Historians have consistently portrayed Hazel's relationship with Collins as a figment of her imagination. Terence de Vere White wrote in his biography of O'Higgins:

Lady Lavery developed a romantic attachment to Michael Collins which was notorious. Rumour gave colour and exaggeration – and Lady Lavery, it must be confessed gave rumour wings — to what was after all, a fancy on her part. Collins was unaware.[100]

Even in 1923 Hazel was anxious to affirm Collins's feelings towards her. Leslie related, 'Hazel was proud of the letters and carried them about ... and was inclined to show Collins's love for her ... she brought them to a party [at Mount Stewart] and was convinced they were rifled by another guest called Dixon. ... She showed men's letters to each other.'[101] This practice, Lady Audrey Morris wrote, 'sprung of course, as did most of her errors, from vanity'.[102] It was to work against her. De Vere White's account, reported third hand,[103] referred to her showing Collins's letters to Lord Birkenhead: 'The occasional romantic passages were interpolated in a woman's handwriting valiantly, if unsuccessfully disguised.'[104] This seems unlikely, as Hazel had Collins's handwritten poetry in her scrapbooks and she was careful that those pieces which she recopied and attributed to him were marked 'copy'.

Aware there were many keen to discredit her, she must have derived ironic pleasure in being mistaken for Kitty Kiernan in August 1923 when she attended the unveiling of a cenotaph to honour Collins and Griffith on Leinster Lawn in Dublin. The Laverys arrived with the Viceregal party. Hazel, sitting in the front row next to Hannie Collins, wore black, except for a tiny band of white flowers on her hat. One columnist wrote:

At one o'clock the whole gathering within the Lawn rose, and stood without a sound, as the President entered, accompanied by the Governor-General, at whose side walked Miss Kitty Kiernan, fiancée of General Collins ... a light, wistful, graceful figure, very charming and sad looking.[105]

The following day a rival newspaper reported, 'Amusing Case of Mistaken Identity':

As a matter of fact, the lady in black was Lady Lavery. ... I think Lady Lavery would have looked even more wistful if she had known what the local word painter was decorously jotting down on his cuff. I may add that Miss Kitty was not present at the ceremony.[106]

Envelope in Collins's hand to Hazel (top), containing a fragment torn from his notebook (middle). The bloodstained fragment of letter from Hazel to Collins (above), found on his body and returned to Hazel by his sister Hannie, reads:

'... how fine and impressive and marvellously organized it all is – I am so so proud Michael how can I say it all! "at all", your letter has just come to me forwarded from London, may God keep you – Hazel'. (Kilmainham Gaol, Dublin)

7th October 1922

Dear Lady Lavery

I am glad my letter reached its real address. You see, I could not very well write to you directly without a certain indelicacy: I had no right to assume — though I knew — that Michael was what I call your Sunday husband. But when a fellow at the Summer School told me that Miss Collins was an old friend of his, and begged me to send her a line, I guessed that the line would get through, and sent it.

And so away with melancholy: you are a very lucky woman.

I have not seen Sir John's portrait ("John's portrait" means Augus-

tus John's) as it has not been sent down to me; and we shall not be in town until Friday, when, by the way, I have a lunch and an evening engagement. We must return here on Saturday afternoon, because there is a serious illness in our London domestic staff, and we have to take meals at our clubs and keep out of the way as much as possible. But we are not out of your reach here — thirty miles by car, or half an hour from Kings+ to Hatfield and then 7 miles hither in our car. Would it amuse you to come out for lunch some afternoon?

Charlotte thought the smile was that of a conqueror. The dead are always triumphant — if they were really alive before.

Thank you for suggesting a dinner; but — if you don't mind, — NOT (Doctor Fogarty in that connexion. On the surface of things, yes — but between you and Michael — somehow — I can't explain; but I couldn't stand it just now, though I like the man well enough.

faithfully

G.B.S.

George Bernard Shaw's letter to Hazel Lavery of 7 October 1922, sympathizing with her loss.

VIII

'that most lovely and cruel country'
[1923-7]

CROMWELL PLACE was now renowned – and in some circles notorious – as a result of the Laverys' involvement with the central figures in the Irish political crisis. One visitor, upon arrival in South Kensington, had difficulty finding the house; the taxi-driver, however, knew precisely where it was, and said in a sinister tone, 'I expect you're going into that Irish place!'[1]

James MacNeill moved to London in 1922 as High Commissioner of the Irish Free State. His wife Josephine recalled: 'When I came to London ... Hazel's house was a most gracious centre of hospitality to Irish political and artistic personalities.'[2] Hazel was proud to count a number of writers among her friends; many, inevitably, had an Irish association. Stephen MacKenna, a journalist and translator of Plotinus, had lived in Dublin; Hazel met him after he moved to London in 1923 and he soon frequented Cromwell Place. Stephen Gwynn and his son Denis (later to wed Alice) were regular visitors, an interest in Irish politics assuring their welcome. The former had been an MP for Galway until 1918 but abandoned politics for writing; and Denis, a former pupil of Patrick Pearse, became a particular favourite of Hazel's. Through the Gwynns, Hazel met Louie Rickard, who was to become her closest female friend in the late twenties and thirties.[3] Rickard, a rector's daughter from Mitchelstown, Co. Cork, made her living as a romantic novelist.

Oliver St John Gogarty first visited in 1922. 'I was shown into a small room in which there were five or six people; one of them rose and with her arms outspread rushed to greet me. I was somewhat taken aback by the impulsiveness of the greeting in a company none of whom I knew. I could not bring myself to think I was so deserving of so warm a welcome.'[4] Gogarty supported the Treaty and in December 1922 sealed his friendship with Hazel by a daring escape from Republicans in which he plunged into the river Liffey. He was a throat surgeon by profession but best known as a skilled conversationalist and writer; Hazel wrote to him that when she gave a reading of his work at Lady Cunard's, 'They declared you were the very wittiest creature ever had come out of Ireland and they intended never to let you leave this dismal London.'[5] After the attempt on his life, he spent increasing amounts of time in London, and Hazel and Lady Leslie ensured his social success.[6]

After one of the Laverys' 'Irish' dinners in June 1923, Andy Cope, Assistant Under-Secretary during the War of Independence and supervisor of the British troop withdrawal, wrote:

I am convinced that these antipathies *can* be removed and that you and Sir John are travelling the *only* road to remove them. ... As for last night. It was magnificent. It *was* an experience for me that will fill my thoughts for weeks to come. There were small men and small women and great men and great women. And among the men stood out *Winston;* ... how pleased I was that although the Irish Treaty was mainly responsible for his fall from office, yet he gave me a cheery welcome. And also among what I feel to be great ones there were Sir John and yourself working with splendid anxiety towards the great end.[7]

Gogarty, also a guest, echoed Cope:

I am borne along by the memory of that most delightful evening at your house last night and of Cope's testimony to the importance and influence of your help for our unfortunate country. ... Your help in the trying transition period from Government to Government cannot be over estimated: my fear is that our native ingratitude may not realize its weight. However that may be, it is a different matter as regards myself: I will not be ungrateful nor forgetful – and your goodwill has helped me more than I venture to say ...[8]

In 1923 John painted the portraits of President W.T. Cosgrave and Vice-President Kevin O'Higgins in London. During these sittings Hazel renewed her acquaintance with O'Higgins, who was drawn to her despite lacking the capacity for small talk and pleasantries.[9] But she had been a close friend of Collins, and O'Higgins had taken on his mantle. He wrote a heartfelt tribute to Collins: 'Mourn people of Ireland for there is gone from amongst you a great-hearted man, who loved you well ... mourn ... read through your tears the lessons of his life – and his death.'[10] By the summer of 1923 O'Higgins had begun to correspond regularly with Hazel:

Your letters are always *very* welcome. Any little driving force I have goes back to the days which your notes always recall – the memory of the little steadfast man [Griffith] and the big dynamic explosive but entirely lovable boy [Collins], whose joint efforts – complementary of one another as they were – lifted Ireland out of the dust and placed her an equal amongst the nations. When they were struck down, both within a fortnight, I resolved that, so far as *I* could effect it, no one was going to profit by their deaths. You can be very sure that I will not let either of them down by word or act.[11]

In August 1923 the Laverys attended the Royal Dublin Society Horse Show, where Hazel's presence in the Royal Box attracted attention. They stayed at O'Higgins's home and the Viceregal Lodge, official residence of the new Governor-General, Tim Healy. As the King's representative the Governor-General had to be acceptable to each side, but the Free State insisted on an Irishman and commoner, while the British wanted an English nobleman. Prime Minister Bonar Law had originally opposed the compromise candidate Healy, accusing him of impulsiveness and drinking too much whiskey, but the support of Hazel and others had helped his cause.[12]

The Laverys were to be frequent guests at the Viceregal Lodge during Healy's tenure. After the first visit to 'Uncle Tim's Cabin' Hazel sent him a signed photograph, at his request, and Healy's daughter Elizabeth wrote, 'It was such a pleasure to us to meet you both; and now when anyone mentions the famous painter or the famous beauty, I shall always boast "I know them!"'[13] Healy's wife had had a stroke shortly after he took office,[14] so the role of hostess fell to Elizabeth, who disliked entertaining. Hazel was therefore occasionally called upon to act as Vicereine.[15] Gogarty remembered her skills as a diplomat:

The leaders were casting about for some indication of Tim's attitude. Would he expect them to curtsey? Would it embarrass them if they did? Lady Lavery's tact saved the situation. She got in the way and led us to His Excellency.[16]

❧∞❧

Irish ministers attended the Dominion Conference as new members in the autumn of 1923. Paddy McGilligan, secretary to the Irish delegation, was 'amazed at the freedom of speech and the trust placed in the Irish ex-rebels' by their Dominion colleagues, of whom they had initially been wary.[17] By the end of the Conference any sense of inferiority had been dispelled, and Desmond FitzGerald, Minister for External Affairs, wrote on his return to Dublin:

On the whole, now it is over, I am very pleased with the result of the Imperial Conference. The lines established with MacKenzie King [Premier of Canada] I think are very good and we certainly made decided advances in the definition of constitutional position – the only thing I was interested in and the only thing the Conference was competent to effect.[18]

In January 1924, a Conference to reach a final settlement over the North was begun. Desmond FitzGerald revealed his hopes and his expectations to Hazel:

President, Kevin and Kennedy are due to confer with British and Northerns on Friday. ... I have just heard that Blythe will probably be with them. By the time you get this you will have seen that Lord Londonderry will be on the Northern side so the whole thing should be very interesting for you. It looks, don't you think, fairly significant that Londonderry comes with Craig? I haven't any very great hopes of the Conference but it may be that they won't exactly come to blows as we like to think that Lord L. [Londonderry] is kindly to us. ... I think our people should make a point of making themselves a nuisance to you as usual! on this trip. With them on one side and Londonderry on the other we certainly should enroll your services.[19]

FitzGerald had misjudged the response of Lord Londonderry, who wrote to Hazel admonishing her for her failure to appreciate the depth of Loyalist feeling: 'I have long since ceased trying to convert you because the tragedy etc. etc. all appeal to you and a banal humdrum happy prosperous Ireland is not the Ireland of your dreams.'[20] A week before the Conference, Londonderry wrote that the Irish attitude

always makes me very impatient because it is cheap and ineffective, and I find it very hard to sympathise with people who having deliberately destroyed a good in some ways beautiful edifice when they know nothing whatsoever about building themselves, then expect sympathy and assistance to erect an unattractive and unserviceable shanty. This is how I compare the possibilities of Ireland in the past with the actualities of the present day. I should like very much to make the attempt to assist and perhaps control your friends, and an outsider, as I call myself to a large extent, has infinitely the best chance.[21]

Hazel's stance over the boundary issue was straightforward: she believed Ireland should be united. The English press considered the boundary to be an Irish domestic issue; she disagreed, and was determined to keep the matter in the public forum. She contacted Geoffrey Dawson, editor of *The Times,* about 'an unpleasant pro-Ulster communication from one Fisher', although she did believe that 'the Free State side has been fairly well put forward in *The Times* lately'.[22] Dawson responded:

I quite see the position. It was, I think, impossible to refuse to publish Fisher's letter, for he is a very responsible and careful, though enthusiastic Ulsterman. I rather expected someone to reply to it much in the sense of your letter; but I am glad on the whole that nothing has reached me so far, for I think a protracted controversy would probably do more harm than good.[23]

In January 1924 Ramsay MacDonald became Britain's first Labour Prime Minister. Hazel soon made overtures to the new Colonial Secretary, J.H. Thomas, inviting him to meet Cosgrave, but Thomas refused, considering he might appear to favour the

South.[24] He later accepted an invitation to luncheon with just the Laverys:

Mr Thomas, Colonial Secretary came to lunch with me yesterday he was tremendously friendly and quite likeable and magnetic but Oh! he is *very vain* ... he had asked to lunch with me in order to 'talk about Ireland' but he did all the talking and it was mostly about himself. ... I discovered that flattery was not unwelcome to him but it rather went against the grain with me even for love of Ireland.[25]

When the Conference began Hazel entertained on behalf of the Irish delegates. She wrote to Hugh Kennedy:

I am hoping that you will be able to come informally to tea on Sunday afternoon at five o'clock. I will try to collect a few people who wish to meet you. I am also hoping the President will come, Kevin O'Higgins and Mr Blythe and Mr O'Hegarty [Secretary of the Free State Executive Council]. I believe neither Joe R. or Mr McGann are here but of course bring any other of your colleagues who would care to come and *surely* come yourself.[26]

The death of Collins had not put an end to Hazel's role as a disseminator of correspondence for Irish politicians. Austen Chamberlain thanked her for allowing him to see letters from Hugh Kennedy and Kevin O'Higgins.[27] When the Free State had difficulties recovering debts. Hazel sought the opinion of Reginald McKenna, a former Chancellor of the Exchequer.[28] Hazel's significance as a go-between is clear from an internal memorandum inadvertently enclosed in a returned letter: 'Lady Lavery who is very thick with the S. Irish Govt. thinks you might like to see this letter from O'Higgins.'[29]

Diplomatic efforts were interrupted by the Irish Army Mutiny on 4 March, when a splinter group within the army presented the government with an ultimatum demanding an end to demobilization and a commitment to Republican ideals. It fell to O'Higgins to quell the mutiny, as Cosgrave was ill at the time. He averted a major crisis by decisive action, informing the Dáil that 'those who take the pay and wear the uniform of the state, be they soldiers or police, must be non-political servants of the state'. Two ministers and several army officials resigned. Desmond

FitzGerald gave Hazel a detailed account of the events: 'I feel that you must be pretty bewildered these days! ... I do feel sorry for you over there with just one disgraceful thing after another here! but don't lose faith or leave us yet.'[30]

That same month unarmed British soldiers at Queenstown (present-day Cobh) were attacked by men in Free State army uniforms. One soldier was killed and twenty injured, but despite a reward offered for information no one was arrested. Tim Healy wrote to Hazel: 'Since your letter came I have been mentally prostrated owing to the Queenstown tragedy. I am quite disabled from writing to you in any sprightly tone, as I should wish. Since the Phoenix Park murders in 1882* I have never felt so downhearted.'[31]

Against this background, the Free State government finally got British government support to get the Boundary Commission off the ground in the spring of 1924. Mr Justice Feetham of the South African Supreme Court was appointed to serve as a neutral chairman and the Free State appointed Eoin MacNeill, Minister for Education, who was an Ulster Catholic, as its representative. The Boundary Commission clause in the Treaty rested on the assumption that the North would appoint a delegate, but Craig refused to co-operate, a dilemma for which the terms of the Treaty had not provided. Instead the British appointed J.R. Fisher, a prominent northern Unionist. For most of the following year the Commission met but kept its findings confidential. In July 1924 Hazel and John travelled to Contrexeville, in France, 'to take the cure'.[32] Eddie Marsh wrote:

I'm delighted that you are *so nearly* enjoying yourself – why not altogether? Do try and forget the Boundary for a fortnight! Things are going as well as they could, and Feetham is making very good progress I'm told ... so do cheer up and enjoy your village de luxe without drawback.[33]

---

* On 6 May 1882 Chief Secretary Lord Frederick Cavendish and Under-Secretary Thomas Henry Burke were assassinated near the Viceregal Lodge in Phoenix Park by a Fenian splinter-group called the Invincibles.

Shortly after their return from France, Hazel and John made their annual visit to Dublin for the Horse Show, and stayed at the Viceregal Lodge with Tim Healy. Other house-guests included G.K. Chesterton and Hilaire Belloc.[34] While at the Lodge, Hazel participated in talks on the subject of the Boundary Commission with Arthur Henderson and J.H. Thomas, who later wrote:

Mr Henderson and I both feel that we and his Majesty's Government owe much to the sympathy and assistance which both sides received from you at yesterday's discussion, and that if, as I believe, we reached on the whole a satisfactory solution, it was partly due to you. Thank you very much.[35]

The Laverys took an automobile tour during August and September, visiting Cork on their journey. Hazel wrote, 'We made a pilgrimage en route to Bealnablath and it was desolate enough in the drenching rain. I almost wished I had not gone.'[36] Ireland was peaceful in the aftermath of the Civil War, and by the end of 1924 the remaining Civil War prisoners, including de Valera, were released. But Hazel's friends in London still considered Ireland unsafe. Lytton Strachey wrote: 'I wonder what you are doing. Shooting things in Scotland? or being shot at in Ireland? Or what or where?'[37]

Hazel found herself in competition for Strachey's attention: 'Please show you like me as well as L—y C—x [Lady Colefax] and come to seek me out even as you always seek her out or is she the "seeker" even as I am.'[38] When Strachey was due to dine with Hazel she feared he would not come, as he 'had ever treated her with coldness and reserve':

Please do not forget that you are dining here on Tuesday ... I have not alas been able to collect a 'Cunardian' party or even a 'Colefaxian' one the gathering will be small and unworthy of both you and me and your last words to me were 'but I *love big* parties'!! When I had suggested an informal but select little dinner I feel consequently rather agitated, especially as I practically used force to make you consent! All the same that very fact should prove to you how greatly I wished you to come, and how warm will be your welcome.[39]

By November 1924 Labour had been swept out on an anti-

Hazel Lavery's charcoal drawings.

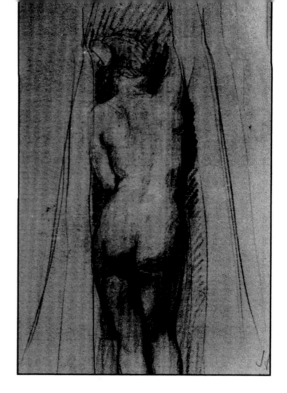

Irish and British delegates to the 1921 Anglo-Irish Treaty negotiations by Sir John Lavery. (Hugh Lane Municipal Gallery of Modern Art, Dublin)

Eamon de Valera, July 1921.
Arthur Griffith, July 1921.

Robert Barton, October 1921.
Eamon J. Duggan, October 1921.

George Gavan Duffy, October 1921.
Michael Collins (the original, presented to Kitty Kiernan, was to be replaced by this 1935 portrait).

Winston Churchill, 1915.
David Lloyd George, 1922.

F.E. Smith, Earl of Birkenhead, 1923.
Austen Chamberlain, n.d.

G.B.S. ON IRELAND

PUNCTUALITY AND FREEDOM.

WHY HE IS RETURNING TO ENGLAND.

Mr. Bernard Shaw, who has been in Ireland for the past fortnight at Rosslare, and returned to London on Saturday night, was asked by a representative of the *Irish Times* to express an opinion on the Irish situation.

"Well," was his reply, "what can anyone say that has not been said already until people are so tired of it that the words have lost all meaning? If you ask me what on earth Mr. de Valera and Mr. Erskine Childers are driving at—what they think they are doing, as the English say—I can only say that I don't know. And that is the weakness of their position from the moment when the elections went against them so completely that the members they were allowed to return by arrangement could not pretend to any representative character, they had either to accept the popular verdict and set to work to convert the Irish people to their views, or to choose between the two other courses open to them. One was to subdue the country by armed force, British fashion, and coerce it to become an independent little republic, whether it liked it or not. The other was to take to the mountains and live more or less merrily by brigandage in the manner of Robin Hood.

"What has happened is that Mr. de Valera and Mr. Childers have attempted the first alternative, but having no war chest and apparently no programme beyond calling Ireland a republic, they have been forced to tell their troops on pay-day that they must live on the country, which means in practice that the leaders are to be republicans contending for a principle and their troops are to be brigands.

"This is an impossible situation. No community can tolerate brigandage, even when it is good-natured. The existing brigandage is not good-natured; and Ireland is obviously on the point of losing its temper savagely with Robin Hood, Alan-a-dale, Friar Tuck, and the rest of them. When the explosion comes, General Collins will be able to let himself go in earnest, and the difficulty of the overcrowded jails and of the disbanded irregular troops who takes to the road again the moment the troops have passed on will be solved, because there will be no prisoners; the strain will be on the cemeteries.

TO LIVE FOR IRELAND.

"General Collins beat Sir Hamar Greenwood at the wrecking game because he had the people behind him. What chance against him has Mr. de Valera without military aptitude or any of Sir Hamar Greenwood's enormous material resources? Of course he can enjoy the luxury of dying for Ireland after doing Ireland all the damage he can. 'What matter if for Ireland dear we fall' is still the idiot's battle song. The idiocy is sanctioned by the memories of a time when there was really nothing to be done for Irish freedom but to die for it; but the time has now come for Irishmen to learn to live for their country. Instead of which, they start runaway engines down the lines, blow up bridges, burn homesteads and factories, and gain nothing by it except such amusements as making my train from Waterford to Rosslare several hours late. Ireland would be just as free at this moment if I had arrived punctually. You see, the cause of Ireland is always dogged by the ridicule which we have such a fatal gift of provoking, and such a futile gift of expressing.

"I suppose it will have to be settled, as usual, by another massacre of Irishmen by Irishmen. If Mr. de Valera had any political genius he might avert it. But with the strongest sentimental bias in his favour I cannot persuade myself that he has any political faculty at all. He has literary talent and that very dangerous plaything, an amorphous ideal; but ever since Arthur Griffith and Michael Collins left him behind when the Treaty was to be negotiated with Mr. Lloyd George, and he himself consented to be left behind, it has been evident that all three were agreed that political negotiation is not his job.

General Michael Collins had a narrow escape from injury on Saturday evening in Kingstown, when the motor car in which he was travelling with other officers, came into collision with a tender containing national troops.

The accident occurred in York street at about [ ] ock. Mr. Collins's car, a Crossley touring [ ], was badly damaged. The tender was driven from the harbour. The crowd which collected round the damaged [ ] recognised the General and cheered [ ] He was escorted to the Harbour barracks [ ] another car was procured.

Photo by [Elliott and Fry]
MR. GEORGE BERNARD SHAW

Dublin for President Griffith's funeral visited the Show on Wednesday afternoon. Lady Lavery in an all-black toilette. S[ ] is very tall and handsome, and is an American. In the evening Mr. Michael Collins dined quietly with them at their hotel.

GENERAL COLLINS.

ATTACK ON HIS MOTOR-CAR.

A BOMB AND RIFLE-FIRE

From Our Own Correspondent.

Dublin, Sunday.

A sensation was created in Dublin by the official statement that General Michael Collins's motor-brougham was attacked.

The occurrence took place on Friday a[ ] n while the car was being driven from Greystones to Dublin. The place selected for the attack is situated about a mile from Stillorgan, at the Dublin side. The brougham is badly damaged.

A bomb was thrown at it, followed by rifle and revolver fire. The driver, a member of the National Transport Service, named Rafter, was wounded in the hip, and is detained in B[ ] street Hospital.

The attack was particularly da[ ]ing, having occurred about one o'clock in the afternoon, in broad daylight. Though the road from Dublin to Stillorgan is rather frequented, opportunity appears to have been availed of to bring off the attack at a point which would be free from public observation.

General Collins was not in the car. The driver and others returned the fire, but it is not known if the attacking party were injured. A social paragraph on Friday stated that General Collins was among the guests entertained by Sir John and Lady Lavery at the Royal Marine Hotel, Dun Laoghaire.

According to further particulars, the brougham was accompanied by an armed escort in another car. They engaged the attackers, on whom they opened fire immediately. Both cars kept quickly on a rapid move and soon got out of the range of the attackers, who also fled after beginning hostilities.

It is apparent the return of the cars from Greystones was awaited, and the attacking party had taken up a sheltered position, as the drivers did not observe anything suspicious about the road, which seemed quite clear.

General relief was expressed in the city when it was known that Mr. Michael Collins was not in the car at the time of the attack.

It has been known for some time that a section of mutineers have harboured designs upon the lives of certain marked members of the Provisional Government.

A page on George Bernard Shaw and Michael Collins from Hazel Lavery's scrapbook.

BEALNABLATHA—THE SCENE OF THE AMBUSH.

The Commander-in-Chief was at the right-hand side of the road when he received the fatal bullet. H
at once removed to the left side. The mark indicates the spot where he breathed his
last, and in the sward close by a Cross is cut.

Forgive her living, - forgive you dead,
Your passion and beauty are clay cold Michael,

AND YOU LIE ALONE IN YOUR DEEP, DARK BE

"MICHAEL COLLINS: KILLED IN ACTION 22ND AUGUST, 1922":
SIR JOHN LAVERY'S MEMORIAL PICTURE OF HIS DEAD FRIEND.

Another page on Collins from Hazel Lavery's scrapbook. The three lines beneath the image of the ambush site at Béal na mBláth are by Hazel. The obscured poem below is by Shane Leslie.

Hazel with the Irish Governor-General, Tim Healy, at the RDS Horse Show.

Kevin O'Higgins, a photograph given to Hazel on 6 November 1926, the eve of her departure for the United States.

The Laverys with Kevin O'Higgins (*left*) at the Royal Dublin Society Horse Show, August 1925.

Left: Jack McEnery and Alice Trudeau, Cannes 1930. *Centre*: Ramsay MacDonald, British Labour Prime Minister; he gave this photograph to Hazel in July 1930. *Right*: Hazel and John on their last Mediterranean cruise, September 1933.

Hazel outside 5 Cromwell Place, *c*.1931, with a 15 h.p. Armstrong Siddeley, given to her for promotional use by the manufacturers.

Hazel Lavery photographed by Cecil Beaton in 1933, one of a series used in *Vogue* magazine.

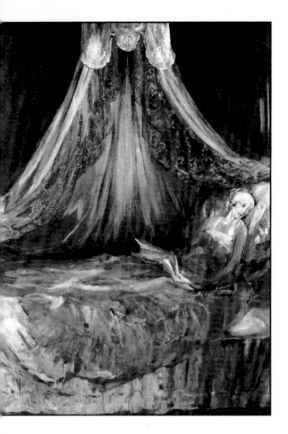

'The Unfinished Harmony', 1934, by Sir John Lavery. This was painted during Hazel's final illness. She died before it was completed. (Hugh Lane Municipal Gallery of Modern Art, Dublin)

'It Is Finished', 5 January 1935, by Sir John Lavery. (Hugh Lane Municipal Gallery of Modern Art, Dublin)

Winston Churchill at Hazel's funeral, Brompton Oratory, London, 7 January 1935.

Soviet tide, and the Conservatives had returned with Stanley Baldwin as Prime Minister. Hazel wrote to Churchill, congratulating him on his appointment as Chancellor of the Exchequer. They continued to hold contrary views on Northern Ireland, and when she raised the question of partition, he responded:

I am glad to know what was the cause of your displeasure because it is certainly *quite unjust*! I have practically always repeated what I said again and again in the House during the passage of the Bill, namely that we never contemplated the 'mutilation' of Ulster. *I* think the Free State are making a frightful mistake in forcing this partition of their country. But of course if they insist, the Treaty must be executed, even though it be to the lasting injury of Irish unity. However, I fear we shall never agree on these subjects. Nevertheless it was very nice hearing from you again.[40]

Despite Hazel's good intentions and social influence, her naive fervour occasionally aroused comment:

One night at the Savoy she saw Lloyd George at one of the tables, advanced on the table where he was smoking a large cigar and said 'I want to settle this Irish dispute tonight.' She then at length propounded the settlement involving the Pope and a French-Canadian Cardinal. Lloyd George began by looking amused but gradually a glaze came over his eyes. The incident only attracted little notice, as Noel Coward, Douglas Fairbanks and another film star were also in the room.[41]

With Ramsay MacDonald out of office, Hazel hoped he might visit Cromwell Place, for she liked the handsome Scot. She had written to thank him for his help over the Boundary Commission negotiations:

I have wished and intended for a long time to write a line of most sincere appreciation and gratitude for all you have done to bring about good feeling and hope in Ireland. I can assure you that Mr Cosgrave and Mr O'Higgins and their Government feel deeply yours and Mr Thomas attitude of courage and fairness in dealing with a problem that was not of your making. I am writing this perhaps rather gratiatingly but Mr Kevin O'Higgins who has just been here asked me to tell you how they felt in case I should see you—the Irish as you know are Conservative in their political sentiments but they are highly sensitive and grateful and quick to honour where honour is due. Which cannot be said of the selfish Conservatives here.[42]

Kevin O'Higgins now became the focus of Hazel's affections, and he visited her frequently in London. As their friendship developed, Hazel would tease him about his moodiness, calling him 'gloomy guss'.[43] Like her other admirers, O'Higgins tried his hand at poetry. Although it is said that he had poems privately printed for her,[44] only one survives:

> H How can I tell you – I unskilled to sing
>
> A All the deep nadirs of despair I know –
>
> Z Zeniths of joy that from remembrance flow
>
> E Evening may fall before our torches glow
>
> L Love of my life, for Time is on the wing.[45]

In early November 1924 O'Higgins told Hazel precisely what her friendship had come to mean:

I got your note of Sunday this morning. I had written to you last night – a queer weary rambling kind of letter which I have destroyed. There was nothing in it which I particularly wanted to say – I was writing simply because I like to hear from you, because your friendship has been for a long time a strength and an inspiration without which I would have crumbled under my load. You *knew* this of course – and it is not any more true or any less true for being written. It is simply a rather stupendous fact. It was on that 'Jumble' I was thinking when I sat tongue tied unable to concentrate on poor Mr Baldwin's difficulties – that queer cruel Jumble with its spikes and broken glass. Yet God knows I would not wish it otherwise. I won't write like this any more, dear Hazel, you will forgive me having written so much. I will get back to the small talk of Irish and Anglo-Irish politics .... Only I can not write of these things now. They don't seem to fit in very well. I had to tell you, *just once*, that you are .not 'a friend of mine' or 'one of my friends' but altogether the sweetest and most wonderful influence in my life. I will not repeat it – after all why should I? – it is true for always ... Yours K.[46]

O'Higgins was known to be a devoted family man. He had a young daughter, Maeve, and that November his wife Brigid, affectionately known as 'Birdie', gave birth to a baby boy. Within twelve days the baby developed pneumonia and died.[47] Before O'Higgins returned to London in December 1924 he wrote to Hazel:

I will see you again before you get this – but I know that when I do see you it will be as it always is, my poor old stunned brain will be unable to send any coherent instruction ... there can be no peace, no happiness for me without you. God help me. I loved the highest when I saw it and Fate has placed it out of reach. You have been so sweet with me.[48]

All of O'Higgins's letters to Hazel after December 1924 were censored by Hazel herself – she clipped out some portions and obliterated others by scribbling over them, then placed the fragments into separate envelopes and dated each one. He wrote frequently, as often as once a week, and sent Hazel copies of several of his political speeches. O'Higgins had fallen in love with Hazel; she was undoubtedly writing just as frequently and accepted his devotion. No correspondence from the period January 1925 to November 1926 survives, but its existence is clear from Hazel's references in later documents.

O'Higgins, indulging Hazel's need to be involved, pressed his Cabinet colleagues to visit Hazel as 'a sort of duty'. Even when Paddy McGilligan wished to remain incognito, O'Higgins took it upon himself to inform Hazel that McGilligan was in London.[49] Desmond FitzGerald, with his portfolio for External Affairs, was often in her debt and in April 1925 Hazel arranged for him to meet with Foreign Secretary Austen Chamberlain. Chamberlain was wary of favouritism and wrote:

It becomes more formal than I intended if I am to 'invite' them over and *might* embarrass me with the representatives of other Dominions. Could you suggest this to Mr C. [Cosgrave] – get them to let me know when Mr FitzGerald or any of the colleagues you name happen to be in London. If by chance any of them happened to be going to call on you (Mr FitzGerald in particular) or were over here for any purpose, I would like to ask them to call. I should feel *no* difficulty about that, but I am a little troubled at the idea of the formal 'summons' to come over apart from the statutory general invitation to all Dominions .. .[50]

After the 'informal' meeting FitzGerald wrote to Hazel that talks 'like the one of Friday evening' were very useful and he would call upon her again.[51]

Hazel provided letters of introduction for dignitaries such as General Sir Sefton Brancker, Director of Civil Aviation, and Professor Emile Ludwig, a German historian, when they were visiting Ireland. On her suggestion Tim Healy invited Leo Amery, the Conservative Colonial Secretary, to the Viceregal Lodge for the 1925 Horse Show. Hazel wrote to Shane Leslie: 'The Viceregal will be rather terrible this year, as Mr Amery is to be there. I advised Tim to ask him as a 'gesture' but never *dreamt* the little Jew would accept! He has and is bringing wife and family!'[52] One newspaper remarked:

It seems perfectly normal to see the Governor-General there in the central box. ... Yet it was recognised as an innovation to see the Minister for the Dominions, Mr Amery, as his guest of honour ... Sir John and Lady Lavery, fortunate people, who can please both North and South in Ireland.[53]

On 5 August O'Higgins invited John and Hazel to visit the Dáil and they listened to the proceedings from the Distinguished Strangers Gallery. On 12 August Gogarty held a garden party and Lennox Robinson recalled that Hazel took him by the arm and insisted he should meet Kevin O'Higgins.[54]

During 1925 O'Higgins went to London at every opportunity. In September he and Desmond FitzGerald spent a week there, as Hazel wrote to a friend:

I was kept busy looking after those young Irish Ministers! and dragging Desmond and Kevin and Mr O'Byrne [the Attorney General] around among the British Statesmen and Press Proprietors. We all spent a week-end with Winston then I took Kevin and Desmond to Sir Horace Plunkett's at Wey-bridge and then to meet Garvin [editor of *The Observer*].[55]

These distractions were welcomed by Hazel, who missed her daughter Alice, now twenty-one and living away from home. Alice had been invited to spend Christmas 1924 in Kilkenny with her school-friend Peggy Moore, whose father hoped that Alice's love of country life would influence Peggy.[56] Alice wrote to her mother:

... [the Irish] are such delightfully kind and amusing people it is nothing like English hunting, either field or country everyone helps everyone else and no one swears at anyone and you're always welcome in the country if you're a stranger. ... I think Ireland is the freshest, simplest, nicest country and people I have ever met and I love every inch of it, so you can say 'I told you so' and crow over me to your hearts content now.[57]

She began visiting Kilkenny for months at a time, staying with the Marks and the McEnerys in Thomastown, Co. Kilkenny. Hazel had often expressed a wish to live permanently in Ireland, and considered buying a house there, but John's work would not permit it.[58] By March 1925 even Alice admitted that the idea was 'a soap bubble'.[59]

John's reaction to O'Higgins's attentions to Hazel are undocumented, but early in 1925 he suggested that the family spend the following winter in America, perhaps in an effort to put distance between O'Higgins and Hazel. Sir Joseph Duveen proposed to exhibit Lavery's interiors, portraits and landscapes in his New York gallery in November and December. It was to be their first visit to America since Dorothy's death fourteen years earlier, and Hazel had been quite content never to visit her native country again. Nor did she want to leave her life in London and her involvement in Irish affairs. She tried to free herself from the journey until Alice decided to accompany them.

For weeks before their departure, Hazel made emotional goodbyes to her friends. George Bernard Shaw wrote:

When Lady Lavery went to New York lately our parting so affected her that ... she kissed me in broad day-light before all the world in Cromwell Place. But it was spoilt by our meeting again next day at lunch at Mary Borden's. When the party broke up Lady Lavery said 'I kissed him yesterday in the middle of the street.' 'Kiss him again by all means,' said Mary. 'I can't' said Lady Lavery; 'he struggles so.'[60]

John, Hazel, Alice, a maid and a valet set sail for New York in November 1925. They stayed at the Ambassador Hotel, while Alice went to Cotton Hill, Connecticut, to stay with Hazel's childhood friend Marie Truesdale, now Mrs Bissell, and then to Saranac Lake to visit the Trudeaus, 'so that they will cease to think me suppressed in any way by cruel mother "who won't let her pining daughter back to her native land"'.[61] Alice had not met her father's family since childhood, and both her paternal grandparents were dead. When in 1915 her grandfather had died, he left her $10,000 in his will.[62]

Hazel and John moved on to the homes of several wealthy families, such as the Yarnells in Philadelphia, to fulfill portrait commissions.[63] John enjoyed America immensely and his commissions enabled them to stay for another two months. Hazel wrote to Eddie Marsh:

It is all far far worse than I anticipated ... suffice it to say I *hate* America! John is a roaring success however and between you and me the pennies are piling up and we shall come back with several bags of this beastly gold only don't mention this too freely it is perhaps indiscreet of me to proclaim the fact particularly to the Exchequer itself! but I know you will be glad to hear that John has been able to take away some of their wealth, which is actually perfectly *amazing* you cannot imagine the strange *sacred importance* that is attached to money ... nothing is tragic or disgraceful or dishonourable save poverty and it is unforgivable as well. John has a great many more portraits and interiors to paint than he can possibly do, but each one fills me with despair because it means a longer stay. We have put off sailing for another two months, alas!

Hazel disdained her husband's American patrons, half-hoping that her aloofness would deter his sitters, but to the contrary, 'the more ungratefully and coldly I behave the more they run after John with open cheque books'.[64] One of John's patrons gave Hazel a diamond bracelet and she wrote: 'It is rather humiliating to my vanity the way wives of my admirers always simply adore me and never suffer a pang of jealousy.'[65]

She feared she was 'getting rather *un Irished*' in America and crudely described Irish-Americans as 'quite awful the worst sort of hyper American even the Jews and Niggers are considered smart in contrast!'[66] John's exhibit travelled on to Pittsburgh, Harrisburgh and Chicago, but the Laverys returned to London in early April 1926.[67] Hazel gleefully wrote to Lady Gregory: 'It is so wonderful to be home again but I shall not really feel at home until I go to Ireland.'[68]

While the Laverys were in America, the Boundary Commission's deliberations came to a premature end: the border established in the Government of Ireland Act was to remain unaltered, with the six counties remaining under the rule of Stormont and Britain. The Free State agreed to increase compensation for property destroyed between July 1921 and May 1923. The Boundary Commission clause, which had persuaded Collins and Griffith to sign the Treaty, had in effect codified the division of Ireland. James MacNeill, Eoin's brother, described the outcome:

As to the result I think that as we could not get more than a few parishes, after much trouble, under an award, we have done better by the settlement. If one believes in eventual and not too remote unity this puts us further on the way. You will probably have heard that there was a hectic week. Cosgrave and Kevin, separately and jointly, did as well as any two men could have done, and I think this success was due primarily to their sincerity and secondarily to their technical competence. ... I think that sincerity and political skill would have been less successful without the goodwill of the P.M. and Winston. As you know, there is a small but sturdy minority in high places who would gladly let us stew. ... In a few years the problem will be changed and the speed of progress towards unification depends mostly on ourselves. ... We shall now settle down like any other dominion to build up a state that is primarily concerned with the welfare of its own people.[69]

O'Higgins had given Hazel his account of the Boundary Commission, as she told Eddie Marsh: 'Kevin says Winston was wonderfully kind and they all liked the PM very much, Thank Heaven, the light seems to be breaking over poor Ireland at last.'[70]

The Laverys' attention now returned to the Hugh Lane controversy. Collins had broached the matter after the Treaty, and several representations were made to the British government for the paintings' return. The Laverys wanted to ask Ramsay MacDonald for the Lane Collection to be returned to Dublin, but were advised to wait until the question was raised in the House of

Commons. A breakthrough had come in 1924 when a committee was appointed to examine the issue. Hazel pressed the issue at every opportunity. In 1929 she wrote to reassure Lady Gregory: 'You must think that because I have delayed answering your charming letter that I haven't been mindful of all the charges because like the Crusader's wife "I too have not been idle."' Hazel had petitioned the Treasurer of the Household, Colonel George Gibbs, who was close to the Royal family and influential with Baldwin's set. She told Lady Gregory that Gibbs was

certainly very sympathetic but so many people are just 'sympathetic!' On Sunday I stayed with Lady Hudson ... the house was full of 'sympathetics' Mr Bir-rell. Sir James Barrie, Sir Arthur Stanley, the Colefaxs, Lady Bonham Carter and so on and on! but really what we want is less sympathy and more tangible proof... although we do so little to help you may be sure we never cease from troubling people here about the beloved country and its welfare ...[71]

The committee decided unanimously against giving Lane's codicil legal effect, having concluded that with knowledge of the Tate Gallery's imminent expansion, he would have certainly destroyed the codicil.[72] The committee also claimed that Sir Joseph Duveen's donation of funds for a new wing was dependent on the paintings remaining in England. Hazel now feared that Lane's gift would be seen as part of the permanent collection. John wrote to Lady Gregory: 'Hazel has been working tooth and heel to get a decision before the official opening but the most she has been able to do has been to prevent an inevitable step being taken. In this she has succeeded and the way is still open.'[73]

While in America John asked Duveen to offer to replace the Lane pictures gradually with comparable works.[74] He believed that 'the pictures arc much wanted for the new Duveen Galleries but as time goes on and other foreign work is accumulated, as it will be, and a new modern Gallery is built in Dublin, there will be a "beau geste" and Hugh Lane's last wish will be fulfilled'.[75] Duveen's wing opened on Saturday, 26 June 1926, and he commissioned John to paint 'The Opening of the Modern Foreign and Sargent Galleries at the Tate Gallery'. John agreed to do it on condition that the Lane paintings were not mentioned as part of the permanent collection at the opening ceremony.[76] John assured Lady Gregory that this meant 'that the authorities are not quite sure of their ground and leaves there an opening, when the time comes, to hand over the pictures'.[77] Hazel thought John overly optimistic but agreed that efforts should be concentrated on building or obtaining a suitable gallery in Dublin, as 'the Tate people and other opponents are forever throwing that in our faces'.[78]

The Laverys returned to the Viceregal Lodge in early August 1926. Alice, now a permanent resident of Thomastown, attended the Horse Show with her parents. While Lavery painted a picture of the judges' box at the Royal Dublin Society, Hazel was with Kevin O'Higgins, who later recalled: 'we sat together at Ballsbridge and looked towards (rather than at) the Horse Show. Do you remember it all, Hazel, every tiny throbbing detail?'[79]

By the end of the year Hazel and O'Higgins were to be parted again. John had had such success in America that he planned to spend a second winter there to work on further commissions. Hazel wrote to Lennox Robinson in despair: 'I leave for America early in November. The idea of another winter in the land of my birth staggers me, especially as I must go to Palm Beach. ...'[80] Desmond FitzGerald, hearing that Hazel would be out of London for part of the Imperial Conference, wrote plaintively:

It is most unfortunate that you will be away then. You know I say that earnestly – not merely selfishly because I like to go to see you sometimes – but because I think your presence in London would be quite important to us at that time particularly. I got quite a shock when I read your letter. I wish Columbus had minded his own business instead of discovering that place. You will at least be in London for the early part of the conference I hope?[81]

At the 1926 Imperial Conference, the Irish delegates were welcomed and courted by London society, with invitations issued for the 'at homes' of Lady Evelyn Guinness, Mrs Kenilworth, the

Duchess of Atholl and the Nobles.[82] The list of official activities for the delegates was extensive. O'Higgins was particularly frustrated by the arduous schedule and Hazel's full diary:

I do know how extraordinarily difficult it must have been for you through all those weeks to fight to keep free from engagements of all kinds which would have encroached upon our [time] ... and yet you managed it, wonderfully, mysteriously as you manage all things ... and oh! I love you for it all.[83]

He dreaded Hazel's departure for America. He had given her a book of poems by Samuel Ferguson and marked 'The Fair-haired Girl: Irish Song', and later wrote 'prophetic of 6 November 1926 K. to H.':

> I through love have learn'd three things,
>
> Sorrow, sin and death it brings;
>
> Yet day by day my heart within
>
> Dares shame and sorrow, death and sin;
>
> Maiden, you have aim'd the dart
>
> Rankling in my ruin'd heart:
>
> Maiden, may the God above
>
> Grant you grace to grant me![84]

Two days before the Laverys set sail, Hazel and O'Higgins parted 'woefully at that horrible station'.[85] The experience was made more unbearable by the arrival of a 'rather motley company': Margot Asquith, Patrick and Lady Ford, William Whyte, and Lord Londonderry.[86] O'Higgins wrote later that day: 'The Spring will bring you back, my beloved and you will bring back the Spring to me. Till then I must set my teeth. ... You are a necessity of existence, like the sun and the air, my own darling. I am yours in time and eternity.'[87]

Hazel and John had agreed to let Alice stay in Co. Kilkenny rather than travel to the United States. She had fallen in love with Jack McEnery, thirteen years her senior and the eldest of twelve children, who lived at 'Rossenarra', in Kilmoganny, with his widowed mother. Alice admired McEnery's skills as a horse-man, but despaired of his shyness and assured an apprehensive Hazel that he was not interested in her.[88]

The Laverys departed from Southampton on 10 November on the S.S. *Majestic*. Hazel wrote to Lennox Robinson while on board: 'Think of me sometimes and do not again write to me that I shall like America better the second time. It is more than I can bear and sounds unsympathetic on your part. I want you to be miserable, to miss me and feel sorry for me.'[89]

O'Higgins in the meantime sent details of the Imperial Con-ference proceedings. The Irish ministers were highly successful, combining with the Canadian and South African delegates to have the Balfour Declaration issued.* O'Higgins was also putting forward a plan for Dual Monarchy, under which a king would be appointed for both North and South of Ireland. At the end of November he described how he approached Carson with the idea:

I bearded the old Lion in his den at Baton Square and talked to him about the 'Kingdom of Ireland' ... the worst he said on the subject was that it might be 'too soon'. Encouraged by this and the fact that Amery (!) Churchill and F.E. are breast-high for the thing, we are taking steps to put it direct to Craig. If he rejects it – as he probably will – his position with the British Govt. will not be improved for undoubtedly the three I have named plus Tom Jones are enthusiastically favour-able. That's as far as the move has gone and a Dublin Coronation is still a long way off....[90]

O'Higgins was miserable without Hazel's company but enjoyed her letters filled with political commentary: 'What a pet you are to make time to give me all that excellent political advice! It was all very very sound too and I'm not smiling at it the tiniest bit.'[91] When he

---

* The Balfour Declaration stated that the Dominions were autonomous communities within the British Empire, equal in status, in no way subordinate one to another in any aspect of their domestic or external affairs, though united by a common allegiance to the Crown and freely associated as members of the British Commonwealth of Nations.

later wrote, 'Whatever I do besides is done with your name in my heart on my lips,' Hazel transcribed the words on the envelope.

O'Higgins emerges in the correspondence in stark contrast to his public persona – the deeply religious hard man of the Cabinet who had considered a vocation to the priesthood and fasted for six months before his marriage. His biographer Terence de Vere White refers to O'Higgins's almost medieval attitude towards women, excluding female stenographers from circuit courts and keeping them from jury duty as they might hear subjects 'one would not wish to discuss with the feminine members of one's family'.[92] But his letters to Hazel reveal the man of flesh and blood:

I am lost and desolate without you ——*I want you ————— all the enchantments ————————sight and sounds and the *touch of you* I want to hold you to me and hear you say again and again and again that you love me and are [mine] forever and that you treasure in your [heart] every golden moment we have spent together in the glory of our [love] [Dear] heart I love you utterly ————————————————you always ————————————— All yours.[93]

The Laverys were in Boston in early December and spent Christmas in New York. John was frantically busy painting portraits of fifteen patrons and later confessed: "I don't think I had two hours left out of three months to enjoy myself."[94] In January 1927 his exhibition of 'Portraits, Interiors and Landscapes' opened in Palm Beach, Florida. Hazel did not 'sound hopeful of happiness', and Alice consoled her: 'Time is so short now that you will not notice American horrors for thinking of home.'[95]

At home O'Higgins was beset by his love for Hazel. His estrangement from his wife and young family is painfully underscored in a letter to Hazel ten days after the birth of his second daughter, Una, in January 1927: 'I am lost and broken. You are my life and my breath my sun and air and wind. Having absorbed everything, having become all life holds for me.'[96]

When the Laverys returned to London in early March O'Hig-

---

* The dashes represent parts of the letter that were redacted by Hazel.

gins wrote that his happiness made his head reel, and he and Hazel planned a reunion on the 21st.[97] Hazel found life demanding on her return: 'The past week has been very crowded and muddled. John's daughter, my step-daughter, has been very ill and although she is slowly recovering it has been an anxious time.'[98] While John joined Eileen, who was in a sanatorium suffering from tuberculosis which would later take her life. Hazel was welcomed home by delighted friends. One newspaper reported: 'Lady Lavery has found herself with very little spare time since she got back with her husband from America. Every artistic venture which society has embarked upon seems to have needed her guidance and advice lately.'[99]

A letter awaited her from Lady Gregory outlining the current status of the Lane paintings. Hazel replied:

I am seeing Edward Hamsworth tomorrow he was quite good in the *Daily Mail* as you know but for some reason has been 'put off not personally I hope but there seems to be a great many hidden hands at work. I have also seen Lady Londonderry who is still keen and Lord Peel who of course is *not* but I have asked him to luncheon on Thursday with the Chamberlains who are great friends of mine and Austen has always been helpful about Ireland. Mr Amery on the other hand seems to have been rather got at. I sat by him at the Irish Dinner when Pagan read the statement about the pictures and it seemed rather to annoy and upset him. ... I did my best to put him right again because at one time he was sympathetic at least for him. ... I am not discouraged though I may sound a trifle that way but I am a little negatified.[100]

Despite Hazel's intentions, the matter progressed no further.

In Dublin O'Higgins was preparing for the general election of June 1927, and described his life to Hazel as 'pretty hideous'.[101]

I am so unhappy and I want you, want you, want you, and it is so miserable to have to pretend that I haven't a wish in the world except to win the elections which is absurd and suggests a convict clamouring for heavier balls of lead about his ankles![102]

A general mood of apathy prevailed. Cumann na nGaedheal, as Cosgrave's party was known, did little to woo the electorate, simply listing their achievements over the previous five years. In

129

March 1926 de Valera had resigned as head of Sinn Féin to form a new political party, Fianna Fáil, which quickly gained support throughout the country. By 10 June O'Higgins was disillusioned and tired:

... is it all worth while, I wonder? this brick-laying of *ours!* Will some fool come along some day when you and I are dead and kick the fabric of our rearing into dust and nothingness? Or will Ireland go forward from strength to strength to find at last Unity and Peace – Peace for her fevered soul?[103]

He was re-elected as the Cumann na nGaedheal candidate to his South Dublin constituency. On 23 June 1927 de Valera and Fianna Fail entered the Dáil but, refusing to take the Oath of Fidelity to King and Commonwealth, were locked out of the chamber.

O'Higgins was quickly appointed Vice-President and Minister for Justice, and also took on the External Affairs portfolio. Within days of taking office he went to Geneva for a conference on the limitation of naval armaments.[104] Hazel thought he looked 'ghastly ill' and wrote:

Kevin lunched with me here en route to Geneva, very pale and powerful looking but very much overdone by the last frightful weeks. Geneva will do him all the good in the world. Everyone here is pleased he has taken on External Affairs. Kevin will keep the English Ministers in their places and put the fear of death into them with his mordant jokes.[105]

Writing from Geneva, O'Higgins was more concerned with affairs in London:

I never found you more utterly, bewilderingly beautiful, more sweetly tender, than when last we met. The deficiency was *mine* and *mine only.* I was utterly spent in mind and body I could only sit and rest in you – listening to your voice rather than your words and trying to get my bearing in the swift transition ... the two of us with our heads in the clouds and the dirty world ever so far below...[106]

O'Higgins returned via London and was with Hazel on 6 and 7 July. Back in Dublin on Sunday 10 July he set out alone to walk the short distance to Mass at Booterstown, without his personal bodyguard. Three Republicans passing through Booterstown chanced upon the unarmed Minister. They fired at him from their car, then got out and shot him again at point-blank range. His assassins reportedly heard him say: 'There has been too much killing in our country. The killing has got to stop. I forgive you.'[107] Hearing the shots, Eoin MacNeill, who lived nearby, was first on the scene. Hazel later said that as O'Higgins died he gave MacNeill a final message for her; MacNeill, perhaps out of propriety, said O'Higgins's dying words were, 'Tell my wife I love her eternally'. He was carried back to his house, still conscious, and lived for five hours. He called out for various people and, according to one report, for Hazel.[108] A few minutes before five o'clock the doctor pronounced him dead.[109]

It was a hot afternoon when word reached Hazel in London. She was sitting on the terrace at Ranelagh watching polo when she received the telegram. She rushed home to find out exactly what had happened. Shane Leslie was summoned by John to comfort her and found her wallowing in 'grief and self-accusation':

I held her for some hours while she shook and sobbed in my arms. She was aghast. She cried out that every man who ever loved her with true love was bound to die. She said she had killed her first husband, Collins and Kevin. She cursed herself as a curse to men.[111]

Hazel expressed her grief to Lennox Robinson:

I can't write, Lennox dear. I feel as though I had been killed too and left broken in the dust. 'Sic itur ad astra'. He was here on Wednesday and Thursday on his way back from Geneva and I had a letter from him written on Friday which was on my breakfast tray Monday morning, so he was dead before it reached me and I've been spared nothing of the lesser stabs of tragic reminder.[112]

She did not attend O'Higgins's funeral, as she wrote to Father Leonard: 'I cannot and do not wish to go to Ireland. I hope I may never see it or any of them again, with the first reaction to shock and pain there comes a curious exaltation that makes one continue to see things with the vision of the dead – but this false sentiment has left me with only bitter contempt for them all.'[113]

Eoin O'Duffy, Commissioner of Guards, had received a message from Hazel the night before the burial, and wrote to her:

I placed the little bunch of flowers at his head that night and I afterwards placed them on his grave at Glasnevin. Being tiny and sweet they were much admired. I intended to place the little bunch of white heather in the coffin but the lid was on when I got there, however I did the next best thing I attached it with a little wire clip to a handle of the coffin. It will be thus with him as you desired.[114]

Letters of condolence arrived from Sibyl Colefax, J.L. Garvin of *The Observer*, Eddie Marsh, Stephen MacKenna and Stephen Gwynn among others. Louie Rickard wrote:

Hazel beloved I have been thinking and think of you without ceasing since I left you and am heartbroken for you. I know the uselessness of words and the folly of any attempt to comfort. The breaking of so much beauty ... shattering blow at the very heart of life goes utterly beyond expression. My Hazel Beloved, you must lift up your dear beautiful head and this tragedy must be glorified .... For some reason or other, and in this terrible way, Kevin died for Ireland. We don't yet know how, or why it had to come like that, but in the end it will be made clear. Dearest, dearest, we only see such a little bit of the whole large purpose and there is nothing one can do except offer up one's broken heart with all the rest.[115]

On 27 July Kevin's widow, Birdie, wrote from Knocklawn in Greystones, Co. Wicklow. She addressed Hazel as 'My dear Lady Lavery':

I want to thank you and Sir John Lavery for your loving messages on the death of our dauntless hero, my beloved Kevin. You were his dear, dear friends – he loved you *both* and he will be with you in life and by your sides when death comes. His own death was an inspiration – quiet – great, beautiful!!!!!!! Sometime I want to tell you about it! I'm sorry you were not here to say adieu to his noble spirit for nothing in his life became him like the manner of leaving it. It was magnificent. He conquered death as he conquered life. He was serene. But Oh! for those who are left ... it is unthinkable – and yet with dying breath he charged us all 'to be brave and to carry on' and 'orders is orders'.[116]

Hazel found these sentiments chilling and showed the letter to Louie Rickard, who was equally aghast.[117] When she sent Birdie O'Higgins' letter to Father Leonard she wrote:

I am enclosing you a card which I have recently received from her on this subject. I make no comment it seems to me too incredible and reveals a point of view and character past my understanding. I have however now received his *last* message *for me* entrusted to another and most truly faithfully delivered to me as he would have desired. Please let me have the enclosed back again indirectly it is a great comfort to me. I have a weakness for irony and the mocking laughter of the Gods! it seems to sting me into a defiant indifference which to my mind seems the only armour against the arrows of fate.[118]

She circulated her letters from O'Higgins freely, just as she had done with Collins's years before.* Lennox Robinson wrote:

It was sweet of you to let me see the letters which I return. I wish I could be wise and take long views and talk of sacrifice not made in vain and all that other bloody rot – I can only wail and turn my face to the wall and hate this mad cruel world.[119]

Hazel wrote subsequently to Desmond FitzGerald, probably to ensure the destruction of her letters to O'Higgins, but as FitzGerald was ill, the surviving reply is from Diarmuid O'Hegarty: '... you need have no further worry. The matter you mentioned has been dealt with. This has been a terrible blow to all of us and I know you must be terribly shocked.'[120]

In the aftermath of O'Higgins's assassination, a Public Safety Act was introduced allowing the government to arrest and impose the death penalty for possession of illegal firearms. An Electoral Amendment Act was passed stating that each candidate for election must swear to take the Oath of Allegiance within a given

---

* In 1949 Terence de Vere White, O'Higgins's biographer, told Thomas Bodkin that he had approached Alice about viewing O'Higgins's correspondence. De Vere White was told that it had all been destroyed and in any case was of little interest. Bodkin wrote: 'Having been shown some of it myself by Lady Lavery, I could only comment cordially on Mrs McEnery's discretion. I have myself a great number of letters ... often amusing things but just as often indiscreet about contemporaries.'

time or vacate his seat. After this the elected representatives of Fianna Fáil finally entered the Dáil. Hazel was furious, describing Fianna Fáil as the party responsible for O'Higgins's murder.[121]

Despite many sympathy letters from Ireland, Hazel still felt ostracized and wrote to Lennox Robinson that she would not make her annual visit to the Horse Show. He replied:

I'm very very sorry that there has been rudeness to you. I know nothing, haven't seen any government people, can't make out from your letter (now burned) what happened, but you're feeling hurt and that's enough for me to feel angry against those who hurt you – I wish to God I could see you and talk to you – we fit each other in a blundering kind of way – blundering I mean on my side. Love and love Lennox.[122]

Although the political face of Ireland was changing rapidly, Hazel's life retained a familiar pattern. She and John visited the Fords in Scotland and later departed for America. John remained in New York, working in Malvina Hoffman's studio on a commissioned portrait of Cardinal Hayes, while Hazel and Alice visited the Bissells in Connecticut. Hazel was suffering from acute shock and John feared another nervous breakdown like the one she had in 1915. Concerned that he would shut her out as he had his first wife, Kathleen, he wrote:

It was a bit empty when I returned and found no-one here ... but I am, as you know, only really serious minded when I work ... I am so occupied with myself that I was on the point of forgetting that you also have feelings that may keep you awake and make you think you are all alone. Don't you believe it. I feel nearer to you this minute than you think.[123]

There is little surviving correspondence from this American visit, but Hazel's despondency is illustrated in a letter from Louie Rickard:

Hazel darling I cannot bear to think of you suffering as you are and can see how this grief has caught you so cruelly. Oh my dear for the sake of all of us who love you so try to swim hard. I know your courage, that wonderful gay courage of yours which is part of your beloved self, and it will return completely. ... Remember that everything gets back to the normal with time however little it seems likely to do so. Steady dearest.[124]

Hazel never went back to the United States after that November, and she was still not prepared to let go of her adopted land. she wrote to a friend: 'I shall come over to Ireland at the first opportunity as I am only happy when I am being made miserable in that most lovely and cruel country!'[125]

The Laverys returned from their winter in America in March 1927.
O'Higgins had been reunited with Hazel in London at the end of that month and wrote this letter shortly after his return to Ireland.

IX

'heartsick of all things Irish'
[1927-9]

I N JULY 1927 John wished to donate his Irish Collection,
which now comprised thirty paintings of Irish figures and
events from the previous decade. Thomas Bodkin, the newly
appointed Director of the National Gallery of Ireland, was asked
to lunch at Cromwell Place to discuss how the collection could
be given to the Free State with as few complications as possible.[1]
Congestion at the National Gallery and the refusal of an extension
by the Board of Works, combined with the Gallery's stipulation that
paintings by living artists must represent deceased Irishmen, made
for difficulties. It was also feared their controversial subject-matter
would incite vandalism.[2] According to Bodkin, Chief Justice Hugh
Kennedy felt that there 'were many grave matters connected the
proposed gift', and that 'Sir John almost certainly did not know
the full facts, but that Lady Lavery probably did'.[3]

Correspondence between Bodkin and President Cosgrave during October, while the Laverys were in America, indicates that the
paintings were on the verge of being accepted. Bodkin wrote to the
Laverys on 3 December that the proposal would be put before the
National Gallery committee in January 1928.[4] Hazel had written
to the President:

... we do not wish to interfere or cause you any disturbance or embarrassment particularly in the matter of the offer of the Irish Pictures to the National Gallery. John
feels that it was perhaps a little premature, his offer, but that was my fault. ... John
does not wish the gift to have any other than an *artistic* and *historical* significance
and to be *hung together* as such whenever the time is suitable. But he feels that he
would not care to have the collection broken up or hung separately as it would lose
the definite sequence which he aimed at. I also wished him to give the pictures before
he presented those to the Belfast Gallery but I am afraid that won't be possible as the
Northern Gallery is almost complete.[5]

John had also painted a collection for the North which was
immediately accepted and housed in a new gallery in Belfast. In
gratitude for this gift to his native city, he would later be awarded
the Freedom of Belfast, becoming the first artist, and first Catholic,
to receive this honour.

As early as 1922 an Irish newspaper had speculated that Lavery would be made official painter to the Free State.[6] Gearóid
McGann had written to Hazel in 1923 saying, 'at present there
is a vacancy on the Board of Governors of the National Gallery
of Ireland and I would like to ascertain privately for the President's information would Sir John care to accept it'.[7] The position never materialized. John's name had also been suggested for
the post of Governor-General in 1922.[8] This rumour circulated
continuously over the next decade. An Irish admirer wrote to
Hazel:

I can only think of one possible man who as Governor-General of the Free State
would have the good will of Republicans, Free Staters, and Ulstermen at once and
that is Sir John. ... I don't of course need to say what a beautiful Lady Lieutenant
I think you'd be in every way, but it's the good will you'd both bring that I think
matters most.[9]

Hazel knew John was an unlikely successor to Tim Healy, and
confided to Lennox Robinson:

I have heard the idea very seriously discussed, but am afraid it will never happen,
much as I would love it. John Lavery would be one to say it would be 'Out of the
question' and 'Absurd'. And Dubliners would object violently to such 'Aliens'. A
Belfast knight and his Irish American lady would never be acceptable. So I don't

let myself dream of playing at being Queen of Ireland, enchanting and delicious as such a dream might be.[10]

O'Higgins had fuelled Hazel's initial enthusiasm, and even John gave the proposal brief consideration: 'I had vague thoughts of Velasquez as Ambassador for Philip IV, Vandyke [*sic*] and other artists in diplomatic positions, but saw the absurdity of it all so far as it concerned me, and told Kevin so.' A few days before O'Higgins's assassination Winston Churchill remarked to John that O'Higgins's idea of the Laverys' getting the Viceregal position had been favourably received in England.[11] John's version of this incident in his autobiography was criticized by the *Irish Independent* in 1940: 'It may be just a non-politician's inaccuracy in these matters; but ... neither the British Ministers nor anybody else in London had any say whatever in the matter, except that the King had the duty to appoint the person who was nominated by the Irish Government.'[12] John had written:

Hazel broke down when Kevin was assassinated. Apart from the tragedy, it shattered her dream of Vice-Regal Lodge. I was terribly sorry for her, for if there ever was a woman qualified for the position of Vicereine of Ireland at that period it was Hazel. When I realized her disappointment I felt I could have given up the paint-brush for the simple joy of seeing her great gifts gloriously framed for the benefit of the Ireland of her own creation, which may indeed have been the real Ireland. At the same time I had a selfish sense of relief that the life I had lived for over half a century, and the one for which I was best fitted, was not to be disturbed.[13]

James MacNeill, former High Commissioner in London, was chosen to be Governor-General in December 1927. Inevitably, Hazel resented MacNeill's wife Josephine, and Alice recalled how her mother had difficulty hiding her disappointment when the MacNeills broke the news.[14] Thenceforth Hazel referred to Josephine as 'the Empress'.

Thomas Bodkin hoped to take MacNeill's place as High Commissioner in London, and asked for Hazel's support.[15] The two became close friends and corresponded frequently. Hazel seized every opportunity to promote his candidacy, whether weekending at

138

Dorking with the Chamberlains or lunching with the Birkenheads. She wrote to Tim Healy, who replied: 'I read in the *Evening Mail* last night that the new High Commissioner was to be a brother of Mr McGilligan [the Minister of External Affairs]. You will, therefore, appreciate why I cannot interpose.'[16]

After O'Higgins's death. Hazel's relations with Irish ministers were strained. Hazel thought her efforts on behalf of Bodkin might be seen as 'intriguing' within the Irish Cabinet,[17] which was now advocating an Irish-Ireland policy that entailed a promotion of Irish culture and language to overcome the influences of English colonial rule. Chief among these was Ernest Blythe, Vice-President and Minister for Finance, whom Hazel had first met in 1924. Hazel had little time for 'all this language movement nonsense' and quipped that the Governor-General would be the only English-speaker left in Ireland. She envisioned a time when the Viceregal Lodge would be the sole place a lonely 'foreigner' could go when he wanted to hire an interpreter or have a cheque cashed into money that could be used in any other country.[18]

Although Hazel was unable to help Bodkin, he was to use his influence to gain lasting recognition for the Laverys. As Director of the National Gallery of Ireland he had been asked to advise the Currency Commission on a design for the new Irish Free State banknotes. In early December 1927 he discussed with Hazel the idea of using her portrait as the central motif on the notes. On 21 December he wrote:

After some futile discussion as to the head to go upon the notes, when all the patriots past and present, and many symbolic figures had been turned down, I suggested that one of your portraits by Sir John should be utilized, and produced the two photographs you gave me. The idea, as you warned me, was scouted at first, but the photographs made a great impression and finally, after a good deal of argument, the meeting agreed that the suggestion was the best one yet laid before them. The difficulties they foresee are (1) that every jealous woman who fancies her looks will ask, Why was Lady Lavery put up on the notes instead of myself? (2) That to reproduce a picture in some Public Gallery would seem to be advertising that Gallery unduly. I then suggested that Sir John might be asked to paint a picture of a beautiful Irish type for the purpose of reproduction on the Notes. ... It is quite understood by us, and will I am sure be understood by the Commission, that Sir John is to select for his type of Irish feminine beauty *the model who most appeals to him*. ... I have only to add that I did not mention to anyone that I discussed the matter with you or Sir John, nor that I had obtained the two photographs from you.[19]

Objections to this scheme focused upon the suitability of Hazel as an Irish figurehead. Frank Lillis, Chairman of the Munster and Leinster Bank, claimed the notes would be called 'Laverys' and that Hazel's image would be recognizable. Bodkin argued that 'Masaryk's daughter appeared on the Czech notes because it was put there simply as a lovely national type.'[20]

Other artists put forward by members of the Currency Commission were rejected by Bodkin, and the group finally agreed to approach Lavery.[21] After Bodkin informed Hazel of the decision, the official request came from Joseph Brennan, head of the Commission. Brennan wrote:

The Currency Commission is at present engaged in the task of settling the designs for the new note issues of the Irish Free State and has sought advice from a few persons of artistic standing in Dublin whose opinions seem likely to be useful. Technical factors connected with the safeguards which should be adopted to frustrate forgery affect the problem of design to some extent but it seems to be quite feasible to find a solution which will give satisfactory results both technically and artistically. ... On protective and artistic grounds the use of a well engraved portrait has a great deal to recommend it. It has been suggested to the Commission that it should invite you to paint a portrait for this purpose ... what we have in mind is that it should be a portrait of a beautiful female head treated in some emblematic fashion which might perhaps have some Irish association.[22]

John modestly suggested that Sean Keating was the ideal choice to design the notes, and proposed an open competition, with the winning design to become the property of the Bank.[23] Bodkin replied to Hazel: 'Sir John's most kind letter to me showed, I thought, a reprehensible desire to do John Keating a good turn.' He also believed that there was not enough time for a competition, and feared that if it took place the Commissioners would wish to act as judges themselves:

Their award would probably favour a portrait of some farmer's daughter. They are men of business, but, emphatically not men of taste. I know them all. So, for the honour of Ireland and the cause of Art, I do hope that Sir John will be asked, and will consent, to do a portrait of you for the notes.[24]

Hazel was delighted:

I really feel you are too kind and generous when you suggest that my humble head should figure on the notes and you know I said from the first that I thought it wildly *improbable, unlikely,* impracticable, *unpopular, impossible*! that any committee would fall in with such a suggestion. Indeed apart from anything else I think a classic head, some Queen of Ireland, Maeve perhaps, would be best. Some one more robust and noble ... although when I describe the type it conjures up a vision of the Marchioness McSwiney or Mrs 'Huge' Kennedy!

Hazel went on to suggest that John paint her as he had in 'The Red Rose', which was an idealized treatment rather than a portrait.[25] John, however, chose to rework an early portrait, 'Mrs Lavery' (1909), into Erin. He began work in January 1928, adding an Irish landscape in the background and renaming the work 'Killarney'. Hazel wrote to Brennan: 'I wanted him to call it "Galway" or "Connemara" I having a weakness for the "West" being a "Martyn" (with a "y") and proud of it!'

She knew she was arousing controversy: 'I shall continue to be very discreet as to the model for the head in the shawl.'[26] John had been quoted in the *Irish Independent* as saying, 'It was not to be a portrait of any particular person', but Hazel's identity was not concealed for long. She wrote to Brennan:

Was it not very disagreeable of the *Express* to publish that comment on the new notes. John asked them where they heard the rumour and they said 'from *Ireland*'. You may *be sure* he denied the statement as to the model and I need not tell you that the story did not come from us. We have really been discreet for your sake and our own.[27]

In May the *Express* attributed the leakage to Hazel. 'Bank Note mystery has been solved", its reporter announced. 'I learn that she is the wife of the famous Irish artist. Lady Lavery has been the model for some of her husband's most successful paintings ... she disclosed to a friend her identity with the head of Erin.'[28] According to a letter from John to Brennan, Hazel indignantly claimed that it was the first time she had 'ever kept a secret absolutely and under great provocation', and that it was 'hard luck to be so rewarded for her single act of discretion'.[29]

The Catholic Herald asserted that Lavery could not have had the 'bad taste' to put his wife's head on the design for the bank notes, and was certain that he was not 'guilty' of so grave a 'breach'. John threatened to reply to the article officially, believing that it had not been 'bad taste' when Rembrandt and others had painted their wives.[30] When the watermark chosen was taken from a portal design by the Irish sculptor John Hogan, of his Italian wife, the irony was not lost on Hazel:

... do find out if the fat female symbolical figure of 'Erin' as the watermark is a portrait of the late Mrs Hogan and whether she was born and bred in Ireland and has no taint of Liverpool, Glasgow or American-Irish in her veins. I should like to be sure of these facts. It would be terrible for Mr Blythe if she should prove to be *not Mrs* Hogan but someone else's wife who sat for the 'Emblematical head'. Forgive me for frivolling but they are funny in their anxiety to disassociate me from any place in the new currency or give me any credit for anything.[31]

Without O'Higgins *to* encourage their visits, the Irish ministers now no longer called to Cromwell Place while in London. Hazel felt this keenly and in March 1928 wrote to Paddy McGilligan, the Minister for External Affairs:

I had hoped so much that you and Mr [Patrick] Hogan might have come to see me when you were in London but I know you were very busy – you may be certain we should have been very pleased and honoured if you could have found time. Please feel that if there is any *little thing* I could do in any way to help, tell me and let me try.[32]

Rumours of Hazel's relationship with O'Higgins may have been responsible for tainting her reputation. Kevin's widow, Birdie, often commented on Hazel, who wrote to Bodkin in exasperation:

I felt inclined to be equally irritated at Birdie's constant sly digs at your wife about me and London visits ... if she continues I shall send her half a dozen of the three hundred odd letters I have from her husband bearing *in no complimentary* manner on married life in general and his own in particular – a fact that only her monumental vanity and cloying sentimentality prevented her from appreciating time and again. But of course, you know, I would do nothing of the sort. I am only sometimes strongly tempted to when she is particularly vulgar and maddening in her technique towards me, and poor, poor Kevin.[33]

As the first anniversary of O'Higgins' death approached. Hazel felt his native land had forgotten him.[34] She recalled:

... it is strange that only a year ago, Tuesday, Wednesday and Thursday of this week he was in London on his way back from Geneva, lovely golden warm summer days. I am glad they were unclouded he had had so few unshadowed hours poor tragic haunted Kevin and thank God he did not guess that in a few hours he would have left the sunlight forever. It is dreadful but I could never think of him save in darkness and tragedy hung about him and lent him that strange fatal dignity like a dark mantle.[35]

In English circles, the Laverys had always defended the Irish position, but after a weekend party at Philip Sassoon's in New Barnet, Trent, Hazel declared: "I'm tired of fighting Irish Battles on English soil! And being blamed by both sides particularly the Irish themselves.'[36]

Josephine MacNeill had not written 'a line' to Hazel since moving to the Viceregal Lodge and Hazel commented, 'I used to think her mad but I think it really is that she suffers from loss of memory only.'[37] In early April an invitation finally arrived from the Lodge, but John declined it.[38] Instead, that month they made their first visit to Alice in Kilkenny. Alice's letters home had told only of her new hunter and an outbreak of foot-and-mouth disease.[39] Hazel found little to her taste in the countryside. Her Ireland of political leaders and the society of the Viceregal Lodge differed utterly from Alice's.

By summer, relations with Josephine MacNeill had improved, and to Hazel's delight she invited the Laverys to the Lodge for

Horse Show week, asking Hazel to suggest other guests. Hazel wrote to Bodkin:

... the Lovats, Birkenheads, Shaws, Chamberlain, Balloe, Churchill, Amery, Londonderry (possibly not the Prince of Wales or the Yorks just yet) would all be welcome I take it, and it is very flattering to feel that she imagines *I* could persuade them to come. It hurts my pride to admit that they most likely would not but I advised her to by all means write or 'command' every class and country – and after all why not, it would startle the Cabinet.[40]

Hazel's proposed guest-list included a lady-in-waiting to Queen Mary, and Josephine chastized her:

... *I think a person immediately connected with royalty would not be exactly the best person*. It is my opinion that the best relations between England and Ireland will be established – *not* on the basis of *throne loyalty* (the *King* is the political badge ... and merely as such that he is acceptable to the great majority here – not for any personal reason of course!) but on the basis of their relationship as partners in the Commonwealth of free nations. On this basis a very real advance is possible, and in fact has already begun. Because of this belief which is purely personal, *though it happens* to *coincide* with the very striking and *true* views put forward in a recent article in the *Government Party Organ*.[41]

Hazel was infuriated and copied the letter for Bodkin, an impulse she later regretted. He replied:

I feel ashamed of my country. The 'Empress' letter is as nasty a morsel of vain, ignorant folly as anything I have ever set eyes on. I cannot begin to understand how anyone can be so devoid of a sense of personal honour as to accept the position of the King's representative, and the prestige and involvements of that office, with the apparent desire of slighting and insulting the King himself. Nor can I see how such conduct is likely to help poor Ireland. ... The attitude of the Government towards England is sickening and every sensible man here, who asks himself what can they expect to gain in honour or in profit by childishly irritating our neighbour, our best customer and our accepted ally, in a silly effort to outbid a discredited bunch of extremists.[42]

Although Josephine's letter turned the Laverys against visiting the Viceregal Lodge in 1928, Tim Healy urged Hazel to accept the invitation, advising that personal diplomacy might achieve what a letter could not.[43] Hazel wrote to Bodkin:

I'm heartsick of all things Irish and although I like to think that you will continue to write and think of me with friendship, I am trying to wipe Ireland out of my mind and heart. Everything that I dreamed and hoped and worked for lies in the dust. No one cares and neither will I.[44]

They went instead to the North to stay with the Londonder-rys at Mount Stewart. From there Hazel wrote forlornly: 'The North bores me to extinction although I am fond of the Londonderrys and they are their very nicest in their Irish demesne, but all the romance is bound up in the South for me.'[45]

While in the North, John was painting portraits for his Northern Collection. His sitters included Dr Grierson (Bishop of Down, Connor and Dromore), Dr D'Arcy (Protestant Primate of all Ireland), Dr McRory (Catholic Primate of all Ireland), Joseph Devlin MP, Sir Edward Archdale (Imperial Grand Master of the Orange Lodge) and Sir Joseph Davison (Belfast Grand Master). Hazel befriended Archdale and D'Arcy and liked to think that she had helped to 'fan and foster' their sympathy for the South.[46] On the whole she disliked

the Black North ... although I must say they all are kindness and attention personified only somehow I can't 'bloom' among them. There is always a 'to hell with the Pope' and 'King Billy' atmosphere that I sense through their most flattering and sympathetic conversation.[47]

By September 1928 the appointment of the Irish High Commissioner was imminent.' When Desmond FitzGerald came to London Hazel lobbied him on Bodkin's behalf, but although she used all her powers of persuasion, ridicule and disapproval, she failed to change his mind.

I did not press the matter but merely said that I thought 'the gentleman in question' was *ideal* and for that reason he 'probably would *not* be appointed judging by the usual procedure of the F.S. [Free State] Cabinet in *always* selecting the wrong man for the highest posts'.[48]

Professor Smiddy, the candidate favoured by the government, was appointed in October. Smiddy had been an economic advisor to Collins during the Treaty negotiations and, after 1923, a permanent government official, lecturer and diplomat in the USA and Canada.[49] Hazel was dismayed: "I am miserable about the H.C. appointment in London – I expect they'll send Dan Breen or de Valera to America or Paris. After the Smiddy choice all things in the way of unsuitability may be expected!'[50]

When in September the Irish Free State notes came into circulation, the design on the lower denominations (10 shilling, £1 and £5) was merely the head of Erin, while the higher denominations (£10, £20, £50 and £100) were of sufficient size to use John's complete picture. Bodkin wrote to Hazel to reassure her of 'an extraordinary success':

There has not been a word of captious criticism. Everyone seems really pleased that your portrait should adorn them. ... There are more people than you perhaps think who would like to be able to say that the lady of the notes was the chief lady of the land in both senses of the word. Prosit omen.[51]

There was in fact a 'bit of a racket' when the notes were released.[52] *The Irish Times* reported that 'the striking resemblance between the colleen painted by Sir John Lavery on the new Irish Free State currency notes and Lady Lavery, has been commented upon by many persons' and that, when questioned, neither Sir John nor his wife had denied the suggestion. Blythe responded: 'The head on the notes is *not* Lady Lavery and does not bear the slightest resemblance to her.'[53] His blunt denial seemed to suggest that Lady Lavery would have been an unwelcome subject. Hazel took her revenge by distributing a flattering studio photograph of herself.[54] One of the recipients was Joseph Brennan, to whom she wrote:

... this photograph is *not* like the head on the notes and presumably *is* like Lady Lavery so Mr Blythe can be reassured that there will be no danger of anyone's recognizing me as the model for the Lady with the Harp which will comfort him I know.[55]

The photograph found its way into *The Irish Times* of 14 September where, printed beside the head from the notes, the resemblance was unmistakable. Reproducing the notes was an offence under the Forgery Act, and the Currency Commission brought the newspaper to court and made it destroy the plates used in making the copy.[56]

Brennan wrote to Dr Willis of *The Journal of Commerce* in New York: 'I may as well explain that the head on the front was painted specially for us by Sir John Lavery. It is intended to be purely emblematic but, as is now generally known, Lady Lavery was the artist's model and the picture bears some resemblance to her although it cannot in any strict sense be considered a portrait of her.'[57] John wrote to Brennan: 'In any case the Irish Free State has paid a high compliment to my wife for the part she took in helping to bring together the unfriendly elements towards the Treaty and to me as an Irish artist.'[58] John obviously still believed that the commission had been given in tribute, despite the fact that Bodkin had orchestrated it almost singlehandedly. His auto-biography gives a confused account of the events surrounding the commission and attributes to Cosgrave the idea of using Hazel as a model. He quotes Cosgrave as saying: 'Every Irishman, not to mention the foreigner who visits Ireland, will carry [her portrait on the banknotes] next to his heart.'[59]

※◌ᴄ※

In November 1928 Hazel, John and Alice travelled to spend the winter in the south of France. Their destination was a cottage on the estate of Brigid Guinness in Mougins, near Cannes, which John rented at an extravagant price.[60] Hazel always referred to the guest-house, called L'Enchantement, as 'Des Enchantement'. She wrote to Lytton Strachey shortly after their arrival:

We have taken this horrid little house for the winter from Mrs Benjamin Guinness who as you have heard from the daily-press is a most energetic and *artistic* lady. She adores discomfort and mediaeval furniture. This cottage in 'Ye olde Provencal' man-ner might have been quite charming with chintz and muslin and simple comfortable chairs but it is like a very gun crack curiosity shop, bits of broken Gothic saints, prie Dieus priest vestments, and Breton beds made into book cases – small high windows and rough plaster and pottery ..I feel like Saint Theresa who always said her prayers on a soft cushion, she said she could not concentrate or be devout with her knees cold and aching. So true of everything.[61]

Hazel complained that the walls were so rough she skinned herself in the bath and that the smell was overpowering.[62] In fact it was a very simple farmhouse which, converted into a comfortable villa, had five bathrooms and central heating. She admitted:

it should make up the sum of human happiness but I'm always wanting something more. I feel lonely here. Everyone is disgustingly rich and callous not intelligent and worst of all very inclined to be 'arty'. Most of the people are Americans and they are at their Yankee worst on the Riviera it seems to me – over eating over drinking and talking about money and their figures from dawn to dark. I feel very far from Ireland the place I love best.[63]

The winter was cold and rarely sunny, the food gave her boils and she worried about the distance from a good doctor. John and Alice, by contrast, were happy in the quiet of the hills looking down over Cannes. A local farmer lent them horses and they became companions as they had been years before in Morocco.[64] Hazel wrote to Father Leonard: 'I don't care for this playing at being a provencal peasant and am more than ever convinced that I am not of the people and the soil.'[65]

Hazel dreaded becoming dull with isolation and longed for visitors to sharpen her wit. Lord Berners, the composer, visited at her request, and Churchill wrote to say that he was bringing his paintbox to Balsans, his house nearby, and suggested that if it was not too cold, they might try a landscape together.[66]

Aside from infrequent visitors. Hazel's only pleasure was in stealing off to the Hôtel Beau Site in Cannes for cups of tea served by the understanding proprietor, Mr Schmid, who listened attentively as she listed her complaints and her dread of Christmas at the mercy of a cook she described as 'a vile one of the lentils and garlic variety'.[67] On Christmas Day the family gloomily awaited their meal, when suddenly a car horn sounded outside, and out stepped three white-capped chefs from the Hôtel Beau Site, each bearing a large covered dish. In later years Alice recalled: 'It was a charming gesture from whatever motive it was done. I never forgot the whole scene and mother's quite infantile delight over it all.'[68] Mr Schmid earned Hazel's eternal gratitude and the Laverys' patronage the following winter.

Shortly after Christmas Alice returned to Kilkenny to announce her official engagement to Jack McEnery. Hazel disapproved and her letters were 'ice-bound and dreadful'.[69] But her humour improved when in the first week of February she and John travelled to the Hotel de Paris in Monte Carlo.[70] Many of their friends were spending the winter there – Admiral and Lady Stanley, the Countess of Wilton and the Duchess of Sutherland, among others. She wrote to Father Leonard: 'I love the glitter and sham and [the] warm sunny hotel and no housekeeping. I shall hate returning to my "artistic" mountain retreat with its cold and discomfort.'[71]

On her return to England Hazel re-opened the red door of 5 Cromwell Place to visitors, who, as always, admired her decorative touch. The dining-room was now all white, prompting one guest to comment that the simplicity was a 'welcome relief after the bizarre decorative schemes one sometimes meets nowadays'.[72] A journalist described leaving the house:

Out through the old flag-stoned hall with its dark, antique furniture, and a glimpse of wide red carpeted stairs behind; out through the red front door, whose colour was picked up again by the half-drawn blinds, and one carried away with one an atmosphere that was not only charming but was characteristic of the warm, kindly hospitality of those within.[73]

Unlike Sibyl Colefax and Syrie Maugham, who set up a decorating business in the 1920s, Hazel never pursued interior design professionally. She did, however, design friends' tables for special events: 'On these occasions she likes single blossoms or beautiful sprays to play with, declining a centre-piece, and using only the slimmest of vases, each holding a single flower in the Chinese fashion'.[74]

Hazel continued to introduce her English acquaintances to Irish figures. At a large dinner party in June 1929, a society columnist wrote, 'Before proceeding to the studio, Sir John and Lady Lavery received the guests in the drawing-room, and then it was noticed what a number of Irish people were present.'[75] The guests included the Londonderrys, Tim Healy, the actress Sarah Allgood, Josephine MacNeill, Lord Donegall, Osbert Sitwell, the Chamberlains, Lady Juliet Duff and Eddie Marsh. After the meal came a rendition of Irish folk songs and Allgood's recital of Yeats's 'The Wandering Aengus'.[76]

Desmond FitzGerald, aware of the breadth of Hazel's social circle, conveniently forgot all previous rancour between himself and Hazel and asked her to extend hospitality and friendship to Professor Smiddy.[77] Hazel was livid. She described her reply as the rudest letter she had ever sent, and was sure that FitzGerald, McGilligan and Blythe would never speak to her again. She admitted to Bodkin, however, that she had enjoyed writing a diatribe condemning the incompetence of the Free State government:

... they *ignore* London and then send a man who is a laughing stock in two countries and unknown in England except through his *anti-English* performances in America. They had better stop gushing out 'ambassadors' to every European capital and pay a decent and mannerly attention to affairs in London.[78]

Hazel's letter was emotional and exaggerated, but she expressed a common view. She complained to Bodkin: 'Mr Blythe may claim not to be "interested" – but that is not good enough for the London end *who are very far* from being dazzled and charmed by the performances in a diplomatic and social role of the "Free State Department of Infernal Affairs", as *Punch* described Mr McGilligan's efforts!'[79] She continued to promote her vision of Ireland:

Ireland *must not* be allowed to destroy herself and we who really love her so tenderly, her wit, her glamour, her wild *free* beauty, must try to hold up the mirror of sanity and light and sweetness, even though by so doing we lose many friends.[80]

Ramsay MacDonald had returned to power with a parliamentary majority and in February Hazel wrote to him about Ireland. He replied: 'Smiddy seems quite pleasant though as you say it is a pity that while Ireland has people who could hold their own with anybody in London from the intellectual point of view that they don't send them.'[81]

When she wrote expressing her views to Mr Boilbester, a journalist in *The Irish Times,* he concurred:

Your attitude towards Mr Blythe and company interests me exceedingly, in view of your thorough knowledge of our new rulers and their ways. ... Most of them – Cosgrave, Hogan, McGilligan for example are decent, unassuming fellows, conscious of their own limitations and anxious to give a square deal to everybody. They have been infernally stupid at times, but on the whole they have done their jobs as well as anybody could have done them in all the circumstances. Blythe and his cultural alter-ego [Richard] Mulcahy are sour-faced Puritans with all the zeal of that type and all its fanatical obstinacy. Blythe is a Lisburn Presbyterian ... Mulcahy's grandparents were Quakers. Both he and Blythe are rabid tee totalers. So there you have the Free Staters' woes in a sentence. ... They are the sea green incorruptables who will not be satisfied, until the British connection – which bred both of them – has been snapped, and until the jabber of the Gaeltacht echoes through a de-Anglicised countryside. Blythe and Mulcahy the Orange convert and the soldier-saint, as poor Kevin O'Higgins used to call them ...[82]

In the summer of 1929 Hazel represented the Irish Dominion in an instructional film produced by the Empire Marketing Board in London. Each Dominion was portrayed by a well-known society woman: Lady Ravensdale (New Zealand), Lady Keeble (Canada), Miss Phyllis Neilson-Jenny (Australia) and Lady Carlisle (South Africa).[83] The film, written by J.M. Barrie and entitled *One Family*, was shot in the Privy Council Chamber in Buckingham Palace. It told the story of a young boy who dreamt he visited the Palace with a friendly policeman, where each 'Dominion' took him to their country to get products for the Christmas pudding. Hazel wrote:

Ireland's only contribution to the Pudding seemed to be a basket of eggs and an enormous wolf-hound who followed me about with embarrassing devotion and insisted upon throwing himself on my six yard train – yon can imagine the difficulty of upholding Irish dignity under the circumstances.

A green Maori-style dress that was "not the least bit "Gaelic" in inspiration' was designed for Hazel. She spoke her few lines in 'a rich brogue'.[84]

Hazel had overcome her scruples about visiting the Viceregal Lodge, and was now concerned about how she might be received during Horse Show Week in August 1929. So much had isolated her from Ireland: 'I feel rather shy about going back this time and sensitive to certain animosities – perhaps I imagine it – but I am not inclined to self consciousness or fancied slights – the Empress said one or two little things that are "upsetting".'[85]

While Hazel opted for the luxury and comfort of the Lodge, John used the opportunity to paint at St Patrick's Purgatory in Lough Derg, Co. Donegal, a place of Catholic penance since medieval times. Patrick Hogan, the Minister for Agriculture, who had been O'Higgins's closest friend, spent time with Hazel, who found him most receptive and understanding:

I suppose 'Birdie' will take him in with her 'bereaved and utterly broken little bird effects', it is a pity because he is the other great hope of Ireland owing to his keen attitude of *common* sense in regard to the benefits of Empire *Trade*, they think highly of him over here ... he would be a tremendous asset all round. I found McGilligan and 'Huge' [Kennedy] less encouraging.[86]

At the Lodge, the MacNeills were caught between their Republican ideals and their status as representatives of the King. When the Irish government formally adopted the 'Soldier's Song' as the national anthem, replacing 'God Save the King' at official functions in Ireland, they felt unable to attend government functions.[87] Hazel saw that they had little actual power[88] and came to realize what a thankless job the Viceregal position would have been: '"Heavy lies the head that wears a *Republican* crown!" alternately with a *Royal* one. They can't *both* suit.'[89]

Rumours circulated that the MacNeills would be removed from the Viceregal post, and the potential successors included the Kennedys, the Blythes, and the Laverys again, as Bodkin attested: 'Opinion here, if I can gauge it at all, is growing more and more in the direction of Sir John and yourself as the best possible occupants of the Lodge.'[90] Birdie O'Higgins reported to the Bodkins 'that the Cabinet are afeared that, if Sir John consented, Lady Lavery would dominate them all'. Bodkin wrote to Hazel: 'I, personally, think that would be a splendid thing for the Cabinet: and I'm sure that, if it were so, the Cabinet would never know that they were being dominated. They would put all good results down to their own natural sagacity.'[91] When a newspaper picked up the story. Hazel remarked, 'I am sorry to see by one newspaper account my pathetic aspirations for the Irish crown have been obvious to all!'[92] But by now she had little real interest in the prospect: 'Oh dear it is all so depressing for me. I feel everything has been in vain. ...'[93]

The Laverys' efforts to donate paintings to the State were again under discussion in September 1929. Bodkin spoke to President Cosgrave, who was anxious that the pictures be secured as soon as possible with a minimum of conditions, but the paintings were never to become part of the National Gallery's collection.[94]

In October 1929 the new gallery in Belfast opened its doors with the Northern Collection housed in a special Lavery Room. Hazel, promoting her husband's work, wrote to the curator, Arthur Deane, disguising her annoyance that Belfast had accepted the collection before Dublin: 'I am really delighted to say that John is sending a very good full length portrait of me called "Hazel in Green and Mauve", it is to my thinking the best one of me he has ever painted'.[95] She was affronted by rumours circulating that John had donated the Dublin paintings to Belfast, and wrote to assure Irish acquaintances that there were in fact two separate collections.[96] She wrote to Bodkin: "John himself is enthusiastic about Dublin's collection being much better than the Belfast and is throwing in several additional masterpieces at least I call them that, he only said "works" to raise the whole collection to the highest pitch of excellence he can attain.'[97]

In Dublin, it was thought the Lavery paintings could be housed in the new gallery of modern art at Charlemont House, recently vacated by the Registrar General.[98] In November 1929 Lady Gregory wrote telling Hazel that a Mr Hannon was to raise the question of the Lane paintings in the House of Commons. 'I don't know Mr Hannon – or if he carries any weight – but anyhow I do hope he will get support.'[99]

Hazel knew that Hannon was "hated in all parties but especially by the Labour people'.[100] Moreover, the political climate was not congenial. 'The English are *not in a mood* to do flattering and generous gestures toward the Free State', Hazel wrote to Bodkin. 'The English Cabinet is not in any mood to introduce a doubtful Bill for the restoration of the Lane pictures to Dublin from the Tate.' Hazel hastily made an appointment with Prime Minister MacDonald and Sir William Jewett, the Lord Chancellor of the Labour Party. MacDonald threatened to squash the Lane case once and for all, and it took two hours for Hazel to calm him down.[101] She wrote to Cosgrave:

I know I ought not write to you, but I want to so much I am indulging myself and giving myself a sort of Christmas present it being the festive season and all. Of course you will realize by now that I've a favour to ask! it is this please have a little talk with Mr Thomas Bodkin about the Lane pictures and the *future procedure* in connection with making 'Representations to the British Government'.[102]

Lady Gregory thanked Hazel effusively for preventing MacDonald from dropping the issue* and spoke of mounting a plaque on the gallery wall in her honour. 'How splendid you have been, I do believe you saved us from that curt "no Sir" that could have

---

* Ownership of the Lane paintings was debated at least six times in the House of Commons between 1948 and 1954. In 1959 an agreement was reached to share the paintings equally between London and Dublin. Under the most recent agreement, signed in 1993, the majority of the paintings are on view in Dublin for a period of twelve years.

sent us back into the valley of discouragement (not despair for this is a word I will never use) — no one but you could have done it.'[103] Hazel described the encounter to Bodkin, who replied:

Your interview with the P.M. certainly seems to have pulled us out of a nasty situation. I guessed that trouble was brewing because the old witch of Coole [Gregory] came to me one day in a state of great enthusiasm for Mr Hannon and the great work he was about to do on behalf of our claim to the Lane pictures. I urged her to have nothing to say to him, that sniping the British Government at the present juncture could be vexatious, that we should save up our power until the time came for a general offensive all along the line, when our Gallery was ready to receive the pictures ... the President ... was displeased at Hannon's intervention, and is all for devoting our energies at the moment to securing the quickest possible completion of the proposed new Municipal Gallery.[104]

With the Imperial Conference pending in December 1929, Hazel endeavoured to maintain Ramsay MacDonald's interest in Irish politics, sending him a copy of the *Irish Statesman* with passages marked for his attention.[105] During the 'thorny and stormy' conference, Thomas, Lord Privy Seal, and Sir William Jewett attended lunch at Cromwell Place with Irish ministers. Hazel wrote to Cosgrave:

You know how many enemies we still have in England and worse still very *half hearted* friends and I am sorry to say that many people who were splendid supporters have been alienated by various unlucky events that really (I quite appreciate) were unavoidable but have given an unhappy and false impression over here.[106]

Josephine MacNeill wrote of 'the inevitable reaction of the English hatred for Ireland'. Hazel despaired: 'Oh! dear every one is to blame of course and the pot calling the kettle black is no solution alas! just the opposite.' She noted:

... the real condition here was not the 'hatred' of England for the Irish but the appalling *lack of interest* and bored *indifference* to Ireland. When they are not annoyed they are laughing, an attitude far more insulting *to my mind* and the press when accused of anti-Irish propaganda simply say 'it's a question simply of Ireland being no longer "news", we can't "sell it".'[107]

This is confirmed by an undated newspaper cutting:

All the world know Lady Lavery is one of the most beautiful women in London, and one of the most charming of hostesses. ... I have known Sir John Lavery to support unpopular causes. Happily for him, the subject of Ireland is now one of permanent indifference to all people outside a few crazy newspaper men who like the Bourbons 'learn nothing and forget nothing'.[108]

Hazel once again became the object of anti-Irish sentiment at weekend parties, and for the first time was resentful. She was asked how her 'traitor Irish' were getting on and was subjected to other 'charming verbal attacks always ending up with a diatribe against the poor MacNeills, who in some oblique way are blamed for everything. Winston leading the chorus always by saying "Your Gov. General is a dirty dog"'. All Hazel could reply was 'Why *mine?*'[109] Alienated from the politics of the place she loved best, her isolation was to become all too apparent during the 1930s.

X

'It Is Finished'
[1930-5]

THE LAVERYS SPENT CHRISTMAS 1929 with the Chamberlains at Polesdon Lacy, Dorking, then set off for the French Riviera to stay at a villa in the grounds of the Hôtel Beau Site, Cannes.[1] They were offered reduced rates and John kept the 'pot boiling' by painting portraits of wealthy visitors.[2] The Cannes visit was far from happy. Hazel and Alice fought constantly over Alice's engagement to Jack McEnery. Hazel wrote to Bodkin: 'I had hoped all her triumphs in tennis and the great goings on and festivities with the young people here for she has many friends in Cannes at the moment would have distracted her mind from the very dull and dismal and altogether unsuitable swain from Kilkenny upon whom she has set her *mind*.'[3]

Hazel refused to recognize that her objections to her daughter's suitor were the same as her own mother's almost thirty years before. She felt Alice could have had the pick of titled young men in their social circle but Alice had chosen an older man outside this set, someone profoundly more suited to her personality. McEnery, an Irish farmer, had nothing in common with Hazel:

[He] has many disadvantages but the one which really breaks my spirit is his complete *lack* of humour or any lightness or charm of outlook in a word he is like a fine

157

blanketing Scotch mist or a shady downpour of rain from a leaden sky with a voice in his collar and a brogue (not a witty one) you could cut with a knife, a sing-song like the tolling of a convent bell. I feel myself going rather mad listening to its monotone (that is when he speaks at all) which is only three or four times a day. I may seem heartless and frivolous but God I *am* unhappy over this marriage! ... This is a matter of quality and breeding and brains of which there is a tragic lack on *his* part and that of his family, the distance in age I do not count how could I? There is over *thirty* years* between John and me but if you knew McEnery you would realize that the twenty years between them** might be 200 ... there really is no link between them save the horse and the church (he is a Catholic) and Alice's insane desire 'to live her own life' the cry of all the daughters of today as a matter of fact they are so obsessed with the wish to 'live their own lives' they are not content unless they rearrange and mess up their parents as well![4]

Alice threatened to run away or enter a convent and John warned Hazel against losing her completely.[5] Alice finally resorted to secretly organizing the marriage bans and all the official details before sending for Jack to come to France. To Hazel's astonishment, she announced the wedding was arranged for 4 March, regardless of parental consent or blessing. Up to the morning of the wedding, Hazel behaved as if the ceremony would not take place.[6] She even slipped a nail-file into Jack's pocket, having heard that a Catholic marriage could be annulled if the groom carried a weapon during the wedding.[7]

The wedding at the church of Notre Dame de l'Espérance, on a hill in the centre of Cannes, was conducted by Father Inglebean, the priest for the English-speaking Catholic community there. Hazel refused to attend and stayed behind to oversee the preparation of the wedding breakfast. John was at the ceremony and gave Alice away. He had always loved her as his own and she often said that she wished he was her real father.[8]

Hazel wrote to Bodkin that she had never 'smiled through a bitterer three days'.

---

* Actually twenty-four.   ** Actually thirteen.

John was too sweet to me and said I behaved with 'great gallantry' which pleased me as much as any tribute 1 have ever had in my life. It is wonderful what one can go through and let no one guess that the grin in the mask costs so dear.[9]

Everyone knew, though, that she had been robbed of the society wedding she wanted for her only child. Alice later wrote: 'I am sorry to have destroyed your dreams like that and Josephine [MacNeill] upset the other, poor Muff.'[10]

The newly-weds spent their honeymoon in Alice's beloved Morocco. Before they departed she wrote:

The more I think over all you and Popsie have done for me all my life, the more unable I feel ever to thank you enough and looking at it like that it does seem very ungrateful of me to have married anyone you don't like, I can only hope that one day you will feel differently about Jack and that our horses may be of some success* and make you a little proud of us one day but it is only a hope and a chance.[11]

Hazel's attention was then taken up by Alain Gerbault, a sitter of John's, who had sailed around the world single-handedly on a thirty-two-foot ketch called *Firecrest*. His three books about the experiences were 'rather thrilling', and she described Gerbault as 'a most wonderful creature, a lone mariner ... a sort of hermit misanthrope, philosopher, quite fascinating intellectually but absolutely detached and "uncharmable"'.[12] Hazel was otherwise dissatisfied with the seasonal visitors at Cannes and thought it a most scandalous town filled with bitter gossips: 'Dublin pales beside them, they live by hate alone, which is rather a bore they probably said that [John] beat me and we both took drugs.'[13] Her humour improved with the arrival of 'Arnold Bennett, Beverly Nicholls, Algernon Blackwood and other nice boy-friends'. Life became more endurable just as she was leaving.[14]

---

* Among the successful horses Jack McEnery bred, owned or trained were Red Park, winner of the Irish Grand National and Galway Plate in 1933, Meadow Fescue, Racketeer, Nasr-er-din and Trubley. Placed in the Irish Classics over the years were Lady Clodagh, Chorlis, Coup de Grace, Chadwick Manor and Hindu Festival (second in the Irish Derby in 1957).

In April Hazel found it 'a joy to come back to London and find that one's friends are *just* the same stupid darlings and far from gossiping most of them have *not* realized you have been away at all!'[5] One of her first social engagements on her return was described by a society columnist as the most amusing luncheon of May:

Lady Gwendeline Churchill and her husband, Lord Londonderry, Lady Colefax, Lady Kenmare, Mr Keating (the Irish artist), Mr Knoblock, and others made up a party of about twenty at four round tables in the famous studio, while the pictures were turned to the walls 'for fear they might be shocked by the talk'.[16]

In his thank-you note the dashing young Lord Donegall wrote: 'It was quite one of the most interesting lunches I have ever been to and I made frenzied notes in my car on the way to the office. Fear not! I noted down the stories for hypothetical memoirs when I am a hoary old man!'[17]

Hazel still had her critics in London. She was considered a 'mettlesome matty' and an *'enfant terrible'*.[18] Many failed to comprehend how the Laverys could remain friendly with opposing factions of the Irish question or befriend members of different political parties. While John was a Liberal, Hazel remained unaffiliated, though she attended a Liberal rally at the Rothschild Manor in 1928. When she opened the Hereford Liberal Bazaar in 1932, the local paper described her as 'an ardent politician and a staunch and unrepentant Liberal'.[19] She once surprised a Tory by praising the Labour Party, adding with candour, 'I like them better when they're in.'[20] Hazel routinely mixed guests of different political beliefs. On one occasion in the early 1930s Randolph Churchill, Winston's son, violently denounced Prime Minister Ramsay MacDonald. Bereft of vocabulary in his fury, he used an expletive which Hazel adroitly fielded, saying, 'A ship, ah yes, a ship of state', and the incident passed off with laughter.[21]

Her interests were still varied. George Bernard Shaw invited her comments on drafts of his *Intelligent Woman's Guide to*

Socialism. She was observed discussing politics with Lady Oxford and literature with Sir Edward Gosse in the same afternoon, the former telling her she should stand for parliament and the latter asking when she was going to write a novel.[22]

In the late 1920s Hazel decided to publish her letters and memoirs, seeking publishers and discussing her ambitions with Tim Healy, among others. The plans never came to fruition. She had already been immortalized as a model for several fictional characters. In her 1927 novel *A Bird of Strange Plumage,* Louie Rickard based the heroine on Hazel. Rickard wrote:

Hazel Beloved, I so loved the Bird of Strange Plumage herself when I was writing the story that I never thought of her as a vampire and am so sad to think that the darling Alice was shocked by it. The story is such nonsense, but every now and then I felt I had actually captured something of your wonderful gay self.[23]

Alice considered a character in James Stephens's 1925 short story 'Here Are the Ladies' of 1925 to be a more accurate portrayal, though it is unclear whether Stephens had Hazel in mind. The novelist Temple Thurston also drew inspiration from Hazel:

My dear Hazel – how deeply sad you looked last night. Do I understand? Beauty is certainly the saddest thing in life. ... There is also that beauty in your story to me and there are moments when I almost feel I dare not touch it closer than the fragments I have from you when we meet – as tho' I had been given more than my deserts, merely in hearing it and that to attempt to retell it would be tempting my own dreams. ... But I can't forget the sadness in your face last night. How am I to express that in words?[24]

The title character in Thurston's *Jane Carroll* was based loosely on Hazel's life during her involvement in Irish affairs, and her portrait as 'Dame en Noir' was on the dustjacket. Alice was again dismayed and wrote, 'How she could have agreed to associate herself, not so much with such a silly story, as with such quite shocking literary style, it is a hopeless book from every angle, poor Temple Thurston such an earnest utterly harmless effort.'[25]

During the 1930s Hazel continued to keep herself well informed on Ireland. She surmised that Ernest Blythe dictated the policies of the Governor-General with his ideas for a Gaelic Ireland, and assumed that he would be the next appointee to the post.[26] When Chief Justice Hugh Kennedy was suggested for the position in 1930, Hazel wrote disbelievingly: 'Well well! "'tis a mad world my masters" but the picture of Clare and Huge dispensing Vice-Regal hospitality really is the maddest idea of all. However I'm glad [the government] isn't doing away with the Post entirely though it will be robbed of any glamour that may have survived.'[27]

The Laverys were invited to the Viceregal Lodge for Easter 1930 but declined, as they were travelling to the North for John to receive the Freedom of Belfast. Hazel had planned to visit Alice in Kilkenny, but her daughter put her off as 'Rossenarra' was in much need of decoration and organization: 'You can't imagine the state of this house ... you could not come without Lucy and if you brought her I am afraid she would have my servants eating the oddest meals.'[28]

Back in London, Hazel continued her social activities, but with diminishing pleasure, as she wrote to Bodkin:

I send you some 'cutting' rubbish to let you see that I have been fast and foolishly wearing myself out doing things for people who really don't care a hang whether I am 'present' or not at these fetes and fairs but one gets 'roped in' for one reason or another – some excellent and some idiotic and then I hate letting other people down even people I don't like and so it goes and in the end one gets no thanks and much blame![29]

She still adored parties and spending weekends with friends, which John only tolerated. At a 'very royal' house party at Mrs Greville's, Hazel wrote: 'John is hopeless on these occasions and when I say "don't you think it is delightfully absurd that we should be here in this galiere?" he always replies "no it is only as boring and awful as any other weekend party as far as I can see" and I suppose he is perfectly right.'[30] John was preoccupied with painting and golf, activities from which Hazel was excluded. She recounted: 'I've been Ascoting yesterday and today. Very exhausting and financially a cruel failure. I've stopped here on the way back to pick up my husband who is playing golf, and the wretched creature is only at the 14th hole miles away and we are late already for dinner and a play.'[31]

Hazel loved going to the theatre, especially opening nights. In one week of September 1930 she attended Lennox Robinson's *The Far-Off Hills* (which she had already seen in Dublin) and Barry Jackson's *The Barretts of Wimpole Street,* and had plans to see a Noel Coward play at the Phoenix and another play which she didn't name.[32]

Her need for attention and admiration grew with age. During the late 1920s and early 1930s she surrounded herself with young men whom she launched into society. Called the 'Hazel Boys' by contemporaries, they accompanied her in her chauffeur-driven brown Renault, which resembled an old French taxi.[33] She encouraged her proteges in their artistic or political activities and received companionship and adoration in return. Douglas Woodruffe later wrote, 'I always felt I was one of her friends she was laying down, as it were, for her old age, which she could not easily envisage.'[34]

The Hazel Boys included Randolph Churchill (Winston's son, in his early twenties and a fledgling journalist), Tom Driberg (journalist with the *Daily Express* 1928-43), Brendan Bracken (MP for North Paddington 1929-45 and Chairman of Union Corporation and *The Financial Times),* Bob Boothby (Unionist MP 1924-58), Douglas Woodruffe (in later years editor of *The Tablet,* 1936-67), Frank Owen (MP for Hereford Division 1929-31 and the youngest member of the House of Commons until he joined the *Daily Express)* and Christopher Hollis (a member of the Oxford University Debating Society and later a writer). They showed her their work and she procured useful introductions for them. In 1927 Rickard wrote that J.L. Garvin of *The Observer* was looking for a sub-editor, and was considering Woodruffe: 'It is all so queer, Hazel, because it is (really) up to you ... I said that you thought him very clever and interesting, and it looks quite as if he can have the job if he wants it. Woodruffe recounted years later:

She was a splendid friend to me, from our first meeting in 1926, and at first it was uphill work for her I am afraid, because it took me some time, being young and new to London, to believe in the friendship of anybody with so many friends and such incessant social activity. Her great steadfastness I had to learn, but I came in the course of seven years to find admiration as well as affection.[36]

Christopher Hollis found she had a better understanding of people than anyone he had ever known.[37] He often sent her his work and she found his books 'attractive'.[38] He once wrote: 'Can the enclosed make you laugh at all? I have hopes that one or two things in it may. At any rate, I hope that you will do me the honour of accepting it.'[39] She accumulated a number of first editions, the vast majority of them signed by their authors. Frank Owen gave her a copy of his first book and wrote, 'You have been a great inspiration to me in all that I have written of Ireland, though I am too clumsy to explain how this has been so.'[40] Hazel asked him for help on her book of letters. Owen was a favourite of Hazel's, perhaps because of his resemblance to Michael Collins.[41]

Brendan Bracken, whom she had met through Winston Churchill, had an open invitation to Hazel's home. 'His conversation, always scintillating, was essentially an essay in self-advertisement,' writes Bracken's biographer Charles Edward Lysaght. 'He dropped names with gay abandon and flaunted his knowledge of history, finance, literature and architecture.' Bracken was happiest bandying words with older women while avoiding those of his own age. Anxious to disassociate himself from the social perils of his Irish background, he fuelled the rumour that he was Churchill's illegitimate son.[42]

The Hazel Boys, invariably single, drifted away as they married. Christopher Hollis wrote:

Hazel dear, I write to tell you that I have got engaged to be married. ... Very *seriously*. Hazel, I am very, very happy indeed and do hope that you will feel able to wish me joy. Your kindness has meant a very great deal to me – *more* perhaps than you have guessed and I am most anxious that this should not in any way interrupt our friendship. I shall be *most* happy if you can write to me and tell me that it will not. I have heard you from time to time say things about your men friends dropping off when they get married.[43]

Hazel was at her happiest with a cause to champion or a man to lavish her attention upon, and among her close companions in the 1930s was the Prime Minister, Ramsay MacDonald. Hazel had written to MacDonald earlier in relation to Ireland, the Boundary Commission and the Hugh Lane controversy, but it was during his second term in office, between 1930 and 1933, that their friendship intensified and they exchanged more than 150 notes and letters.* The friendship appears to have begun in May 1930 at a party in MacDonald's honour. He noticed Hazel's presence and wrote, 'My dear Lady Lavery, Thank you very much for enlivening the party of yesterday.'[44] Less than a fortnight later the Laverys were guests at Chequers.

By July MacDonald was addressing Hazel as 'My dear Hazel' and signing his correspondence 'Hamish', his given name at Lady Londonderry's 'Ark' parties.

Hamish let it be. James is the original. But, Hamish implies youth and dash, and alas the sere and the yellow leaf is now mine. My friends have got into the habit of addressing me as J.R. which is a costume befitting such of the seven ages of man. But take your choice, and when you are inclined to come to tea at Chequers never waver. Just ring up and see if the kettle is to be boiled ... Yours JRM.[45]

In mid-July Hazel and MacDonald exchanged photographs. Hazel placed his handsome studio-portrait in her scrapbook (*see plate*); he called it 'an indifferent photograph which will only frown upon you when it looks at you. I was too shy to ask for yours. Make good my defect, pray ...'.[46]

MacDonald's wife Margaret had died in 1911 and he never remarried. Over the years he developed a number of close friend-

---

* Most of the notes are undated. Those that have dates are mainly from 1931.

ships with women such as Lady Margaret Sackville, Molly Hamilton, Cecily Gordon-Cummings, Lady Edith Londonderry and Marthe Bibesco. According to his biographer David Marquand, 'he got on better with women than with men – partly, no doubt, because they sensed his inner loneliness and need for reassurance ... he was a lonely and overworked old man whose wife was dead .and whose children were growing up, who sometimes preferred frivolous gossip to serious political discussion, and who occasionally enjoyed a wistful flirtation across a dinner table'.[47] Even in old age, he was strikingly good-looking and attractive to women.

His correspondence with Edith Londonderry, Cecily Gordon-Cummings and Marthe Bibesco developed alongside that with Hazel, yet in Marquand's biography, which chronicles these friendships.' Hazel is not mentioned. MacDonald had kept Hazel's early letters, but nothing remains in his collection from their weekly exchanges of the 1930s. He once wrote to her: 'To keep letters is like to collect thumb prints and I abhor it.'[48] He was, of course, corresponding with a woman whose hobby was to collect letters. 'You need not burn when the letters are only chaff, but I have a horror of letters lying about and perhaps published when I am dead and in my grave and all my bones are rotten (that will not happen, as a matter of fact, because I am to be burned).'[49] MacDonald was well aware of the dangers of loose talk:

Gossip is a forked tongued jake who spares no-one and who is most devoted in her attentions to figures on pedestals. Her kindness is tipped with an arrow and her thoughts are inspired by mischief. Heed her not. I shall refuse to talk to any lively person, for it seems to be too dangerous for either of our reputations. I shall become a Pape and go into a monastery. Even you must be careful![50]

In 1930 MacDonald was sixty-four. Two years of minority government and mounting unemployment had taken their toll, and he found great solace in his visits to Cromwell Place:

You gave me today such a lunch as I in most vainest moments hope I may have in the dining rooms of Paradise with company, of which you were chief, such as I dream that I might meet there when kind heart will say 'Poor Devil! He had a hard time below, let us give him cheer here' ... you were really very dear today. I *loved* meeting your guests especially those I had known but not met.[51]

MacDonald often only had time to 'rush out and in',[52] but despite his shortage of leisure time he agreed to let John paint his portrait in September 1930.

Even after years of political involvement, Hazel was still indiscreet. She wrote to Thomas Bodkin: 'I know you think I am frail and not to be depended upon to keep a secret! (along with the rest of my sex!). Well I'm very loyal believe it or not once I am fond of people.'[53] MacDonald still had to chide her: 'I was overcoming my prejudices until I heard that you had given me away in that dinner conversation.'[54]

She enjoyed being a confidant of the Prime Minister. An anonymous note in her scrapbook states: 'They report to me that your latest success is Ramsay and that Lady C.H. [the initials are indistinct] is worried about it.'[55] Their association was noted by the press:

The beautiful Lady Lavery, wife of the famous artist, seems to be taking an interest in politics. She is continually seen at the House of Commons these days. One night last week she was holding court on the terrace. ... Lady Lavery being one of the few people whose witty conversation delights the Premier's scanty moments of leisure.[56]

The Irish ministers came to London for the Imperial Conference in October 1930 and the Laverys attended the opening reception at Lancaster House. Hazel held an 'Irish' luncheon on 3 October, with guests including MacDonald, Bernard Shaw, Sir Joseph Duveen, Douglas Woodruffe, Paddy McGilligan, Patrick Hogan and Desmond FitzGerald.[57] John, now seventy-four, was ill with prostate problems in late October but this did not prevent Hazel from continuing to entertain the delegates. John's condition worsened and on 12 November he had two operations. He was forced to remain at the Empire Nursing Home for almost six weeks. Hazel wrote to Lady Gregory on 24 November:

Thanks be to God and all the saints John *is really,* after his two hideous months of suffering, steadily and surely gaining he has had such a cruel suffering illness but he has been so brave as a fine little lion and his *good life* and healthy peasant blood have stood him in good stead and he has come through *most* triumphantly this operation.[58]

MacDonald enquired daily about John's health, usually on Downing Street paper, but his letters show more concern for Hazel and her exhaustion.

In December Alice gave birth to a red-haired boy, christened Martyn. Early in 1931 Hazel went to Kilkenny to see Alice and her new grandson. She wrote to Mrs Bodkin, 'I've just returned from my flying visit to Ireland. (I had nearly put "Iceland!") I found them both very flourishing but oh! the cold of her great unheated house was arctic. I feel I shall be months thawing.'[59]

Alice was determined to be independent. She concealed the fact that Martyn spent his first week sleeping in a drawer, as she knew Hazel would rush out and buy him too expensive a layette.[60] Relations had been improving between Hazel and Jack McEnery and she finally admitted he was 'quite a good fellow'. Alice's happiness came first, 'So I smile sweetly at my son-in-law and see Alice *without* him whenever possible! so on the surface all is blissfully serene.'[61]

Soon after Hazel's return from Kilkenny she and John left for Cannes, though Hazel was reluctant to travel as MacDonald was now her abiding interest. Undoubtedly Hazel had fallen a little in love with him and she may have proclaimed her feelings to him before her departure, as he replied:

Now! now! now! My dear Hazel, if you are in love don't show signs of it. And one of the worst signs is to be annoyed for small causes and unreal troubles. ... You will go away and forget it all in the air of Cannes, where you will feast, dance and be merry, and return with the Spring flowers and sun and scents. You will dream of Frenchmen of debonair appearance and gallic gallantry, and will be sick of anyone whom you have accused of coldness. You may dream of him, but in the morning you will upbraid yourself for your bad taste. ... In a remote place the poor man will spend dolorous hours reading 'In Search of Ireland', 'Hazel's Wand' [*sic*] and the 'Golden Treasury of Irish Verse' and if he is rude enough to dream of you ... You will lecture him on all the virtues and show him that you have turned over a new fig leaf. All this Cannes will do. Bon Voyage! And the Saints attend you and bless you and above all keep you in your sense of humour and preserve you from thinking unhappy things about yourself. Under that heading you sometimes write awful nonsense. Obey the dictates of a human being, now honey pot and now moth, and put it all down to the good Lord who made you and who destined you to be included in 'The Book of Beauty'.[62]

The Laverys took a villa in the grounds of the Hôtel Beau Site. Though the weather was cold, the break from London gave John an opportunity to recover. Hazel described their fellow visitors as 'an American wife who dresses in tweeds and blows her nose in a masculine manner, a novelist who is the most perfect embodiment of the petit bourgeoisie of our day and generation, a politician who should have kept a bucket shop'.[63] To dispel her gloom, MacDonald painted a bleak picture of the English winter – but also revealed that he was gloomy without her:

... the snow falls here to-day, the wind howls and I sit by the fire as a lover warms himself by his love. I must have a hot-water bottle in bed. ... Only in my dreams do I hear the palms rustling and converse with people clad in air and the feathers of their wings because the sun is hot. I must to bed and leave this cold world. Happily I may dream that there is a warmer one, and you may find me wandering somewhere in Cannes. If you do, let me know, and I shall send a paragraph of my whereabouts to the Society column of the Times.[64]

The Laverys, as usual, attended the important social events of the season.[65] Hazel was noted watching tennis at the Carlton Club 'wrapped in a pale grey broadtail coat', carrying a fur rug while 'her escort carried another'.[66] The escort was probably J. Lyttleton Rogers, the Irish international tennis champion in Cannes at the time; he had coached Alice the previous year and she reached the final of the Cannes Handicap.'[17]

By April 1931 the Laverys were back home and sittings

resumed for MacDonald's portrait. Lennox Robinson recalled

one luncheon – Lord and Lady D'Abernon, Ramsay MacDonald, Max Beer-bohm, James Stephens and Fred O'Donovan. We lingered at the table after lunch; Ramsay was talking spiritualism and his experiences with beautiful siren German spies during the war. He tore himself away at four o'clock to go to the House – he was Prime Minister – and we others went upstairs to look at the portrait Sir John was painting of him. Someone made the trite, often-repeated comment that MacDonald was vain. Max Beerbohm, looking at the portrait, observed very gently, 'Well, I suppose if you got up in the morning and started to shave that handsome face and reflected that you were a humble Scotswoman's son and that you were now Prime Minister of England – and it is *something* to be Prime Minister of England — you might feel a little vain.'[68]

In 1931 Hazel and Lady Diana Cooper, both still renowned beauties, appeared in advertisements for Ponds Cold Cream. Beneath Hazel's portrait read 'The Greatest Beauty since Lady Hamilton'[69] a fanciful tribute to a favourite character of Hazel's. MacDonald teased Hazel that if his portrait was attractive he would 'use it for a face cream too'.[70]

MacDonald and Hazel carried on a flirtatious correspondence, supplemented by frequent telephone conversations. He enjoyed Hazel's letters and waited eagerly for the next instalment. One night at midnight he wrote, 'I ought to be in bed but your unacknowledged letter is on my conscience. What days of log sawing! No Irishman from Galway in the Canadian backwoods hews and hacks harder or thinks more of his colleen.'[71] At another time, 'I asked for you ... but I saw not a fold of your frock, not a flap of your hat not a gleam of your eye. If you do not send a drawing at once I shall have forgotten you – and this week is hopeless unless you are going to one or other of those official dinners I have to attend.'[72]

Hazel gave him a few odd little gifts: Edward Martyn's biography, a purse, an autograph-book. MacDonald nicknamed Hazel 'the applewoman':

I am jealous, and doubt if you care as much for me as sometimes appears to be the case. I must just be philosophical and remind myself in every muscle of my heart that I must take things as I find them and not worry. When God created man *and* woman he did a stupid and a dangerous thing. It is the most upsetting feature of creation and I often wonder whether the deed was not really done by the Serpent in the Garden as the first Act in the Apple Drama. The truth is plain: "No woman, no apples', and humanity has been suffering from Apples ever since. Physically the doctors say an apple a day keeps the doctor away. But psychologically I have a repulsion against apples on account of the part they play in history. Moths, candles and apples form an inseparable companionship to me. Therefore, all women are apple women to me.[73]

Like Collins and O'Higgins before him, MacDonald took to writing Hazel poems, including 'Renewal':

> When I get back from journeying,
> And hear your voice once more,
> I am as storm-toss'd sailorman,
> That makes the smiling shore,
>
> Or as thrice thirsty traveller
> From desert parch'd and drear
> That sees the clustered palm trees stir,
> O'er wells of water clear.
>
> And when at last I meet you,
> And gaze into your eyes,
> I am a pilgrim entering,
> Raptures of Paradise.[74]

Hazel was annoyed to find MacDonald's affections were not exclusively focused on her and requested the names of others to whom he wrote poetry. MacDonald replied:

Who told you of songs? I wish people would mind their own business and not spend time making free for others. This is the classical kind of lines I write. I'm writing you dong as well as a ding. And in order to rhyme will end with a ring. Did Tennyson or Keats ever write anything better? Are you now the 12th lady to whom I address verses? Or the 4th? or the 22nd? Now do be a philosopher and not so gusty. A March wind is not ladylike and old gentlemen with lumbago and work do not like it. Wives were made to stir you up and blow you about; friends to smooth you down.[75]

MacDonald warned Hazel not to expect too much. Clearly she took their correspondence more seriously than he wished:

171

You really must control your sentiments, however your pencilled note of today flames like your head. ... I shall ring you up on Monday but meanwhile clothe yourself in philosophy. These outbursts are the attributes of the applewoman and we must keep her under control so far as we can. I expect to see her again in all her glowing splendour and perhaps more enticing than ever. ... Hazel, behave yourself or I shall pull your leg and make you feel uncomfortable. I shall dip you in buckets of cold water and hang you out to dry.[76]

The Prime Minister's letters became less frequent after 1931, as his work load grew more intense. In October 1931 MacDonald made a controversial decision to break with Labour, and to form a National Government with the Liberal and Conservative parties. It was hoped that a combined government could overcome the economic recession of the 1930s. The Laverys remained friendly with him, visiting his home at Lossiemouth in Scotland in August 1933. John, at Hazel's request, painted a group portrait of MacDonald, his daughter Isabel and his housekeeper Jeannie, in the kitchen setting the table for tea, entitled 'The Prime Minister at Lossiemouth, 1933'.[77]

⚓

During 1931 Hazel befriended Evelyn Waugh 'at a time when he had very few friends in London'.[78] Hazel was twenty-three years older than Waugh and encouraged him, in turn sharing in his success. He dedicated his first travel book, *Remote People*, to her* and they exchanged letters while Waugh was on his travels throughout the 1930s. In this period Hazel was becoming increasingly unhappy and lonely. She craved attention, and in her eagerness to please she often told white lies, one of which Waugh detected:

You can't possibly have bought two copies of *Black Mischief* because it isn't out. So that is one of your misstatements (lies). In fact you will know as soon as it is out by receiving a copy of a v. grand edition-de-luxe with illustrations.[79]

---

* Waugh also dedicated *When the Going Was Good* (1946) to the memory of Hazel Lavery.

In his biography of Waugh, Martin Stannard suggests Hazel unsuccessfully pursued Waugh in the summer of 1932 – 'She was ardent and he was cool, vaguely embarrassed by it all' – and quotes an incident from Waugh's diary to illustrate Hazel's ardour: 'Found several telephone messages from Hazel, and Hazel herself sitting in the vestibule of the Savile. She drove me to North End Road, where I collected clean clothes, and to a passport photographer's for photograph for Venezuelan visa.'[80] The implication that Hazel's interest was unreciprocated is misleading, as Waugh had written to her prior to his return, reminding her that he would be at the Savile: 'Mind you keep some time free for me.'[81]

Whether sincere or not, Waugh wrote to Hazel of his 'longing' to see her: 'I think I will come to London again in a fortnight ... will tell you when and we will make whoopee. No concerts this time. '[82] He appeared to treat their relationship lightheartedly and dismissively, as the following newspaper report indicates:

Lady Lavery turned with one of her gracious smiles to greet Lord Berners when he arrived with Mr Evelyn Waugh. 'How nice to see you,' she said 'and Mr Wuff too.' A few minutes later she turned to Lord Berners again. 'Where is Mr Wuff?' 'Mr Wuff,' said Lord Berners, 'has left for Abyssinia.'[83]

Waugh, typically, wrote in harsh terms of Hazel, complaining that her attentions were suffocating. On his return from Brazil and British Guiana in May 1933 he instructed fellow-novelist Henry Yorke: 'Don't tell Hazel I'm back.'[84] Yet within the same week he wrote to Hazel, 'Just back. Longing to see you. ... Please come small cocktail party ... at 13 Belgrave Square.'[85]

Her practice of giving small gifts, which others found thoughtful, irritated Waugh. He recalled, 'I remember long ago, when I had no home and spent my life globe-trotting, being furious with Hazel Lavery for giving me a glass swan, thinking (rightly) that it is better to be forgotten than so little remembered.'[86] He steadily had less and less time for Hazel, perhaps exemplifying what MacDonald called her frequent 'gusty' friendships, which undermined her faith in her looks and charms.*

One admirer remained constant. Sir Patrick Ford continued to write poetry and send presents to Hazel. His gifts became more and more eccentric. He sent Alice a cheque as a wedding gift and she wrote to her mother with relief: 'I was nervous he might send a Chinese chicken or stuffed puppies in a basket.'[87]

Hazel now began to suffer increasingly from depression that was exacerbated as friends died – Lord Birkenhead in 1930, William Orpen and Tim Healy in 1931. She wrote of her life to Bodkin: 'Yours is to some purpose, but mine I feel is complete inefficiency to cope with things in general.'[88] Those who knew Hazel well commented on the aura of sadness about her. Alice recalled:

Through all her eager joy in life there ran this strange vein of melancholy ... she had a curious and unwarranted air of tragedy about her, of course sad things did happen to her ... I do not believe it was the sorrows, or losses in her life that gave her the curious tragic quality, but something within her own nature ... she was most amusing, witty and lots of fun at times, but the sadness was there like a theme in her being, even as a child.[89]

Hazel was intensely sensitive to people and their moods, and afflicted if she felt she was not liked. Douglas Woodruffe wrote of her in this period:

When we met she was very often in her 'vanitas vanitatum' moods, surveying the social scene in which she shone and asking with comical bewilderment what it was all about and why we were so much like mice in a cage ... continuously active and having nothing to show in the end. People who thought from the constant printing of her photograph that first nights and parties were sufficient for her, little knew her, while she embraced and enjoyed all these things, she lived on a much wider front, full of heart and intelligence, so that there is no milieu where she would not have enriched and adorned.[90]

---

* When Waugh heard of Hazel's death, he wrote to Lady Mary Lygon: 'I feel sad at Hazel being dead on account of having been very Dutch to her and so I feel a shit. So to beat myself I am having a mass said at 7.30 which means being called at 6.30 and driving 6 miles in the cold and dark but the person who gets the most beating by that is poor Lord Oxford because he has to get up to drive me and he was never dutch to Hazel so that is unfair' (Mark Amory [ed.]. *The Letters of Evelyn Waugh* [London 1980], p.92).

Hazel was now in her fifties, and continued to keep her age a closely guarded secret. As her youthful beauty faded, make-up became an obsession, and she spent hours in front of the mirror. Patrick Ford's youngest son, Sherrif Harold Ford, recalled seeing Hazel cry, her tear making a tunnel down her cheek.[91] When visitors came to Cromwell Place and asked for Hazel, John would answer that she was in her bedroom painting.[92] Alice wrote: 'I used to feel miserable about my mother when she used to gaze into the mirror ... and I could see her thoughts in the reflection, "it is going, it has almost gone, the thing I cherished all my life, that meant such joy to me and those who loved me ... beauty has faded away".'[93]

John's last formal portrait of Hazel was 'The Gold Turban', painted in 1929, which shows a gaunt Hazel whose eyes are almost obscured. She still featured in her husband's work, a figure seen from behind, watching tennis or swimming, turning away from the public eye, hiding her ageing visage. She told a reporter of the curse of famous beauties: 'They are so talked about that in the end people just say "I can't see why they say she's beautiful: Anyhow she won't last long!" It's frightening the way the world waits to see a beautiful woman fade away.'[94]

Yet she did not completely shun publicity and was delighted when another young male friend, Cecil Beaton, photographed her for *Vogue*. Beaton wrote in his autobiography that Hazel was one of the biggest stars of his adolescent days, and he was astounded and gratified by her interest in him when he came to London: 'Hazel was one of the first to overwhelm me with encouragement and kindness. She did all she could to help me. She sent notes, drawings, criticisms and suggestions. She sympathized with my despairs.'[95] Hazel featured in his *Book of Beauty*, published in June 1930, where he wrote:

Lady Lavery, the possessor of that strikingly Gaelic and easily recognizable mask, that goatish Luini mask, with the ravishingly chiselled, rabbity nose, ruby lips cloven into a pout, wistful hare eyes, pink lids. ... She is different from the other beauties – melancholy, wise – a rare and romantic being.[96]

Beaton organized a *tableau vivant* entitled 'The Pageant of Stars' with a theme of 'Beauty As I See It'. One reporter claimed that "no artist could ask for a more attractive subject than Lady Lavery in a box at the opera'.[97] Beaton wrote: 'Heavenly Hazel, Thank you *so* much for being so sweet. Everyone thought you perfect and a ravishing sight and I am so grateful. Thank you 999999999999999 times.'[98]

He asked her to pose for Vogue again in March 1933, and the photograph bore the caption: "Lady Lavery, wife of Sir John Lavery, the celebrated painter, here wears one of the little white fur jackets which are so chic for early Spring and so becoming to her dark Irish elegance."[99] Hazel responded with delight:

My picture in *Vogue* is dazzling. How rich I look and how smart. My Irish elegance has the ring of a horse in the Grand National and an Irish friend of mine has decided to call his new filly 'Irish Elegance'. The pictures are lovely, but many people resent the total absence of chin and think that the face is too much elongated. I have explained that my face is not being perpetuated and that there are too many furrows, dewlaps, pouches ... hollows, blemishes, moles and other horrors due to advancing years. Diana Cooper and I had a consultation the other day and decided that the new hats should have veils like the Khu [*sic*] Klux Klan, the face entirely hidden. How deliciously mysterious it would be, an almost eerie collection of features would be a charming surprise when the mask was lifted.[100]

Hazel's natural fashion flair may, paradoxically, have been augmented by the financial constraints which dictated that she 'dressed to type' irrespective of the prevailing mode. She would claim that about every ten years she was in the fashion,[101] and once remarked that because she was 'triste financially' she would havee to wear a sackcloth for her spring attire. 'It being Lent it is not too conspicuous but what feathers I shall deck out after Easter I cannot imagine.'[102] The Laverys' finances were precarious during the Depression as art patronage dwindled. While recuperating in Scotland John wrote to Hazel about his exhibition in London: 'Perhaps something may hit and encourage future sitters to pay through the nose.'[103] Hazel was more optimistic and wrote to Bodkin, 'John Lavery is in good health and is (fortunately for us financially) working very hard. I am glad to say that vanity still endures in the human race and aldermen ... and their wives still have their portraits! painted by R.A.s' [Royal Academicians].[104] At an international exhibition of pewter, which Hazel had been invited to open, she selected a few items and was overheard persuading her husband, 'This is practical, Johnnie, labour saving, you know.'[105]

Her Armstrong Siddeley motor-car was nicknamed by the family 'The White Elephant' as it used so much petrol. The company had given her the car to advertise it, and Hazel loved its red-leather interior and posed with it for numerous photographs (*see plate*). She had investments in the automobile company and was always expecting her shares to pay a dividend, but by the 1930s she had had few returns.[106]

❧❧

Hazel was disappointed by the victory of Fianna Fáil and Labour in the Irish general election of 1932, which led to de Valera replacing Cosgrave as President. She wrote to Bodkin:

I feel sometimes a great uneasiness over the Irish happenings but for good or ill there is nothing I can do to help, this election has been a disappointment to us over here but I see your papers seem to think it is not a calamity but surely it would have been better ... people here feel that a vote for Fianna Fáil *is* rather distressing! particularly as it means the policy of non-payment of land *annuities* but we 'hope it will be all right' as that seems to be the only philosophy about everything now.[107]

James MacNeill was still Governor-General when de Valera acceded to power, and he and his wife soon were publicly at odds with the new President. One English newspaper, unaware of the complexity of the Irish situation, suggested:

If Mr de Valera really wanted a pacifier, who is not a politician, Sir John Lavery should be the ideal man. An Irishman, he makes friends with everybody. ... Perhaps the fact that Sir John and Lady Lavery are so popular with the Governor-General and Mrs McNeill [*sic*] and with Mr Cosgrave would rule him out![108]

MacNeill soon resigned, and de Valera appointed Domhnall ua Buachalla as his replacement. Ua Buachalla never occupied the Viceregal Lodge, living at 108 Rock Road, a private residence in Blackrock.[109] The government eventually abolished the post completely. When de Valera took office he set about dismantling the Treaty, removing the oath of allegiance and, as promised, ending payment of land annuities.* Hazel was horrified. She felt the Anglo-Irish diplomacy she had helped to forge was being destroyed. Watching Fianna Fáil gain political strength after their decisive victory in the general election of 1933, she finally closed Ireland out of her mind: 'I don't dare to think about you all in Ireland! as for hoping I haven't any hope left it makes me so anxious the way even God seems to [be] fighting for that old de V.'[110]

Throughout 1933 the Laverys suffered from various ailments and in September embarked on a restorative cruise on the S.S. *Kraljica Marija,* surrounded by friends including Evelyn Waugh and Lady Lovat.[111] John wrote nostalgically to Cunninghame-Graham: 'We have just returned from a Mediterranean pleasure cruise passing Tangier in the twilight. I felt quite sad recalling the past.'[112] No record remains of Hazel's reaction to the cruise, but it was the last time she left Britain. Soon after her return she became seriously ill.

The removal of a wisdom tooth in November 1933 was the catalyst for Hazel's final illness, myocarditis, an inflammation of the walls of the heart. For John's portrait of their dentist, Conrad Ackner, in 1929, Hazel had posed as his patient. A journalist described the picture: 'A lady – a noted lady, rumour says – reclines in the fateful chair stoically submitting her teeth to expert probings.'[113] Hazel later described the difficult extraction: 'They had to really blast the horrid thing out. They gave me gas and local anaesthetic ... I had been given so much dope it poisoned me and my heart, tummy, lungs etc. all went wrong and

---

* The annuities were due to the British government on holdings purchased by Irish tenants under the Land Acts, 1887 to 1923.

they have put me to bed until I get quite recovered.'

She was forbidden visitors or telephone calls, as excitement might weaken her heart. Hazel, who spent hours on the phone gossiping, naturally found the new regime a great bore. As seasons passed, she continued to be bedridden. One letter to the sick-room read:

It is so sunny that I think you will be feeling almost 'Hazelish' again – you make so much difference that I hope you are striving to regain your lone pinnacle of lovely vitality and beautiful exquisite feminineness from which you were wont to thrill us all.[115]

Her inability to fight the myocarditis, John believed, was brought on by her loss of zest for life and the nephritis which flared up once again. She still refused to go to a nursing-home so a permanent nursing staff had to be moved into Cromwell Place, and Hazel loathed the invasion of her privacy: 'I hate all illness, all nurses, doctors, all the dreadful lack of personal privacy to have one's face washed and other dreadful liberties taken by "gamps" and that terrible familiarity of the sick room conversations. I detest the paraphernalia of it all.'

Months passed with no improvement. Weak and prone to infection, she contracted 'a bout of pleurisy and double pneumonia' from one of her nurse's slight colds.[116] Her loneliness was compounded by her daughter's absence. On 11 February 1934 Alice gave birth to her second child, a baby girl named Mary, but contracted septic phlebitis, an infection of the veins not uncommon after childbirth. Due to fear of an embolism like the one that had killed her father, she was bedridden for three and a half months,[117] and wrote to her mother:

I was so happy to get father's letter because I was thinking so much of you, all week lying in bed, one has so much time to think and often it makes me worry unduly and things assume a wrong proportion often, little things anxieties big and so on.[118]

In early May 1933 the Laverys moved to the playwright Edward Knoblock's seaside house at Clifton Terrace, which seemed ideal for recuperation: 'We hope to get to Brighton as soon as I am strong enough for the journey at present I look like something fallen out of the nest and am very weak but they all say I'll get fit and fat in Brighton air.'[119] The journey was taken by ambulance: 'I went down to Brighton yesterday by ambulance, the most comfortable way of travelling, I shall never use any other method of conveyance.'[120] Knoblock, nicknamed 'the period-hound' because of his love of the eighteenth century, had filled his house with exquisite *objets d'art*. Hazel described it as a Regency gem with a panoramic view of the town.[121]

Her sole contact with her old life was now by letter, and she never failed to draw an astute, witty sketch of her surroundings:

I am still a bit bed-ridden so you'll have to come and see me when I get back and tell me all your news. I get bulletins from Lady Colefax which are pleasant and kind but quite illegible; I've tried everyday to make them out, using both secretaries and John's spectacles, the various regency relics in this house, including an Admiral's spy glass, opera glasses of the period, lorgnettes be longing to a Regency Beau, quizzing glasses of a regency wit etc. etc. No use! — can't read one word excecpt 'divine party, greatest fun, all one's friends'. I suppose that should be enough. But in my loneliness I crave detailed gossip.[122]

Knoblock needed the use of his house in order to write his new play and Hazel reluctantly returned to London. The newspapers hailed her recovery and friends came to Cromwell Place once again, but she was far from well. 'Her illness made her restless and hysterical,' wrote Cecil Beaton. 'She became "poor Hazel". She had always talked too much – of her young beaux and of Michael Collins, of Lady Colefax and Lady Cunard. But now she refused to allow a conversation to take its natural course.'[123]

The slight improvement in Hazel's health did not cheer her up, as a friend recalled: 'I am convinced that Hazel did not want to live very much towards the end of her life. One day we were lunching at the Ritz. Hazel said suddenly, "How I hate the world I don't want to live anymore".'[124] Hazel now returned to her bedroom, which John dubbed her 'boudoir prison', but refused to live in the atmosphere of a sick room. The room was decorated in shades of pink and purple, the colour of her bedclothes, and filled with flowers.[125] When Thomas Bodkin sent roses. Hazel wrote to 'Tom, dear *and* lavish': 'I had just begun this letter to you when John came up bearing the lovely Tea Roses so I added the "lavish" for indeed it is sweet of you to realize how I love the sight and smell of them.'[126]

Cromwell Place now felt empty and all remaining activity centred upon the patient's room. The phone rang for Hazel, but friends were told she was unable to see them. Collins's sister Hannie wrote:

On Sunday when I woke I saw your face in the photograph on my bedroom mantel shining in the darkness: a stray gleam of sunshine had come through the curtains lightening up your face and head, making a very charming effect. I thought (and hoped) it must be a good omen so I am looking out for better news of you. I think of you so much and so often that you must feel it. I even try to pass on my strength to you through the ether, but it seems I'm not much good as an air transmitter! But I am looking forward to the time when you will be well again and able to break the silence which soon will have lasted during a whole year. ...[127]

Hazel was alone with John, and the silent house they had longed for in their early married days was now theirs. On their twenty-fourth wedding anniversary. Hazel wrote:

In fact I love you and admire you much more truly and completely than on that far off 22nd of July when we went to the Oratory together. So please accept this very modest gift with my dear dear love and the prayer that we may have many anniversaries yet together even though I am a puir wee thing but Thine own.[128]

John spent most of the day amusing Hazel in her room, but, never idle, he also began a huge canvas of his wife in her sickbed. Hazel regretted such a sad souvenir and 'The Unfinished Harmony', in pink and green, depicts her as a waif lost in her large canopy bed (*see plate*). Her looks were ravaged by illness and she described herself as 'the imaginary child of Mahatma Gandhi and Lady Oxford'.[129] The public Hazel had gone and only her immediate family were allowed to see her unadorned.

Alice arrived at Cromwell Place as soon as she was well enough to travel.

John consulted eighteen doctors over Hazel's last months in a desperate effort to find a cure. Leeches were applied to her skin but only heightened her suffering. Hazel, delirious, cried out that she didn't want to die.[130] Memories of the past returned to haunt her, and she was heard repeating, 'My house is built with straw. My house is built with sticks.'[131] She finally died in her sleep on Thursday 3 January 1935 at 9.40 p.m.

As his wife lay in her coffin, John selected a small canvas and painted 'It Is Finished – 5 January 1935' (*see plate*). Flowers colour the top and base of the coffin. The bare dressing-table, designed by Hazel, is visible in the background. A tall candle is reflected in the mantel mirror. With ritual intent, John had completed the cycle: as he himself stated, it was the final chapter of a beautiful life.[132]

Hazel's funeral mass took place in Brompton Oratory on 7 January 1935. In Dublin a memorial service was held at St Andrew's Church in Westland Row, at the request of former members of Cosgrave's government. Among those who paid tribute to her from Ireland, England and America was her young protégé Cecil Beaton:

Poor Hazel has been laid in her coffin. ... A living spirit has become a thing of the past. Those who loved her will perhaps make a legend of her, decorating her memory with the tuberoses, orchids and crimson roses that she surrounded herself with in life. But soon, and inevitably, even these dearest friends will be busy going out to lunch with someone else.[133]

List of Floral tributes.

1. Sir John Lavery.
✓2. Mr. & Mrs. McEnery.
✓3. Lord Sempill.
. 4. Lady Sempill.
✓5. The Hon. Misses June & Anne Sempill.
✓6. Gwendoline Lady Sempill & Mrs. Forbes-Sempill
    Fintray House, Aberdeenshire.
✓7. Rear-Admiral & Mrs. Lionel Forbes-Sempill,
    "Dummer Grange"
✓8. Lord & Lady Londonderry, Londonderry House, Park Lane, W.
✓9. Lord & Lady Duveen, 4 Grafton Street, W.1.
✓10. Lord Lonsdale, 14 Carlton House Terrace, S.W.
✓11. Lord Darling & Miss Diana Darling, 81 Albert Hall Mansions, S.W.7.
✓12. Sir Patrick & Lady Ford, 8 Morray Place, Edinburgh.
✓13. Sir William & Lady Jowitt, 35 Upper Brook Street, W.1.
✓14. Sir Archibald & Lady Sinclair, 1 Thorney Court, Kensington Gore, W.
✓15. Sir Ian & Lady Hamilton, 1 Hyde Park Gardens, W.
✓16. Sir Paul & Lady Latham, 4 Hyde Park Gardens, W.
    Street.
. 17. Lady Birkenhead, 4 Chester Street, Belgrave Square, S.W.
✓18. Lady Diana Cooper, 90 Gower Street, W.C.
✓19. Lady Juliet Duff, 3 Belgrave Square, S.W.
20. Lady Colfax, Argylle, 211 King's Road, S.W.3.
✓21. Lady Castlerosse, Rupert Hazon Ryack Park
✓22. Lady Gwendoline & Mr. John Churchill, 41 Cromwell Houses, S.S.7.
✓23. The Count & Countess McCormack, Moore Abbey, Monastrevan, Co. Kildare
✓24. Lady Cunard, 7 Grosvenor Square, W.

[2]

✓25. The Hon. Lionel & Mrs. Flora Guest, Ferring-on-Sea, Sussex.
✓26. The Countess Howe, 35 Curzon Street, W.
✓27. Leopold von Hoesch, German Embassy, Carlton House Terrace, S.W.
✓28. Capt & Mrs. Caselot, Fairlawne, Tonbridge, Kent.
    Phillimore Gardens, W.
✓29. Capt. Geoffrey Crawshay, C/o E. Cremlyn-Jones Esq., 19 Upper /
✓30. The Rt. Hon. J. Ramsay McDonald, 10 Downing Street, S.W.1.
✓31. Mr. & Mrs. Winston Churchill, Chartwell, Westerham, Kent.
32. Mr. Randolph Churchill, Mayfair Hotel, W.
33. Mr. & Mrs. Nevin Dumont, 5 Carlton Gardens, S.W.
✓34. Mr. & Mrs. Doyle-Jones, 2 Wentworth Studios, Manresa Road, Chelsea
✓35. Mr. & Mrs. Lawson-Johnstone, 7 Park Lane, W.1.
✓36. Mr. & Mrs. Rea Price, 19a East Heath Road, Hampstead, N.W.
✓37. Mr. & Mrs. Ackner, 47b Welbeck Street, W.
✓38. Mr. & Mrs. Bates, 15a Rabley Mews, Stafford Rd, Kensington.
✓39. Mrs. David Nicoll, Littlehurst, The Ridgeway, Gerrards Cross, Bucks
✓40. Mrs. Haddon, 6a Overstrand Mansions, Battersea, S.W.
✓41. Mrs. Gilbert Russell, 23 Cavendish Square, W.
✓42. Mrs. Watmore, ??? ??? ???
✓43. Mr. Frank Salisbury, Sarum Chase, West Heath Road, Hampstead, N.W.
✓44. Mr. Edward Knoblock, 21 Ashley Place, Westminster, S.W.
✓45. Mr. Samuel Courtauld, 12 North Audley Street, W.
✓46. Mr. E.W. Creslyn-Jones, 19 Upper Phillimore Gardens, W.
✓47. Mr. Derek Patmore, 28 St. James's Square, S.W.
✓49. Mr. Ludovic Ford, ??? ??? 19 St. L Terrace, Chelsea, S.
✓50. Mr. Benjamin Guinness, [handwritten]

[3]

Miss Wiborg, Ritz Hotel, Piccadilly, W.1.
Miss Haslatcher, 3 Kensington Park Gardens, Nottinghill, W.
Miss Hogg, 26 Eaton Mansions, Sloane Square, S.W.1.
Miss Olga Lynn, 11 Harrowby Court, Seymour Place, W.
Miss Lucy Lauder, C/o Miss Jacobs, Harcourt House, Cavendish Square.
Misses Mary & Virginia Carter, 41 Portman Square, W.1.
May Byrne, ??? ???
Patsy Flevins, ??? ???
Miss Christine Knowles, 6 Cheyne House, Embankment Gardens, S.W.3.
"LAURIE" ??? ???
The Staff, 5 Cromwell Place, S.W.7.
The Royal Society of Portrait Painters.
The Chelsea Arts Club.
The South Kensington Fruit Stores.
Mr. & Mrs. Garvey, ??? ??? 169, Wellington Buildings, Ebury Bridge Road, Pimlico, S.W.
Mr. & Mrs. Reville Terry, 50 Grosvenor Street, W.1.
Miss Johanna Collins, 77 Perryn Road, Acton, W.3.
Czechoslovakian Minister, 9 Grosvenor Place, S.W.
"FELICITY" ??? ???
. Miss Mortimer, C/o Messrs Reville-Terry Ltd., 50 Grosvenor Street, W.1.
. Lady Glentanar, 11 Hill Street, W.
. Mrs. James Johnston Ford, St. Colms, North Berwick.
. "SYRIE" ???? ???. [handwritten]

List of Telegrams & Cablegrams.

1. - T.M. The King & Queen
2. - The Prince of Wales.
3. - The Prince George.
4. - Lord & Lady Louisburg.
5. - Schmidt (Beauville Count)
6. - Crosley (Belfast)
7. - Professor & Mrs. MacNeill
8. - Donoughmore.
9. - Kate
10. - Emmet Dalton
11. - Paul Henry.
12. - Mr & Mrs Ackner
13. - Emile & Angela Mond.
14. - Stanmore.
15. - Oxford.
16. - Reading.
17. - Bowen Davis.
18. - George Enner
19. - Maurice
20. - Romaine Walker
21. - Benjamin
22. - Marie Courtenay Milieu.
23. - Dora & Denham Ross.
24. - Lobre (Paris)
25. - Lannon
26. - Superiores Concert Listern.
27. - D'Abernon.
28. - Laura.
29. - De Laylo.
30. - Molly Hodgson.
31. - D'Erlanger
32. - Sir John Lacy
33. - Donbrough.
34. - Mr & Mrs Bain

35. - Lady Sempill
36. - Leslie (Glasslough)
37. - Lemlin Sandsoon
38. - Georgia & Sadie.
39. - ??? from Monte Carlo
40. - Lady Shannon
41. - Cissie Dempsey.
42. - Norah (L. Lindsay)
43. - Macaulay.
44. - Mackay (U.S.A)
45. - Greenleaf (U.S.A)
46. - Carpenter (U.S.A)
47. - Murray-Baker (U.S.A)
48. - Balfour Ross (U.S.A)
49. - Arthur Young (U.S.A)
50. - Ginney (U.S.A ??)
51. - Dicken Marie (U.S.A)
52. - Jocelyn (U.S.A)
53. - Bender (Monte Carlo)

Epilogue

JOHN OUTLIVED HAZEL by six years. After her death he continued to paint. Devoted to the memory of his wife, he distributed portraits of Hazel as gifts to her friends. Some of the paintings were portrait sketches, others were painted posthumously, and recipients included Lady Cunard, J.M. Barrie and Edward Marsh. He also fulfilled one of Hazel's ambitions when in June 1935 he donated his Irish Collection in her memory to the Hugh Lane Municipal Gallery of Modern Art, Dublin. W.B. Yeats visited the gallery in August 1937 and described the paintings of Hazel in his poem 'The Municipal Gallery Re-visited':

> Hazel Lavery living and dying, that tale
> As though some ballad-singer had sung it all

In 1936 John travelled to America, visiting Hollywood and painting Shirley Temple among others, and in 1937 he visited Palm Springs. In 1940 he published his autobiography. *The Life of a Painter.* The Second World War had just begun and no longer wishing to stay in Cromwell Place, he wrote to Alice: 'London is no place for the old or the young, we are only in the way, will you take me till it is over?'[1] He went to live in Kilkenny where he died a few months later, on 10 January 1941.

Alice and Jack McEnery had two other children after Martyn and Mary: Robin in 1937 and Jacqueline in 1940. Jack died in his mid-sixties after a short illness in 1957, and Alice sold Rossenarra and moved with her family to Malahide, Co. Dublin. In 1963 she married Professor Denis Gwynn, whom she had known since childhood. He had recently retired from lecturing in the Department of Modern History at University College Cork, and they settled in Malahide until his death in 1971. Alice spent the last years of her life at Rosenalis, in Beauparc, Co. Meath, until her own death at the age of eighty-six on 19 April 1991.

Abbreviations

LAMC: Lady Audrey Morris Collection
Lavery, *Life: The Life of a Painter* by John Lavery
Leslie MS: 'A Memoir of Hazel Lavery' (undated) by Shane Leslie, in the Leslie
    papers in Georgetown University Library, Washington D.C.
LLC: Lady Lavery Collection
Morris MS: unpublished biography of Lady Lavery by Lady Audrey Morris
NLI: National Library of Ireland
TBP: Thomas Bodkin Papers in Trinity College Dublin, MS 6942.
TCD: Trinity College Dublin
UCDA: University College Dublin Archives

Notes and Sources

PREFACE
1   Shane Leslie, 'A Memoir of Hazel Lavery' (undated) – Leslie papers in Georgetown University Library, Washington D.C. (herein Leslie MS).
2   John Lavery, *The Life of a Painter* (London 1940) (herein Lavery, *Life*), p. 198,
3   John Lavery to Louie Rickard (6 March 1940) – Lady Lavery Collection (herein LLC).
4   Lennox Robinson, *Curtain Up* (London 1942), p. 206.
5   Alice McEnery to Father Leonard (10 January 1936) – Father Leonard papers in All Hallows College, Dublin.
6   Leslie MS.
7   Alice McEnery to Father Leonard (12 June 1936) – Father Leonard papers in All Hallows College, Dublin.
8   *Ibid.* (10 January 1936).
9   Shane Leslie to Alice McEnery (12 January 1949) – Alice McEnery Gwynn papers.
10   Shane Leslie to Audrey Morris (18 June 1950) – Leslie papers in Georgetown University Library, Washington D.C.
11   Leslie MS.

CHAPTER I
1   Lavery, *Life*, pp. 195-6.
2   The census of 1880 for Cook County, Illinois.
3   Lady Audrey Morris's unpublished biography of Lady Lavery (herein Morris MS), p. 26.
4   *The Chicago Tribune* (13 April 1897), p. 4.
5   E.R. Prichard (cd.), *Illinois of to-day and its Progressive Cities* (Chicago n.d.), p. 19.

6   I am grateful to Thomas J. O'Gorman for this reference.
7   *The Daily Ocean* (13 April 1897), p. 4.
8   Moms MS, p. 27.
9   G.V. Martyn to Hazel Lavery (May 1923) – LLC.
10 I am grateful to Thomas J. O'Gorman for this reference.
11 *The Chicago Tribune,* Sunday supplement (30 April 1950), p. 5.
12 Hazel Lavery to Lytton Strachey (3 December 1928) – Strachey papers in the British Library, London (MS 60676).
13 Roger Butterfield, *The American Past* (New York 1966), p. 315.
14 *The Chicago Times-Herald,* (13 April 1897), p. 5.
15 *Ibid.*
16 Morris MS, p. 34.
17 *Ibid.,* p. 28.
18 *Ibid.* p. 29.
19 *The Chicago Daily Journal* (4 May 1904), p. 4.
20 *Kenosha Evening News* (25 May 1917).
21 *Kenosha News (*11 November 1973).
22 *Kenosha Evening News* (21 May 1970).
23 *Kenosha News* (3 November 1945).
24 Alice Gwynn to author (10 November 1990).
25 Hazel Martyn's application to the Miss Masters School, Dobbs Ferry, New York.
26 *The Alumnae Record of the Miss Masters School* (New York 1913), p. 25.
27 The Minute Book (1894-7), St Chrysostom's Church, Chicago, Illinois.
28 The school fees amounted to $1149.71 between September 1897 and June 1898. The Martyns were billed $70 for Hazel's singing lessons and $12 tor her use of the school piano. (The School Ledger 1897-8, Miss Masters School, Dobbs Ferry, New York).
29 Unidentified press cutting (undated 1930s) – Lady Lavery's scrapbooks -LLC.
30 Alice Gwynn to author (10 November 1990).
31 *The Daily Ocean* (13 April 1897), p. 4.
32 *Town Topics* (12 May 1904), p. 9,
33 Edward Livingston Trudeau, *An Autobiography* (New York 1916), p. 272.
34 *Indianapolis Star* (14 January 1899), p. 9, quoted in John Wilmerding, *American Art* (Middlesex 1976), p. 144.
35 Whitney Chadwick, *Women, Art and Society* (London 1990), p. 197.
36 *The Sunday Inter Ocean* (25 July 1909), p. 6.
37 Hazel Trudeau to John Lavery (2 May 1905) – LLC.
38 *The Chicago Tribune* (26 November 1899), p. 42.
39 *The Sunday Inter Ocean* (12 November 1899), p. 18.
40 *The Chicago Tribune* (12 November 1899), p. 37; (29 November 1899), p. 17.
41 Lady Anita Leslie reminiscences in the possession of Eoghan Harris, Monkstown, Co. Dublin.
42 *The Chicago Record-Herald* (22 July 1909), p. 1.
43 *The Chicago Tribune* (17 April 1897), p. 9.
44 The last will and testament of Alice Louise Martyn – Probate Office,

Chicago City Hall.
45   *The Chicago Tribune* (30 May 1902), p. 13.
46   *The Chicago Inter-Ocean* (25 July 1909), p. 6.
47   Thomas J. O'Gorman, 'Madonna at a Bullfight', in *The World of Hibernia*, Vol.1, No.1 (Summer 1995), p. 169.
48   *The Sunday Inter-Ocean* (25 July 1909), p. 6.
49   O'Gorman, *op. cit.*, p. 169.

CHAPTER II
1   Richard R. Brettell, Scott Schaefer, Sylvie Gache-Padn, and Francoise Heil-brun, *A Day in the Country, Impressionism and the French Landscape* (Los Angeles 1984), p. 300.
2   Lavery, *Life*, pp. 128–9.
3   Kenneth McConkey, *John Lavery* (Edinburgh 1993), p. 13.
4   Lavery, *Life*, p. 49.
5   Kenneth McConkey, *John Lavery Retrospective Exhibition Catalogue 1985* (Belfast 1984), pp. 23-5 (herein *Catalogue*).
6   *The New York Times (13* January 1941) – LLC.
7   Lavery, *Life*, pp. 128-9.
8   *Ibid.*, p. 128.
9   *Ibid.*, pp. 128-9.
10   This drawing is in Lady Lavery's scrapbooks – LLC.
11   *The Chicago Tribune* (29 December 1903).
12   Lavery, *Life*, p. 128.
13   *Ibid.*, p. 129.
14   Hazel Martyn to John Lavery (27 September 1903) – LLC.
15   Hazel Martyn to John Lavery (29 October 1903) – LLC.
16   Hazel Martyn to John I.avery (27 September 1903) – LLC.
17   *Ibid.*
18   Lavery, *Life*, p. 68.
19   John Lavcry to Hazel Martyn (28 September 1903) – LLC.
20   *Ibid.*
21   John Lavery to Hazel Martyn (undated, October 1903) – LLC.
22   Hazel Martyn to John Lavery (5 October 1903) – LLC.
23   John Lavery to Hazel Martyn (undated, October 1903) – LLC.
24   Hazel Martyn to John Lavery (15 October 1903) – LLC.
25   Hazel Martyn to John Lavery (5 October 1903) – LLC.
26   *Ibid.*
27   Hazel Martyn to John Lavery (11 October 1903) – LLC.
28   John Lavery to Hazel Martyn (undated, October 1903) – LLC.
29   John Lavery to Hazel Martyn (24 October 1903) – LLC.
30   Hazel Martyn to John Lavery (24 October 1903) – LLC.
31   John Lavery to Hazel Martyn (undated, October 1903) – LLC.
32   Alice Martyn to John Lavery (23 October 1903) (1) – LLC.
33   Alice Martyn to John Lavery (23 October 1903) (2) – LLC.
34   Alice Gwynn to author (10 November 1990).
35   Hazel Martyn to John Lavery (24 October 1903) – LLC.
36   Hazel Martyn to John Lavery (23 October 1903) – LLC.

37   Hazel Martyn to John Lavery (29 October 1903) – LLC.
38   Alice Gwynn to author (10 November 1990).
39   Certificate in the Adirondack Collection – Saranac Lake Free Library, Saranac Lake, New York.
40   Trudeau, *An Autobiography,* p. 274.
41   The Trudeau Little Rapids Visitors Book – Adirondack Collection – Saranac Lake Free Library, Saranac Lake, New York.
42   Hazel Martyn to John Lavery (15 November 1903) -LLC.
43   John Lavery to Hazel Martyn (1 December 1903) – LLC.
44   John Lavery to Alice Martyn (3 December 1903) (1) – LLC.
45   John Lavery to Alice Martyn (3 December 1903) (2) – LLC.
46   *The Chicago Tribune* (3 December 1903), p. 17.
47   *The Chicago Tribune* (4 December 1903), p. 21.
48   *The Chicago Record-Herald* (22 July 1909), p. 1.
49   Lavery, *Life,* p. 130.
50   *The Chicago Evening Post* (28 December 1903).
51   *The Chicago Tribune* (29 December 1903).
52   *Ibid.*
53   Register at St Chrysostom's Church, Chicago.
54   Trudeau, *op. cit., p.* 24.
55   Hazel Martyn to John Lavery (28 December 1903) – LLC.

CHAPTER III
1   *The Chicago Tribune* (28 December 1903), p. 7.
2   *Town Topics* (17 March 1904).
3   *New York Charities Directory* (New York 1905).
4   *The New York Times (*2 May 1904).
5   *The New York Daily Tribune* (4 May 1904), p. 9.
6   *The Daily News* (4 May 1904), p. 17.
7   Alice McEnery to Audrey Morris (undated 1950s) – Lady Audrey Morris Collection (herein LAMC).
8   Hazel Trudeau to John Lavery (16 November 1904) – LLC.
9   Alice Martyn to John Lavery (10 November 1904) – LLC.
10   Hazel Trudeau to John Lavery (16 November 1904) – LLC.
11   Hazel Trudeau to John Lavery (2 May 1905) – LLC.
12   Hazel Trudeau to John Lavery (1 July 1905) – LLC.
13   Hazel Trudeau to John Lavery (16 July 1905) – LLC.
14   Hazel Trudeau to John Lavery (26 July 1905) – LLC.
15   Hazel Trudeau to John Lavery (1 July 1905) – LLC.
16   Hazel Trudeau to John Lavery (22 July 1905) – LLC.
17   Hazel Trudeau to John Lavery (12 July 1905) – LLC.
18   Hazel Trudeau to John Lavery (9 August 1905) – LLC.
19   Hazel Trudeau to John Lavery (26 July 1905) – LLC.
20   Richard R. Brettell (*et al.*), *op. cit., p. 276.*
21   Hazel Trudeau to John Lavery (8 August 1905) – LLC.
22   Hazel Trudeau to John Lavery (13 August 1905) – LLC.
23   *Ibid.*
24   Hazel Trudeau to John Lavery (undated, August 1905) – LLC.

25   Alice Martyn to John Lavery (undated, August 1905) – LLC.
26   Hazel Trudeau to John Lavery (19 October 1905) – LLC.
27   Hazel Trudeau to John Lavery (27 October 1905) – LLC.
28   Hazel Trudeau to John Lavery (28 October 1905) – LLC.
29   John Lavery to Alice Martyn (2 November 1905) – LLC.
30   *Ibid.*
31   John Lavery to Alice Martyn (8 November 1905) – LLC.
32   John Lavery to Alice Martyn (2 November 1905) – LLC.
33   Alice Martyn to John Lavery (6 November 1905) – LLC.
34   Hazel Trudeau to John Lavery (10 February 1906) – LLC.
35   Alice Martyn to John Lavery (6 November 1905) – LLC.
36   Lavery, *Life*, p. 39.
37   *Ibid.*, pp. 68-9.
38   John Lavery to Alice Martyn (8 November 1905) – LLC.
39   Hazel Trudeau to John Lavery (14 November 1905) – LLC.
40   Hazel Trudeau to John Lavery (28 November 1905) – LLC.
41   John Lavery to Hazel Trudeau (29 November 1905) – LLC.
42   Hazel Trudeau to John Lavery (8 December 1905) – LLC.
43   Hazel Trudeau to John Lavery (12 December 1905; ?21 December 1905)
      – LLC
44   Hazel Trudeau to John Lavery (1 January 1906) – LLC.
45   Hazel Trudeau to John Lavery (25 December 1905) – LLC.
46   Hazel Trudeau to John Lavery (8 December 1905; 10 February 1906; 12
      December 1905)-LLC.
47   Hazel Trudeau to John Lavery (12 December 1905) – LLC.
48   Hazel Trudeau to John Lavery (?16 January 1906) – LLC.
49   John Lavery to Hazel Trudeau (11 January 1906) – LLC.
50   Hazel Trudeau to John Lavery (?16 January 1906) – LLC.
51   *Yale Classbook* (1901), p. 69 – Yale Club Library, New York.
52   *The 'National Cyclopaedia of American Biography*, pp. 433-4.
53   Hazel Trudeau to John Lavery (14 February 1906) – LLC.
54   Hazel Trudeau to John Lavery (24 February 1906) – LLC.
55   Hazel Trudeau to John Lavery (28 February 1906) – LLC.
56   John Lavery to Hazel Trudeau (undated, March 1906) – LLC.
57   Hazel Trudeau to John Lavery (19 March 1906) – LLC.
58   Hazel Trudeau to John Lavery (20 March 1906) – LLC.
59   Margaret Canover to Audrey Morris (undated 1950s) – LAMC.
60   Hazel Trudeau to John Lavery (20 November 1906) – LLC.
61   John Lavery to Hazel Trudeau (2 February 1907) – LLC.
62   Hazel Trudeau to John Lavery (undated, March 1907) – LLC.
63   John McCutheon, *Drawn from Memory* (New York 1950), p. 225.
64   Chicago Art Institute 1907-1908 Circular of Instruction *(Chicago 1908);*
65   Records in the Chicago Art Institute.
66   *The Inter Ocean* (5 October 1911).
67   *Ibid.* (5 October 1911).

CHAPTER IV

1   *The Chicago Tribune* (14 October 1911), p. 1.
2   *The Chicago American* (21 June 1909). The death certificate noted the cause of death as 'appendicitis 39 days exhaustion'.
3   Alice Gwynn to author (10 November 1990).
4   Hazel Trudeau to John Lavery (25 June 1909) – LLC.
5   John Lavery to Hazel Trudeau (undated 1909) – LLC.
6   John Lavery to Hazel Trudeau (undated June 1909) – LLC.
7   Dorothy Martyn to John Lavery (21 July 1909) – LLC.
8   *The Chicago Daily News* (22 July 1909), p. 12.
9   Alice Gwynn to author (10 November 1990).
10 *The Chicago Daily News* (22 July 1909), p. 12.
11 Hazel Lavery to Thomas Bodkin (1 July 1928) – TBP \587).
12 Hazel Lavery to John Lavery (undated, July 1909) – LLC.
13 Morris MS, p. 52.
14 Lavery, *Life*, p. 119.
15 Morris MS, p. 58.
16 John Lavery to Hazel Lavery (6 Angust 1909; 11 August 1909) – LLC.
17 Hazel Lavery ro John Lavery (undated, August 1909) – LLC.
18 *Ibid.*
19 *Ibid.*
20 John Lavery to Hazel Lavery (undated, August 1909) – LLC.
21 Hazel Lavery to John Lavery (9 August 1909) – LLC.
22 *The Chicago Tribune (*11 August 1909).
23 Hazel Lavery to John Lavery (undated August 1909) – LLC.
24 Hazel Lavery to John Lavery (11 August 1909) – LLC.
25 Hazel Lavery to John Lavery (13 August 1909) – LLC.
26 Hazel Lavery to John Lavery (11 August 1909) – LLC.
27 John Lavery to Hazel Lavery (24 August 1909) – LLC.
28 Hazel Lavery to John Lavery (13 August 1909) – LLC.
29 Hazel Lavery to John Lavery (16 August 1909) – LLC.
30 Hazel Lavery to John Lavery (14 August 1909) – LLC.
31 Hazel Lavery to John Lavery (13 August 1909) – LLC.
32 Hazel Lavery to John Lavery (23 August 1909) – LLC.
33 Hazel Lavery to John Lavery (14 August 1909) – LLC.

CHAPTER V

1   Morris MS, p. 54.
2   *Evening Standard* (11 July 1941) – LLC.
3   Lavery, *Life*, p. 46.
4   Leonore Davidoff, *The Best Circles: Society, Etiquette and the Season* (London 1973), pp. 59-70.
5   Unidentified press cutting (undated) – Lady Lavery's scrapbooks – LLC.
6   Lady Cynthia Asquith, *The Diaries of Lady Cynthia Asquith 1915-1918* (London 1987), p. 362. (Entry: 6 November 1917).
7   Michael and Eleanor Brock, *H.H. Asquith letters to Venetia Stanley* (Oxford 1982), p. 1.
8   Herbert Henry Asquith (typed) (1910)-LAMC.

9   Morris MS, p. 21.
10   Unidentified press cutting (undated) – Lady Lavery's scrapbooks – LLC.
11   Morris MS, pp. 17-18.
12   Cecil Beaton, *The Wandering Tears, 1922-1939* (London 1961), p. 271.
13   Alice Gwynn to author (10 November 1990).
14   Unidentified press cutting – (undated, prior to 1918) – Lady Lavery's scrapbooks – LLC.
15   Alice Gwynn to author (10 November 1990).
16   *The Inter Ocean* (15 October 1911), p. 4.
17   Lavery, *Life,* pp. 231, 236.
18   Alice Gwynn to author (21 November 1990).
19   Dorothy Martyn, *Grove Eden* (Chicago 1912).
20   *The Inter Ocean* (15 October 1911), p. 4.
21   *The Chicago Tribune* (15 October 1911), p. 15.
22   *The Inter Ocean* (15 October 1911), p. 4.
23   *Chicago Record-Herald* (19 October 1911), p. 4.
24   Alice Gwynn to author (10 November 1990).
25   *Ibid.*
26   John Lavery to Alice McEnery (1 September 1930) – LLC.
27   Unidentified press cutting – (undated) – Lady Lavery's scrapbooks – LLC.
28   *Ibid.*
29   Lavery, *Life,* pp. 180-1.
30   Unidentified press cutting – (undated) – Lady Lavery's serapbooks – LLC.
31   Michael Curtin, 'A Question of Manners: Status and Gender in Etiquette and Courtesy', *Journal of Modern History,* Vol. 57 (September 1985), p. 419.
32   Hazel Trudeau to John Lavery (12 July 1905) – LLC.
33   Beaton, *The Wandering Years,* p. 271.
34   *The Northern Whig* (April 1930) – Lady Lavery's scraphooks – LLC.
35   McConkey, *Catalogue,* p. 73.
36   McConkey, *John Lavery,* p. 121.
37   Lavery, *Life,* pp. 96-7.
38   Alice McEnery to Audrey Morris (undated 1950s) – LAMC.
39   Lavery, *Life,* p. 130.
40   Alice McEnery to Audrey Morris (undated 1950s) – LAMC.
41   *Ibid.*
42   Alice McEnery to Hazel and John Lavery (20 March 1930) – LLC.
43   Alice McEnery to Audrey Morris (undated 1950s) – LAMC.
44   Hazel Lavery to Eddie Marsh (undated 1914), Marsh papers in the Berg Collection, New York Public Library, New York.
45   *Ibid.*
46   Alice McEnery to Audrey Morris (undated 1950s) – LAMC.
47   Lavery, *Life,* p. 131.
48   Alice McEnery to Audrey Morris (undated 1950s) – LAMC.
49   Alice McEnery to Audrey Morris (undated 1950s) – LAMC.
50   Alice Gwynn to author (10 November 1990).
51   Unidentified press cutting (undated) – Lady Lavery's scrapbooks – LLC.
52   Lavery, *Life,* p. 77.

53   Alice Gwynn to author (21 November 1990).

54   Unidentified press cutting (undated) – Lady Lavery's scrapbooks – LLC.

55   Hazel Lavery to Eddie Marsh (undated 1914), Marsh papers in the Berg
      Collection, New York Public Library, New York.

56   *Vogue* (undated); *Lady's Pictorial* (13 December 1919) – Lady Lavery's
      scrapbooks – LLC.

57   Unidentified article entitled 'The Butterfly Fashion' – Lady Lavery's scrap-
      books – LLC.

58   *Vogue* (undated) – Lady Lavery's scrapbooks – LLC.

59   Lavery, *Life*, pp. 197-8.

60   David Beatty to John Lavery (22 March 1918) – Lavery Collection in the
      Tate Gallery Archive, London (TGA. 7245.218).

61   Lavery, *Life*, p. 195.

62   *Lady's Pictorial* (13 December 1919) — Lady Lavery's scrapbooks – LLC.

63   Morris MS, p. 135.

64   Unidentified press cutting (1916) – Lady Lavery's scrapbooks – LLC.

65   Harold Acton, 'Lady Cunard' in Peter Quennell (ed.). *Genius in the Draw-
      ing Room* (London 1980), pp. 175-6.

66   Lavery, *Life*, p. 195.

67   *Ibid.*, pp. 152-3.

68   Lady Edith Londonderry, *Retrospect* (London 1938), p. 143.

69   Asquith, *Diaries.*, p. 409. (Entry: 4 February 1918).

70   Leslie MS.

71   Lavery, *Life*, p. 197.

72   Shane Leslie, *Long Shadows* (London 1966), p. 228.

73   Stephen Roskill, *Admiral of the Fleet: Earl Beam, The Last Naval Hero*
      (London 1980), p. 46.

74   Shane Leslie to Hazel Lavery (undated 1920s) – Leslie papers in George-
      town University Library, Washington D.C.

75   Lady Anita Leslie reminiscences in the possession of Eoghan Harris,
      Monkstown, Co. Dublin.

76   *The Chicago Tribune*, Sunday supplement (30 April 1950), p. 5. Robin
      Londonderry wrote to Audrey Morris: 'I cannot vouchsafe for the story.
      I only heard of it from Shane. My reason for doubting it ... he also said
      my father gave her some family jewels. He was far too mean for that' (10
      November 1950).

77   'Shane Leslie to Audrey Morris (undated 1950s) – LAMC.

78   Kenneth McConkey, 'Hazel in Black and Gold', *Irish Arts Review*, Vol. 1,
      No.3 (Autumn 1984), p. 16.

79   Unidentified press cutting (April 1930) – Lady Lavery's scrapbooks – LLC.

80   Alice Gwynn to author (21 November 1990).

81   Hazel Lavery to Arthur Deane (8 May 1929) – Ulster Museum, Belfast.

82   Morris MS, p. 106.

83   Unidentified press cutting – Lady Lavery's scrapbooks – LLC.

84   Bruce Arnold, *Orpen: Mirror to an Age* (London 1981), pp. 302-3.

85   Terence Pepper, *Camera Portraits by E.O. Hoppé (1878-1972) – Exhibition
      Catalogue* (London 1978), p. 6 (herein *Hoppé Catalogue*).

86   *The Daily Graphic* (undated) – Lady Lavery's scrapbooks – LLC.

87   *Duff* Cooper to Hazel Lavery (5 August 1914) – LLC.
88   Lavery, *Life*, pp. 131-3, 138-9.
89   H. Montgomery Hyde, *The Londonderrys, A Family Portrait* (London 1979), p. 132.
90   The member's name either rhymed or began with the first letter of their Christian name or surname. Lady Londonderry was known as Circe the Sorceress with the ability to turn men into beasts. Her husband Charley, whose vast fortune enabled her to entertain in such style, was aptly known as the Treasurer of the Ark. (Londonderry, *Retrospect,* p. 247).
91   Morris MS, p. 84.
92   Winston Churchill, *Thoughts and Adventures* (London 1990), p. 224.
93   John Colville, *The Churchillians* (London 1981), p. 118.
94   Lavery, *Life,* pp. 140,142-3.
95   *Chicago Daily Journal* (1916) – Lady Lavery's scrapbooks – LLC.
96   Alice Gwynn to author (10 November 1990).
97   Lavery, *Life,* p. 141.
98   Morris MS, p. 86.
99   McConkey, *Catalogue,* p. 79.
100   Unidentified press cutting (1916) – Lady Lavery's scrapbooks – LLC.
101   *Ibid.*
102   Asquith, *Diaries,* p. 178. (Entry: 21 June 1916).
103   Unidentified press cutting (undated) – Lady Lavery's scrapbooks – LLC.
104   Asquith, *Diaries,* p. 175. (Entry: 15 June 1916).
105   Unidentified press cutting (1916), Lady Lavery's scrapbooks – LLC.
106   Alice Gwynn to author (26 March 1991).
107   Terence Pepper, *of. cit., p. 7.*
108   Lavery, *Life,* pp. 141-2.
109   McConkey, *John Lavery,* p. 127.
110   John Lavery to Robert Cunninghame-Graham (28 May 1915), cited in *ibid.,* p. 130.
111   Walter H. Page to John Lavery (6 January 1918)-LLC.
112   William Orpen to John Lavery (1 January 1918)- LLC.
113   *Daily Express* (7 April 1941) – LLC.
114   Alice McEnery to Audrey Morris (undated 1950s) – LAMC.
115   Lavery, *Life,* p. 148.

CHAPTER VI
1   Lavery, *Life,* p. 221; Unidentified press cutting – (undated) – Lady Lavery's scrapbooks – LLC.
2   Robinson, *Curtain Up,* p. 207; Unidentified press cutting (undated) – Lady Lavery's scrapbooks – LLC.
3   Lady Anita Leslie reminiscences in the possession of Eoghan Harris, Monkstown, Co. Dublin.
4   Lavery, *Life,* p. 221.
5   *The Chicago Tribune,* Sunday supplement (30 April 1950), p. 5.
6   Lavery, *Life,* p. 208.
7   *United Ireland* (13 January 1935), p. 6. *The Irish Independent* (Easter Week 1966) reported that the canvas was purchased for £800.

8   Letter quoted in Lavery, *Life*, p. 189.
9   *The Weekly Dispatch* (22 October 1916) – Lavery Collection in the Tate Gallery Archive, London (T.G.A. 7245.8).
10   Lavery, *Life*, pp. 189-90.
11   *Ibid.*
12   Margaret Gavan Duffy to John Lavery (16 November 1916) – Lavery Collection in the Tate Gallery Archive, London (T.G.A. 7245.1).
13   McConkey. *John Lavery*, pp. 149-50.
14   Thomas Bodkin, *Hugh Lane and his Pictures* (Dublin 1956), pp. 7-43.
15   Lavery, *Life*, p. 221.
16   De Valera had escaped execution due to his American citizenship, although he argued that the administration had decided that enough was enough by the time he was to be executed. (F.S.L. Lyons, *Ireland since the Famine* (Suffolk 1981) p. 376).
17   Lavery, *Life*, p. 133.
18   *Ibid.*, p. 212.
19   *The Chicago Tribune*, Sunday supplement (30 April 1950), p. 5.
20   Shane Leslie to Alice McEnery (25 February 1949) – Alice McEnery Gwynn papers. Although Leslie repeated this story widely and wrote of it to Londonderry's children, no documentary evidence survives to prove that the challenge ever took place. Leslie had a reputation for embellishing tales.
21   Lavery, *Life*, p. 209.
22   John Lavery to Eileen Lavery Sempill (undated 1920) quoted in Morris MS, p. 109; Lavery, *Life*, pp. 209-10.
23   Lavery, *Life*, p. 211.
24   *Ibid.*, pp. 211-12.
25   Ivor, Lord Wimborne to Audrey Morris (1950s) – Lady Audrey Morris research.
26   Morris MS, p. 113.
27   *Ibid.*
28   Lavery, *Life*, p. 213.
29   Hazel's Teacher's Bible is in the LLC.
30   Alice Gwynn to author (10 November 1990).
31   I am grateful to Thomas *J.* O'Gonnan for this reference.
32   Lavery, *Life, p. 208.*
33   John Lavery to Mrs Duncan (14 July 1921) in the Collection of the Hugh Lane Municipal Gallery of Modern Art, Dublin.
34   Claud Cockburn research in the possession of Eoghan Harris, Monkstown, Co. Dublin.
35   Oliver St John Gogarty to Audrey Morris – (undated) – LAMC.
36   Lord Longford (Frank Pakenham), *Peace by Ordeal* (London 1972), p. 74.
37   Lavery, *Life*, p. 213.
38   Shane Leslie Diaries (1914–44) (Entry: 16 July 1921) – NLI , Dublin (MS 22,863).
39   Longford, *op. cit., p. 77.*
40   Margery Forester, *The Lost Leader* (London 1972), p. 217.
41   John Lavery to Art O'Brien (6 October 1921) – Childers papers in TCD (MS 7796/1/1).

42   *Ibid.*

43   Piaras Beaslai, *Michael Collins and the making of a new Ireland (Vol. 11)* (Dublin 1926), p. 299.

44   Hazel Lavery to Thomas Bodkin (26 March 1929) – Thomas Bodkin papers in Trinity College, Dublin, MS 6942 (herein TBP) (600).

45   Anonymous letter (undated 1921) – LLC.

46   Shane Leslie Diaries (1914--44) (Enrry: 11 October 1921) – NLI , Dublin (MS 22,863).

47   Morris MS, p. 113.

48   Lavery, *Life*, p. 213.

49   This portrait eventually found its way into Kitty Kiernan's possession. 'Michael's letters, were, of course. Kitty's most treasured souvenirs, but almost of equivalent importance was the portrait of Collins that Sir John Lavery painted 'in London, and which she set up on an easel in the principal living room.' (Leon O'Broin, *In Great Haste* [Dublin 1984], p. 222). 'Regrettably the painting is not in our possession and we have no knowledge of its whereabouts.' (Felix Cronin [Kitty's son] to author, 16 April 1992). In 1935 John gave another portrait of Collins to the Hugh Lane Municipal Gallery of Modern Art to complete their collection.

50   Michael Collins to Kitty Kiernan (16 November 1921), O'Broin, *In Great Haste*, p. 58.

51   Christopher Hassall, *Edward Marsh, Patrons of the Arts* (London 1959), p. 489.

52   Forester, *The Lost Leader*, p. 25.

53   Frank O'Connor, *The Rig Fellow* (Dublin 1979), p. 159.

54   Lavery, *Life*, p. 165.

55   Hazel Lavery to Clare Kennedy (9 October 1922) – Kennedy papers in University College Dublin Archive (herein UCADA) p4\1434.

56   Longford, *op. cit.*, p. 107.

57   Elizabeth, Countess of Fingall, *Seventy Years Young* (Dublin 1991), p. 403.

58   Hazel Lavery to Lytton Strachey (10 July 1924) – Strachey papers in the British Library, London.

59   Shane Leslie to Audrey Morris (undated 1950s) – Lady Audrey Morris research.

60   Robinson, *Curtain Up, p.* 208.

61   Hazel Lavery to Michael Collins (10 December 1921) in O'Broin, *In Great Haste*, p. 78.

62   Shane Leslie to Audrey Morris (1950s) – Lady Audrey Morris research.

63   Lady Diana Cooper reminiscences in the possession of Eoghan Harris, Monkstown, Co. Dublin.

64   Lady Anita Leslie reminiscences in the possession of Eoghan Harris, Monkstown, Co. Dublin.

65   Alice Gwynn to author (10 November 1990).

66   Longford, *op. cit.*, p. 146.

67   *Ibid.*, pp. 100-1.

68   *Ibid., p.* 150.

69   *Ibid., p. W.*

70   R. Erskine Childers to Molly Childers (8 November 1921), R. Erskine

Childers papers in TCD (MS 7855/1205).

71   R. Erskine Childers Diaries (6 December 1921) – R. Erskine Childers papers in TCD (MS 7814/1102).

72   Longford, *op. cit.,* p. 207.

73   *Ibid.,* p. 215.

74   *Ibid.,* p. 217.

75   In his account of the Treaty, Lord Longford states that Collins met Lloyd George on the morning of 5 December, but a meeting between them on Sunday night, 4 December is borne out by C.P. Scott's diary entry for that night (see *The Political Diaries of C.P. Scott 1911-1928,* Trevor Wilson [ed.], [London 1970] pp. 410-11).

76   Fingall, *op. cit.,* p. 402.

77   Lavery, *Life,* pp. 213-14.

78   *Ibid.,* p. 214.

79   Morris MS.

80   Clemmie Churchill to Audrey Morris (1950s) – Lady Audrey Morris research.

81   Longford, *op. cit.,* p. 221.

82   *Ibid.,* pp. 239-40.

83   R. Erskine Childers to Molly Childers (6 December 1921) – R. Erskine Childers papers in TCD (MS 7855/1264).

84   Meda Ryan, *The Day Michael Collins Was Shot* (Dublin 1989), p. 13.

85   Alice Gwynn to author (10 November 1990).

CHAPTER VII

1   Hazel Lavery to Michael Collins (10 December 1921), O'Broin, *In Great Haste,* p. 78.

2   *Ibid.* (14 December 1921), pp. 79-80.

3   *Ibid.*

4   *Ibid.*

5   Shane Leslie to Audrey Morris (15 June 1950) – Leslie papers in Georgetown University Library, Washington D.C.

6   Michael Collins, Dáil Éireann, public session (19 December 1921), *Official Report Debate on the Treaty between Great Britain and Ireland,* p. 32.

7   Speech given by Kevin O'Higgins at the Irish Society at Oxford University, 1924, cited in D.W. Harkness, *The Restless Dominion The Irish Free State and the British Commonwealth of Nations, 1921-1931* (New York 1970), p. 26.

8   Juliet Duff to Leonie Leslie (23 January ?1922) – Leslie papers in Georgetown University Library, Washington D.C.

9   Edgar Holt, *Protest in Arms, The Irish Troubles 1916-1923* (London 1960), p. 265.

10   Lady Lavery's scrapbooks (1922) – LLC. Hazel Lavery recorded 'meetings of Irish delegates' at 5 Cromwell Place on 21 January, 5 and 15 February, 29-31 March, 1 April, 27-31 May, and 1-13 June. All the dates correspond to the times when Collins wrote from London to Kitty Kiernan. Further assemblies in Dublin are listed as 15, 16, 17, 18, 19 (?June).

11   Shane Leslie Diaries (1914-1:4) (Entry: 27 May 1922) – NLI (MS

22,863).

12 O'Connor, *The Big Fellow*, p. 187.

13 Una O'Higgins O'Malley, 'Rumour of Women, *Irish Times* (*I* October 1990).

14 Montgomery Hyde, *The Londonderry!*, p. 150.

15 On the basis of the letter from Michael Collins to Edith Londonderry, Montgomery Hyde assumes that this meeting was organized by Edith Londonderry. It was more likely to have been arranged by Hazel Lavery. (I am grateful to Deirdre MacMahon for bringing this to my attention.)

16 Montgomery Hyde, *op. cit.*, pp. 151-2.

17 Robin Londonderry to Audrey Morris (10 November 1950) – LAMC. When Lady Morris asked to view these letters Robin Londonderry replied: 'The only letters I have are of no value. They are purely private. One does suggest that she would like to see more of my father again. There is also a box from her with a note saying he was to keep her letters in it. However, he was not so rash as that.' (27 November 1950).

18 Shane Leslie to Margaret Londonderry (19 January 1950) (copy) – LAMC.

19 Shane Leslie to Hazel Lavery (undated 1923) – Leslie papers in Georgetown University Library, Washington D.C.

20 Hazel Lavery to Father Leonard (20 March 1924) – Father Leonard papers in All Hallows College, Dublin.

21 Shane Leslie to Audrey Morris (18 June 1950), Leslie papers in Georgetown University Library, Washington D.C.

22 Unidentified press cutting (undated) – Lady Lavery's scrapbooks – LLC.

23 Harold Nicolson, unidentified press cutting (undated 1941) – LLC.

24 *Evening Standard* (11 January 1941).

25 Michael Collins to Kitty Kiernan (4 February 1922) in O'Broin, *In Great Haste*, p. 110.

26 *Ibid.* (23 February 1922), p. 127.

27 Hazel Lavery to Marie Belloc Lowndes (undated) – The Harry Ransom Humanities Research Center, University of Texas at Austin.

28 Michael Collins to Kitty Kiernan (28 May 1922) in O'Broin *In Great Haste*, p. 166.

29 Oliver St John Gogarty, Memoir (undated) – LAMC.

30 Shane Leslie to John Lavery (June 1922) – Kilmainham Gaol, Dublin.

31 Michael Collins to Hazel Lavery (in Lady Lavery's hand, marked 'copy') (22 June 1922) – Lady Lavery's scrapbooks – LLC.

32 Michael Collins to Hazel Lavery (?13 June 1922) – Lady Lavery's scrapbooks – LLC.

33 Lord Cavan to Hazel Lavery (13 June 1922) – LLC.

34 Michael Collins to Hazel Lavery (11 June 1922) (fragment) – LLC.

35 Winston Churchill to Hazel Lavery (copied by Shane Leslie) – Leslie papers in Georgetown University Library, Washington D.C.

36 Michael Collins to Kitty Kiernan (30 May 1922) in O'Broin, *In Great Haste*, p. 166.

37 Derek Patmore quoted in Leslie MS.

38 Hazel Lavery to Hugh Kennedy (24 June 1922) – Kennedy papers in UCDAp4/1430(l).

39 Shane Leslie Diaries (1914-44) (Entry: 22 June 1922) – NLI (MS22,863).

40 Poem by Hazel Lavery – Lady Lavery's scrapbooks – LLC.

41 Hazel Lavery to Marie Belloc Lowndes (6 December 1922) – Tlie Harry Ransom Humanities Research Center, University of Texas at Austin.

42 Hazel Lavery to Hugh Kennedy (8 August 1922) – Kennedy papers in UCDA p4/1432 (4).

43 Hugh Kennedy to Hazel Lavery (rough copy of original) (undated) – Kennedy papers in UCDA p4/1429 (2).

44 Hazel Lavery to Hugh Kennedy (24 June 1922) – Kennedy papers in U.C.D.Ap4/1430(l).

45 John Lavery to Andy Cope (30 June 1922) – Kennedy Papers, in UCDA p4/1428(l).

46 Hugh Kennedy to John Lavery (1 July 1922) – Kennedy papers in UCDA p4/1428(2).

47 Kitty Kiernan to Michael Collins (?3 July 1922), O'Broin, *In Great Haste*, pp.186-7.

48 Michael Collins to Kitty Kiernan (?5 July 1922), in O'Broin, *op. cit.,* p. 188.

49 Michael Collins to Hazel Lavery (10 July 1922) in Hazel's handwriting but noted 'copy' – Lady Lavery's scrapbooks – LLC.

50 Charley Londonderry to Hazel Lavery (5 August 1922) – LLC.

51 Charley Londonderry to Hazel Lavery (7 August 1922) – LLC.

52 Charley Londonderry to Hazel Lavery (5 August 1922) – LLC.

53 Hazel Lavery to Hugh Kennedy (8 August 1922) – Kennedy papers in UCDAp4/1432(3).

54 Hazel Lavery to Hugh Kennedy (8 August 1922) – Kennedy papers in UCDAp4/1432(4).

55 Tim Pat Coogan, *Michael Collins* (London 1990), p. 399.

56 Confidential source.

57 Claud Cockburn research in the possession of Eoghan Harris, Monkstown, Co. Dublin.

58 Lord Longford reminiscences in the possession of Eoghan Harris, Monkstown, Co. Dublin.

59 Coogan, *Michael Collins,* p. 294.

60 Shane Leslie to Audrey Morris (15 June 1950) – Leslie papers in Georgetown University Library, Washington D.C.

61 Alice Gwynn to author (26 March 1991).

62 Horace Plunkett to Hazel Lavery (17 August 1922) – LLC.

63 Daniel J. Murphy (ed.). *Lady Gregory's Journal,* Vol. 1, October 1916-February 1925 (Buckinghamshire 1978), p. 388.

64 Lavery, *Life,* p. 216.

65 Hassall, *Edward Marsh,* p. 488.

66 Fingall, *Seventy Tears Young,* p. 409.

67 Trevor West, *Horace Plunkett, Co-Operation and Politics* (Washington D.C. 1986), p. 198.

68 Lavery, *Life,* p. 216.

69 Hassall, *Edward Marsh,* p. 488.

70 Report to the Director of Publicity for the press, Kathleen MacKenna

Napoli (19 August 1922) – NLI (MS 22,779).

71 Shane Leslie Diaries (1914-44) (Entry: 11 July 1927) – NLI (MS 22,863).
72 Lavery, *Life*, pp. 216-17.
73 Ryan, *The Day Michael Collins Was Shot*, pp. 103-7.
74 Lavery, *Life*, p. 217.
75 Fingall, *Seventy Years Young, p.* 409.
76 Terence de Vere White, *Kevin O'Higgins* (Dublin 1986), p. 93.
77 J.B. Lyons, *Oliver St John Gogarty the Man of Many Talents* (Dublin 1980), p. 125.
78 Lavery, *Life*, p. 217.
79 HassaU, *Edward Marsh*, p. 489.
80 Lady Sempill to Thomas J. O'Gorman, quoted in O'Gorman, 'Madonna at a Bullfight', p. 174
81 Hassall, *Edward Marsh*, p. 489.
82 Sean O'Connell to Hazel Lavery (11 October 1923) – LLC.
83 Hazel Lavery to Marie Belloc Lowndes (14 September 1922) – The Harry Ransom Humanities Research Center, University of Texas at Austin.
84 Lady Lavery's scrapbooks – LLC.
85 *Ibid.*
86 Gearóid McGann to Hazel Lavery (undated 1922) – LLC.
87 Hannie Collins to Audrey Morris (undated 1950s) – LAMC.
88 Michael Collins to Hazel Lavery (undated) – Kilmainham Gaol Museum, Dublin.
89 Philip Sassoon to Hazel Lavery (30 August 1922) – LLC.
90 Edward Marsh to Hazel Lavery (23 August 1922) – LLC.
91 George Bernard Shaw to Hazel Lavery (7 October 1922) – LLC.
92 Audrey Morris to author (May 1992).
93 Kevin O'Higgins to Hazel Lavery (1 September 1922) – LLC.
94 Hazel Lavery to Winston Churchill (29 October 1922), quoted in Martin Gilbert, *Winston Churchill (Companion IV 1917-1922)* (London 1977), pp.2096-7.
95 De Vere White, *Kevin O'Higgins*, pp. 128, 257.
96 Shane Leslie to Hazel Lavery (undated) – LLC.
97 Anonymous (undated, ?1923) – LLC.
98 Emmet Dalton to Hazel Lavery (15 November 1922) – LLC.
99 Kevin O'Higgins to Hazel Lavery (5 July 1923) – LLC.
100 De Vere White, *Kevin O'Higgins*, p. 93.
101 Shane Leslie to Audrey Morris (15 June 1950) – Leslie Papers in Georgetown University Library, Washington D.C.
102 Morris MS, p. 132.
103 Terence de Vere White to author (1991).
104 De Vere White, *Kevin O'Higgins*, p. 93.
105 Unidentified press cutting (August 1923) – Lady Lavery's scrapbooks – LLC.
106 Unidentified press cutting (August 1923) – Lady Lavery's scrapbooks – LLC.

CHAPTER VIII
1   Beverly Nichols to Hazel Lavery (undated) – LLC.
2   Josephine MacNeill to Audrey Moms (27 July 1951) – LAMC.

3 Alice Gwynn to author (26 March 1991).

4 Oliver St John Gogarty memoir – LAMC.

5 Hazel Lavery to Oliver St John Gogarty (22 May 1923), quoced in Lyons, *Gogarty,* p. 333.

6 Lyons, *op. cit., p.* 131.

7 Andy Cope to Hazel Lavery (30 June 1923) – LLC.

8 Oliver St John Gogarty to Hazel Lavery (undated, June 1923) – LLC.

9 De Vere White, *Kevin O'Higgins,* p. 168.

10 Unidentified press cutting (undated ?1923) – Lady Lavery's scrapbooks – LLC.

11 Kevin O'Higgins to Hazel Lavery (5 July 1923) – LLC.

12 Keith Middlemas (ed.) *Thomas Jones's Whitehall Diary,* Vol. III *Ireland 1918-25* (London 1971) p. 2 IS. Hazel's involvement in Healy's selection was referred to in *The United Ireland* (12 January 1935), which was known to reflect Cosgrave's views.

13 Elizabeth Healy to Hazel Lavery (7 September 1923) – LLC.

14 Brendan Sexton, *Ireland and the Crown 1922-1936 The Governor-Generalship* (Dublin 1989) pp. 99-100.

15 Audrey Morris to author (May 1992).

16 Oliver St John Gogarty in Morris MS, p. 159.

17 Harkness, *The Restless Dominion,* p. 53.

18 Desmond FitzGerald to Hazel Lavery (17 November 1923) – LLC.

19 Desmond FitzGerald to Hazel Lavery (30 January 1924) – LLC.

20 Charley Londonderry to Hazel Lavery (1 November 1922) – LLC.

21 Charley Londonderry to Hazel Lavery (6 November 1923) – LLC.

22 Hazel Lavery to Hugh Kennedy (undated 1924) – Kennedy papers in UCDA p4\1436.

23 Geoffrey Dawson to Hazel Lavery (5 February 1924) – LLC.

24 Eddie Marsh to Hazel Lavery (undated 1924) – LLC.

25 Hazel Lavery to Hugh Kennedy (undated 1924) – Kennedy papers in UCDAp4/1437.

26 Hazel Lavery to Hugh Kennedy (undated 1924) – Kennedy papers in UCDAp4/1435.

27 Austen Chamberlain to Hazel Lavery (7 November 1923) – LLC.

28 Reg McKenna to Hazel Lavery (12 June 1923) – LLC.

29 Anonymous note (undated) – Lady Lavery's scrapbooks – LLC.

30 Desmond FitzGerald to Hazel Lavery (24 March 1924) – LLC.

31 Tim Healy to Hazel Lavery (25 March 1924) – LLC.

32 Alice Trudeau to Hazel Lavery (5 July 1924) – LLC.

33 Eddie Marsh to Hazel Lavery (9 July 1924) – LLC.

34 Tim Healy to Annie Healy (16 July 1924) – Healy papers in UCDA p6/a/96.

35 J.H. Thomas to PLi/.el Lavery (6 August 1924) – LLC.

36 Hazel Lavery to Father Leonard (9 September 1924) – Father Leonard papers in All Hallows College, Dublin.

37 Lytton Strachey to Hazel Lavery (14 September 1924) (copy) – Leslie papers in Georgetown University Library, Washington D.C.

38 Hazel Lavery to Lytton Strachey (10 July 1924) – Strachey papers in the

British Library, London MS 60676.

39   Hazel Lavery to Lytton Strachey (31 May 1924) – Strachey papers in the British Library, London MS 60676.

40   Winston Churchill to Hazel Lavery (12 November 1924) -LLC.

41   N. Butler to Ramsay MacDonald (?28 July) – MacDonald papers in the Public Record Office, London (MS 30/69/1184).

42   Hazel Lavery to Ramsay MacDonald (4 November 1924) – MacDonald papers in the Public Record Office, London (MS 1433/73-4).

43   Alice Gwynn to author (10 November 1990).

44   Shane Leslie's Diaries (1914-44) (Entry: 11 July 1927) – NLI, MS 22,863.

45   Written in Shane Leslie's hand, Kilmainham Gaol Museum, Dublin.

46   Kevin O'Higgins to Hazel Lavery (4 November 1924) – LLC.

47   De Vere White., *Kevin O'Higgins, p.* 177.

48   Kevin O'Higgins to Hazel Lavery (17 December 1924)-LLC.

49   Thomas Bodkin to Hazel Lavery (4 October ? 1928) – LLC.

50   Austen Chamberlain to Hazel Lavery (22 April 1925) – LLC.

51   Desmond FitzGerald to Hazel Lavery (6 May 1925) – LLC.

52   Hazel Lavery to Shane Leslie (undated, July 1925) – Leslie papers in Georgetown University Library, Washington n.c.

53   Stephen Gwynn – Unidentified press cutting (August 1925) — Lady Lavery's scrapbooks – LLC.

54   Robinson, *Curtain Up,* p. 209.

55   Hazel Lavery to Father Leonard (undated, September 1925) – Father Leonard papers, in All Hallows College, Dublin.

56   Alice Gwynn to author (10 November 1990

57   Alice Trudeau to Hazel Lavery (5 January 1924) – LLC.

58   Unidentified press cutting (undated) – Lady Lavcry's scrapbooks – LLC.

59   Alice Trudeau to Hazel Lavery (25 March 1925) – LLC.

60   Dan H. Laurence (ed.), *Bernard Shaw Letters,* Vol. 4, 1926-50 (London 1988), p. 8.

61   Alice Trudeau to Hazel Lavery (25 March 1925) – LLC.

62   The Last Will and Testament of Edward L. Trudeau, Franklin County Surrogate's office. New York.

63   Morris MS, p. 196.

64   Hazel Lavery to Eddie Marsh (26 January 1926) – Marsh papers in the Berg Collection, New York Public Library, New York.

65   Robinson, *Curtain Up,* p. 207.

66   Hazel Lavery to Eddie Marsh (26 January 1926) – Marsh papers in the Berg Collection, New York Public Library, New York.

67   McConkey, *Catalogue,* p. 92.

68   Hazel Lavery to Lady Gregory (26 April 1926) – Gregory papers in the Berg Collection, New York Public Library, New York.

69   James MacNeiU to Hazel Lavery (11 December 1925) – LLC.

70   Hazel Lavery to Eddie Marsh (26 January 1926) – Marsh papers in the Berg Collection, New York Public Library, New York.

71   Hazel Lavery to Lady Gregory (26 April 1926) – Gregory papers in the Berg Collection, New York Public Library, New York.

72   Barbara Dawson, 'Hugh Lane and the Origins of the Collection' in *Images*

and Insights, Hugh Lane Municipal Gallery of Modern Art Catalogue (Dublin 1993), p. 29.

73   John Lavery to Lady Gregory (27 June 1926) – Marsh papers in the Berg Collection, New York Public Library, New York.

74   *Ibid.* (2 October 1926).

75   *Ibid.* (27 June 1926).

76   Hazel Lavery to Lady Gregory (26 June 1926) – Gregory papers in the Berg Collection, New York Public Library, New York.

77   John Lavery to Lady Gregory (27 June 1926) – Gregory papers in the Berg Collection, New York Public Library, New York.

78   Hazel Lavery to Lady Gregory (26 June 1926) – Gregory papers in the Berg Collection, New York Public Library, New York.

79   Kevin O'Higgins to Hazel Lavery (12 November 1926) – LLC.

80   Robinson, *Curtain Up,* p. 207.

81   Desmond FitzGerald to Hazel Lavery (31 August 1926) – LLC.

82   FitzGerald papers in the UCDA, MS p80/591(49).

83   Kevin O'Higgins to Hazel Lavery (12 November 1926) – LLC.

84   *Poems by Sir Samuel Ferguson* (Dublin, undated) pp. 49-50 – LLC.

85   Kevin O'Higgins to Hazel Lavery (27 November 1926) – LLC.

86   Hazel Lavery to Father Leonard (30 November 1926) – Father Leonard papers in All Hallows College, Dublin.

87   Kevin O'Higgins to Hazel Lavery (8 November 1926) – LLC.

88   Alice Trudeau to Hazel Lavery (?August 1926) – LLC.

89   Hazel Lavery to Lennox Robinson (?November 1926), Morris MS p. 175.

90   Kevin O'Higgins to Hazel Lavery (27 November 1926) – LLC.

91   Kevin O'Higgins to Hazel Lavery (12 January 1927) – LLC.

92   Dc Vere White, *Kevin O'Higgins,* p. 168.

93   Kevin O'Higgins to Hazel Lavery (27 November 1926) – LLC.

94   *The Star* (11 January 1941).

95   Alice Trudeau to Hazel Lavery (undated February 1927) – LLC.

96   Kevin O'Higgins to Hazel Lavery (4 February 1927) – LLC.

97   Kevin O'Higgins to Hazel Lavery (18 March 1927; 19 March 1927) – LLC.

98   Hazel Lavery to Lady Gregory (26 March 1927) – Gregory papers in the Berg Collection, New York Public library. New York.

99   Unidentified press cutting (undated) ~ Lady Lavery's scrapbooks – LLC.

100   Hazel Lavery to Lady Gregory (26 March 1927) – Gregory papers in the Berg Collection, New York Public Library, New York.

101   Kevin O'Higgins to Hazel Lavery (14 May 1927) – LLC.

102   Kevin O'Higgins to Hazel Lavery (6 May 1927) – LLC.

103   Kevin O'Higgins to Hazel Lavery (10 June 1927) – LLC.

104   De Vere White, *Kevin O'Higgins,* p. 237.

105   Morris MS, p. 177.

106   Kevin O'Higgins to Hazel Lavery (3 July 1927) – LLC.

107   Roger Gannon, son of one of the assassins, in a Radio Telifis Eireann interview (July 1991).

108   Terence de Vere White to Josephine MacNeill (16 February 1949) (copy) -Alice McEnery Gwynn papers.

109   De Vere White, *Kevin O'Higgins,* pp. 241-2.

110   Shane Leslie Diaries (1914-44) (Entry: 11 July 1927) – NLI (MS 22,863).

111   Shanc Leslie to Audrey Morris (15 June 1950) (copy) – Leslie papers in Georgetown University Library, Washington D.C.

112   Robinson, *Curtain Up,* p. 210.

113   Hazel Lavery to Father Leonard (undated, July 1927) – Father Leonard papers in All Hallows College, Dublin.

114   Eoin O'Duffy to Hazel Lavery (1 September 1927) – LLC.

115   Louie Rickard to Hazel Lavery (14 July 1927) – LLC.

116   Birdie O'Higgins to Hazel Lavery (27 July 1927) – LLC.

117   Louie Rickard to Hazel Lavery (2 August 1927) – LLC.

118   Hazel Lavery to Father Leonard (10 August 1927) – Father Leonard papers in All Hallows College, Dublin.

119   Lennox Robinson to Hazel Lavery (undated 1927) – LLC.

120   Diarmuid O'Hegarty to Hazel Lavery (14 July 1927) – LLC.

121   Hazel Lavery to Paddy McGilligan (31 March 1928) – McGilligan papers inUCDAp35/d/134.

122   Lennox Robinson to Hazel Lavery (undated 1927) – LLC.

123   John Lavery to Hazel Lavery (19 September 1927) – LLC.

124   Louie Rickard to Hazel Lavery (22 August 1927) – LLC.

125   Hazel Lavery to Thomas Bodkin (31 August 1927) – TBP (573).

CHAPTER IX

1   Thomas Bodkin to W.T. Cosgrave (28 July 1927) – National Archive, Dublin, S5503.

2   Thomas Bodkin to Hazel Lavery (24 April 1929) – LLC.

3   Thomas Bodkin to Hazel Lavery (28 September 1927) *(copy)* TBP in TCD MS 6942/575.

4   Thomas Bodkin to Hazel Lavery (3 December 1927) – LLC.

5   Hazel Lavery to W.T. Cosgrave (28 December 1927) (copy) – National Archive, Dublin S5503.

6   Unidentified press cutting (undated 1920s) – Ladv Laverv's scraphooks – LLC.

7   Gearóid McGann to Hazel Lavery (21 December ? 1923) – LLC.

8   Shane Leslie Diaries (1914-44) (Entry: 10 November 1922) – Leslie papers in NLI, MS 22,863.

9   Thomas McDeering to Hazel Lavery (26 October 1925) – LLC.

10   Hazel Lavery to Lennox Robinson (undated November 1926) in Morris MS,p.174.

11   Lavery, *Life,* pp. 220-2.

12   *Irish Independent* (13 February 1940) – LLC.

13   Lavery, *Life,* p. 222.

14   Alice Gwynn to author (26 March 1991).

15   Hazel Lavery to Thomas Bodkin (20 December 1927) – TBP (577).

16   Tim Healy to Hazel Lavery (22 December 1927) – LLC.

17   Hazel Lavery to Thomas Bodkin (20 December 1927) – TBP (577).

18   Hazel Lavery to Thomas Bodkin (10 March 1929) – TBP (599).

19   Thomas Bodkin to Hazel Lavery (21 December 1927) – LLC.

20 Thomas Bodkin to Hazel Lavery (25 December 1927) – LLC.
21 *Ibid.*
22 Joseph Brennan to John Lavery (copy) (30 December 1927) – Brennan papers in NLI (MS 26,020).
23 John Lavery to Thomas Bodkin (30 December 1927) – TBP (547).
24 Thomas Bodkin to Hazel Lavery (4 January 1928) – LLC.
25 Hazel Lavery to Thomas Bodkin (26 December 1927) – TBP (578).
26 Hazel Lavery to Joseph Brennan (3 March 1928) – Brennan papers in NLI (MS 26,020).
27 *Ibid.* (6 April 1928).
28 *The Express* (April 1928) – Lady Lavery's scrapbooks – LLC.
29 John Lavery to Joseph Brennan (25 May 1928) – Brennan papers in NLI, MS 26,020.
30 Hazel Lavery to Joseph Brennan (undated, April 1928) – Brennan papers in NLI, MS 26,020.
31 Hazel Lavery to Thomas Bodkin (26 September 1928) – TBP (592).
32 Hazel Lavery to Paddy McGilligan (31 March 1928) – McGilligan papers inUCDAp35/d/134.
33 Hazel Lavery to Thomas Bodkin (19 February 1929) – TBP (597).
34 Hazel Lavery to Thomas Bodkin (16 July 1928) – TBP (588).
35 Hazel Lavery to Thomas Bodkin (1 July 1928) – TBP (587).
36 Hazel Lavery to Thomas Bodkin (16 July 1928) – TRP (588) .
37 *Ibid.* (24 February 1928) – MS 6942/580.
38 Hazel Lavery to Thomas Bodkin (6 April 1928) – TBP (584).
39 Alice Trudeau to Hazel Lavery (undated, February 1928) – LLC.
40 Hazel Lavery to Thomas Bodkin (1 July 1928) – TBP \587).
41 Josephine MacNeill to Hazel Lavery (11 July 1928) – LLC.
42 Thomas Bodkin to Hazel Lavery (21 July 1928) – LLC.
43 Tim Healy to Hazel Lavery (31 July 1928) – LLC.
44 Hazel Lavery to Thomas Bodkin (16 July 1928) – TBP (588).
45 Hazel Lavery to Lennox Robinson (26 July 1928) in Morris MS, p. 183.
46 *Ibid.*
47 Hazel Lavery to Thomas Bodkin (8 August 1928) – TBP (590).
48 Hazel Lavery to Thomas Bodkin (22 January 1928) – TBP (579).
49 Harkness, *The Restless Dominion*, p. 63.
50 Hazel Lavery to Thomas Bodkin (2 December *1925)* –TBP (595).
51 Thomas Bodkin to Hazel Lavery (22 September 1928) – LLC.
52 Hazel Lavery to Joseph Brennan (10 September 1928) – Brennan papers in NLI, MS 26,020.
53 Maurice Moynihan, *Currency and Central Banking in Ireland 1922-1960* (Dublin 1975), p. 126.
54 Copies of the photograph are in the Bodkin papers in TCD and the Brennan papers in NLI.
55 Hazel Lavery to Joseph Brennan (10 September 1928) – Brennan papers in NLI, MS 26,020.
56 Joseph Brennan to Hazel Lavery (22 September 1928) – LLC.
57 Joseph Brennan to Dr H. Parker Willis (22 September 1928) (copy) – Brennan papers in MS 26,020.

58 John Lavery to Joseph Brennan in Moynihan, *op. cit.*, p. 126.
59 Lavery, *Life*, p. 222.
60 Hazel Lavery to Father Leonard (11 November 1928) – Father Leonard papers in All Hallows College, Dublin.
61 Hazel Lavery to Lytton Strachey (3 December 1928) – Strachey papers in British Library, London, MS 60676.
62 Alice McEnery to Audrey Morris (undated 1950s) – LAMC.
63 Hazel Lavery to Thomas Bodkin (2 December 1928) – TBP (595).
64 Alice McEnery to Audrey Morris (undated 1950s) – LAMC.
65 Hazel Lavery to Father Leonard (14 December 1928) – Father Leonard papers in All Hallows College, Dublin.
66 Hazel Lavery to Thomas Bodkin (2 December 1928) – TBP (595); Winston Churchill to Hazel Lavery (27 February 1929) – LLC.
67 Hazel Lavery to Father Leonard (14 December 1928) – Father Leonard papers in All Hallows College, Dublin.
68 Alice McEnery to Audrey Morris (15 May 1950) – LAMC.
69 Alice Trudeau to Hazel Lavery (21 January 1929) – LLC.
70 Alice Trudeau to Hazel Lavery (undated February 1929) – LLC.
71 Hazel Lavery to Father Leonard (5 February 1929) – Father Leonard papers in All Hallows College, Dublin.
72 Derek Patmore in unidentified press cutting (16 May 1931) – Lady Lavery's scrapbooks – LLC.
73 Unidentified press cutting (undated) – Lady Lavery's scrapbooks – LLC.
74 Unidentified press cutting (undated) – Lady Lavery's scrapbooks – LLC.
75 Unidentified press cutting (undated) – Lady Lavery's scrapbooks – LLC.
76 Unidentified press cutting (undated 1929) – Lady Lavery's scrapbooks – LLC.
77 Hazel Lavery to Thomas Bodkin (undated 1929) – TBP (598).
78 *Ibid.*
79 *Ibid.*
80 Hazel Lavery to Thomas Bodkin (19 February 1929), MS 6942/598.
81 Ramsay MacDonald to Hazel Lavery (26 February 1929) – LAMC.
82 Mr Boilbester (journalist with *The Irish Times*) to Hazel Lavery (29 March 1929) – LLC.
83 Unidentified press cutting (July 1929) – Lady Lavery's scrapbooks – LLC.
84 Hazel Lavery to Thomas Bodkin (28 July 1929) – TBP (601).
85 *Ibid.*
86 Hazel Lavery to Thomas Bodkin (15 August 1929) – TBP (603).
87 Sexton, *op. cit.*, pp. 118-19.
88 Hazel Lavery to Thomas Bodkin (6 September 1929) – TBP (605).
89 *Ibid.* (24 December 1929), MS 6942/610.
90 Thomas Bodkin to Hazel Lavery (19 October 1929) – LLC.
91 *Ibid.* (30 March 1928).
92 Hazel Lavery to Thomas Bodkin (1 December 1929) – TBP (608).
93 Hazel Lavery to Thomas Bodkin (12 December 1929) – TBP (609).
94 Saorstat Eireann Notes: Lavery Pictures 1927/1928 – National Archive, Dublin (MS S5503).
95 Hazel Lavery to Arthur Deane (8 May 1929) – Belfast Museum Archive.

96   Hazel Lavery to W.T. Cosgrave (2 March 1928) – National Archive, Dublin (MS S5503).
97   Hazel Lavery to Thomas Bodkin (23 October 1929) – TBP (606).
98   Barbara Dawson, *op. cit.,* p. 30.
99   Lady Gregory to Hazel Lavery (13 November 1929) – LLC.
100   Hazel Lavery to Lady Augusta Gregory (18 November 1929) – Berg Collection, New York Public Library.
101   Hazel Lavery to Thomas Bodkin (1 December 1929) – TBP (608).
102   Hazel Lavery to W.T. Cosgrave (9 December 1929) – National Archive, Dublin, MS S9987.
103   Lady Gregory to Hazel Lavery (24 December 1929) – LLC.
104   Thomas Bodkin to Hazel Lavery (7 December 1929) – LLC.
105   Rose Rosenberg to Hazel Lavery (23 November 1929) – LLC.
106   Hazel Lavery to W.T. Cosgrave (9 December 1929) – National Archive, Dublin MS S9987.
107   Hazel Lavery to Thomas Bodkin (24 December 1929) – TBP (610).
108   Unidentified press cutting (undated 1920s) – Lady Lavery's scrapbooks – LLC.
109   Hazel Lavery to Thomas Bodkin (12 December 1929) – TBP (609).

CHAPTER IX
1   Hazel Lavery to Thomas Bodkin (24 December 1929) – TBP (610).
2   Hazel Lavery to Thomas Bodkin (20 February 1930)-TBP (613).
3   *Ibid.*
4   Hazel Lavery to Thomas Bodkin (12 March 1930) – TBP (614).
5   Hazel Lavery to Thomas Bodkin (20 February 1930) – TBP \613).
6   Alice McEnery to Audrey Morris (undated 1950s) – LAMC.
7   Lady Anita Leslie reminiscences in the possession of Eoghan Harris, Monkstown, Co. Dublin.
8   Alice Gwynn to author (10 November 1990).
9   Hazel Lavery to Thomas Bodkin (12 March 1930) – TBP (614).
10   Alice McEnery to Hazel Lavery (27 March 1930) – LLC.
11   Alice McEnery to Hazel Lavery (13 March 1930) – LLC.
12   Hazel Lavery to Thomas Bodkin (12 March 1930) – TBP (614).
13   Hazel Lavery to Thomas Bodkin (30 December 1929) – TBP (611).
14   Hazel Lavery to Lennox Robinson (undated April 1930) in Morris MS, p. 201.
15   Hazel Lavery to Thomas Bodkin (30 December 1929) – TBP (611).
16   Unidentified press cutting (undated) – Lady Lavery's scrapbooks – LLC.
17   Lord Donegall to Hazel Lavery (3 May 1930) – LLC.
18   Morris MS, p. 135.
19   *Hereford Journal* (19 September 1931) – Lady Lavery's scrapbooks – LLC.
20   Morris MS, p. 211.
21   *Ibid.,* p. 65.
22   Unidentified press cutting – (undated 1930s) – Lady Lavery's scrapbooks – LLC.
23   Louie Rickard to Hazel Lavery (30 September 1927) – LLC.
24   Temple Thurston to Hazel Lavery (undated) – LLC.

25   Alice McEnery to Audrey Morris (undated 1950s) – LAMC.

26   Hazel Lavery to Thomas Bodkin (6 September 1929) – TBP (605).

27   Hazel Lavery to Thomas Bodkin (16 June 1930) – TBP (616).

28   Alice McEnery to Hazel Lavery (9 May 1930) – LLC.

29   Hazel Lavery to Thomas Bodkin (1 December 1929) – TBP \608).

30   Hazel Lavery to Thomas Bodkin (1 July 1928) – TBP \587).

31   Hazel Lavery to Lennox Robinson (undated) in Morris MS, p. 193.

32   Hazel Lavery to Thomas Bodkin (21 September 1930) – TBP (619).

33   Morris MS, p. 1.

34   Douglas Woodruffe to John Lavery (12 January 1935) – LLC.

35   Louie Rickard to Hazel Lavery (2 August 1927) – LLC.

36   Douglas Woodruffe to John Lavery (12 January 1935) – LLC.

37   Louie Rickard to Alice McEnery (14 March 1940) – Alice McEnery Gwynn Papers.

38   Morris MS, p. 196.

39   Christopher Hollis to Hazel Lavery (31 August 1930) – LLC.

40   Frank Owen to Hazel Lavery (26 June 1934) – LLC.

41   Morris MS, p. 219.

42   Charles Edward Lysaght, *Brendan Bracken* (London 1979), pp. 68, 82, 88.

43   Christopher Hollis to Hazel Lavery (undated) – LLC.

44   Ramsay MacDonald to Hazel Lavery (21 May 1930) – LLC.

45   Ramsay MacDonald to Hazel Lavery (June 1930) – LLC.

46   Ramsay MacDonald to Hazel Lavery (15 July 1930) – LLC.

47   David Marquand, *Ramsay MacDonald* (London 1977), p. 406.

48   Ramsay MacDonald to Hazel Lavery (undated 1930s) – LLC.

49   Ramsay MacDonald to Hazel Lavery (31 January 1931) – LLC.

50   Ramsay MacDonald to Hazel Lavery (25 July 1930) – LLC.

51   Ramsay MacDonald (24 September 1930) – LLC.

52   Ramsay MacDonald to Hazel Lavery (undated 1930s) – LLC.

53   Hazel Lavery to Thomas Bodkin (8 January 1933) – TBP (630).

54   Ramsay MacDonald to Hazel Lavery (undated 1930s) – LLC.

55   Anonymous note to Hazel Lavery (undated) – LLC.

56   Unidentified press cutting – Lady Lavery's scrapbooks – LLC.

57   Desmond FitzGerald to Mabel FitzGerald (3 October 1930) – FitzGerald papers in UCDA p80/1411.

58   Hazel Lavery to Lady Gregory (24 November 1930) Berg Collection, New York Public Library, New York.

59   Hazel Lavery to Aileen Bodkin (10 January 1931) – TBP (625).

60   Morris MS, p. 205.

61   Hazel Lavery to Thomas Bodkin (21 September 1930) – TBP (619).

62   Ramsay MacDonald to Hazel Lavery (undated 1931) – LLC.

63   Ramsay MacDonald to Hazel Lavery (25 January 1931) – LLC.

64   Ramsay MacDonald to Hazel Lavery (31 January 1931) – LLC.

65   Unidentified press cutting – Lady Lavery's scrapbooks – LLC.

66   Unidentified press cutting – Lady Lavery's scrapbooks (January 1931) – LLC.

67   McConkey, *John Lavery*, p. 186.

68   Robinson, *Curtain Up,* pp. 210-11.

69 Lady Lavery's scrapbooks (undated) – LLC.
70 Ramsay MacDonald to Hazel Lavery (undated 1931) – LLC.
71 Ramsay MacDonald to Hazel Lavery (undated 1930s) – LLC.
72 Ramsay MacDonald to Hazel Lavery (undated 1930s) – LLC.
73 Ramsay MacDonald to Hazel Lavery (undated 1930s) – LLC.
74 Ramsay MacDonald to Hazel Lavery (15 June 1931)- LLC.
75 Ramsay MacDonald to Hazel Lavery (undated 1930s) – LLC.
76 Ramsay MacDonald to Hazel Lavery (undated 1930s) – LLC.
77 Lavery, *Life*, pp. 183-4.
78 Morris MS, p. 2.
79 Evelyn Waugh to Hazel Lavery (16 August 1932) – LLC.
80 Martin Stannard, *Evelyn Waugh, The Early Years 1903-1939* (London 1986), pp. 300, 306.
81 Evelyn Waugh to Hazel Lavery (undated, December 1932) – LLC.
82 Evelyn Waugh to Hazel Lavery (undated) – LLC.
83 *Daily Express* (8 October 1930) – Lady Lavery's scrapbooks – LLC.
84 Mark Amory (ed.). *The Letters of Evelyn Waugh* (London 1980), p. 71-2.
85 Evelyn Waugh to Hazel Lavery (undated May 1933) – LLC.
86 Evelyn Waugh to Clarissa Churchill (8 January 1951) in Amory, *op. cit.*, p. 363.
87 Alice McEnery to Hazel Lavery (9 May 1930) – LLC.
88 Hazel Lavery to Thomas Bodkin (8 November 1932) – TBP (628).
89 Alice McEnery to Audrey Morris (undated 1950s) – LAMC.
90 Douglas Woodruffe to John Lavery (12 January 1935) – LLC.
91 Sheriff Harold Ford to Kenneth McConkey (March 1993) – I am grateful to Kenneth McConkey *for* this reference.
92 Morris MS, p. 190.
93 Alice McEnery to Audrey Morris (May 1955) – LAMC.
94 Derek Patmore memoir – LAMC
95 Beaton, *The Wandering Tears,* pp. 270-1.
96 Cecil Beaton, *The Book of Beauty* (London 1930), p. 40.
97 Unidentified press cutting (undated 1930s) – Lady Lavery's scrapbooks – LLC.
98 Cecil Beaton to Hazel Lavery (undated) – LLC.
99 *Vogue* (8 March 1933) – LLC.
100 Morris MS, p. 225.
101 Unidentified press cutting (undated 1930s) – Lady Lavery's scrapbooks – LLC.
102 Morris MS, p. 219.
103 John Lavery to Hazel Lavery (undated April 1933) – LLC.
104 Hazel Lavery to Thomas Bodkin (8 January 1933) – TBP (630).
105 Unidentified press cutting (undated 1930s) – Lady Lavery's scrapbooks – LLC.
106 Moms MS, p. 219.
107 Hazel Lavery to Thomas Bodkin (undated 1930s) – TBP (615).
108 Unidentified press cutting (undated 1930s) – LLC.
109 J.J. Lee, *Ireland 1912-1985* (Cambridge 1989), p. 177.
110 Hazel Lavery to Thomas Bodkin (8 January 1933) – TBP (630).

111 Amory, *op. cit.,* p. 79.
112 McConkey, *John Lavery,* p. 104.
113 Unidentified press cutting (October 1929) – Lady Lavery's scrapbooks – LLC.
114 Hazel Lavery to Thomas Bodkin (undated, ?December 1933) – TBP (636).
115 Anonymous note to Hazel Lavery (undated 1934) – LLC.
116 Hazel Lavery to Thomas Bodkin (5 April 1934) – TBP(635).
117 Morris MS, p. 222.
118 Alice McEnery to Hazel Lavery (March 1934) – LLC.
119 Hazel Lavery to Thomas Bodkin (5 April 1934) – TBP (635).
120 Lennox Robinson, *Curtain Up,* p. 206.
121 Morris MS, p. 223.
122 Hazel Lavery to Cecil Beaton, quoted in Morris MS, pp. 223—4.
123 Beaton, *The Wandering Years,* p. 272.
124 Derek Patmore memoir – LAMC.
125 *Daily Express* (25 August 1934) – LLC.
126 Hazel Lavery to Thomas Bodkin (undated, ?1934) – TBP (639).
127 Hannie Collins to Hazel Lavery (12 November ? 1934) – LLC.
128 Hazel Lavery to John Lavery (22 July 1934) – LLC.
129 Moms MS, p. 224.
130 Morris MS, p. 228.
131 John Lavery to Enid Richards (1940) -LLC.
132 Unidentified press cutting – (January 1935) – LLC.
133 Beaton, *The Wandering Tears,* p. 272.

EPILOGUE
1   McConkey, *Catalogue,* p. 91.

SELECT SECONDARY SOURCES

Acton, Harold, 'Lady Cunard', in Peter Quennell (ed.). *Genius in the Drawing Room* (London 1980).
Arnold, Bruce, *Orpen: Mirror to an Age* (London 1981).
Asquith, Lady Cynthia, *The Diaries of Lady Cynthia Asquith 1915—1918* (London 1987).
Beaslai, Piaras, *Michael Collins and the Making of a New Ireland (Vol. 11)* (Dublin 1926).
Beaton, Cecil, *The Wandering Tears, 1922-1939* (London 1961).
Bodkin, Thomas, *Hugh Lane and his Pictures* (Dublin 1956).
Brettell, Richard R., Scott Schaefer, Sylvie Gache-Patin, and Francoise Heilbrun, *A Day in the Country: Impressionism and the French Landscape* (Los Angeles 1984).
Brock, Michael and Eleanor (eds), *H.H. Asquith Letters to Venetia Stanley* (Oxford 1982).
Butterfield, Roger, *The American Past* (New York 1966). Chadwick, Whitney, *Women, Art and Society* (London 1990).
Churchill, Winston, *Thoughts and Adventures* (London 1990).

Colville, John, *The Churchillians* (London 1981).

Coogan, Tim Pat, *Michael Collins* (London 1990).

Davidoff, Leonore, *The Best Circles: Society, Etiquette and the Season* (London 1973).

de Vere White, Terence, *Kevin O'Higgins* (Dublin 1986).

Elizabeth, Countess of Fingall, *Seventy Years Young* (Dublin 1991).

Forester, Margery, *The Lost Leader* (London 1972).

Harkness, D.W., *The Restless Dominion: The Irish Free State and the British Commonwealth of Nations, 1921-1931* (New York 1970).

Hassall, Christopher, *Edward Marsh, Patron of the Arts* (London 1959).

Holt, Edgar, *Protest in Arms: The Irish Troubles 1916-1923* (London 1960).

Hyde, H. Montgomery, *The Londonderrys, A Family Portrait* (London 1979).

Lavery, John, *The Life of a Painter* (London 1940).

Lee, J.J., *Ireland 1912-1985* (Cambridge 1989).

Leslie, Shane, *Long Shadows* (London 1966).

Londonderry, Lady Edith, *Retrospect* (London 1938).

Lord Longford (Frank Pakenham), *Peace by Ordeal* (London 1972).

Lyons, "F.S.L., *Ireland Since the Famine* (Suffolk 1981).

Lyons, J.B., *Oliver St John Gogarty* (Dublin 1980).

Lysaght, Charles Edward, *Brendan Bracken* (London 1979).

Marquand, David, *Ramsay MacDonald* (London 1977).

McConkey, Kenneth, 'Hazel in Black and Gold', *Irish Arts Review,* vol. 1, no. 3 (Autumn 1984).

McConkey, Kenneth, *John Lavery* (Edinburgh 1993).

McConkey, Kenneth, *John Lavery Retrospective Exhibition Catalogue 1985* (Belfast 1984).

McCutheon, John, *Drawn from Memory* (New York 1950).

Moynihan, Maurice, *Currency and Central Banking in Ireland 1922-1960* (Dublin 1975).

Murphy, Daniel (ed.). *Lady Gregory's Journal* (Buckinghamshire 1978).

O'Broin, Leon, *In Great Haste* (Dublin 1984).

O'Connor, Frank, *The Big Fellow* (Dublin 1979).

O'Gorman, Thomas J., 'Madonna at a Bullfight', in *The World of Hibernia,* vol. 1, no. 1 (Summer 1995).

Pepper, Terence, *Camera Portraits by E.O. Hoppe (1878-1972) – Exhibition Catalogue* (London 1978).

Pritchard, E.R., (ed.), *Illinois of to-day and its Progressive Cities* (Chicago n.d.).

Robinson, Lennox, *Curtain Up* (London 1942).

Roskill, Stephen, *Admiral of the Fleet: Earl Beatty, The Last Naval Hero* (London 1980).

Ryan, Meda, *The Day Michael Collins Was Shot* (Dublin 1989).

Sexton, Brendan, *Ireland and the Crown 1922-1936: The Governor-Generalship* (Dublin 1989).

Stannard, Martin, *Evelyn Waugh, The Early Years 1903-1939* (London 1986).

Trudeau, Edward Livingston, *An Autobiography* (New York 1916).

West, Trevor, *Horace Plunkett, Co-Operation and Politics* (Washington, D.C. 1986).

Wilmerding, John, *American Art* (Middlesex 1976).

Index

INDEX

113; overtures to MacDonald's Colonial Secretary 113–14; entertains during Dominion Conference 114; disseminates political correspondence 114, 133; and Boundary Commission 116; visits Beal na mBláth 116; disagrees with Churchill 117, 156; accosts Lloyd George 117; writes to MacDonald on Ireland 117, 155; considers buying house in Kilkenny 121; resists trip to America 121; fears 'getting un-Irished' 122; alienated from Ireland 131, 156,178; resents Fianna Fáil 133,178; ostracized by Irish 134, 139, 142; only happy in Ireland 135; writes to Cosgrave on Irish Collection 137; on rumours of JL being named Governor-General 137–8; desire to be Vicereine 138; resents Josephine MacNeill 138, 143, 144; promotes Bodkin for High Commissioner 138–9, 145; disdains Irish-Ireland 139; image on Irish currency 139–42, 146–7; subjected to anti-Irish sentiment 143,156; suggests guests for Horse Show 144; dislikes the North 145; opposes Smiddy 145–6, 150–1; continues to entertain Irish and English together 149-50; critical of Free State government 150–1, 160–1; represents Irish Dominion in Empire Marketing film 150–1; bemoans marginality of Ireland 155-6; hosts Imperial Conference delegates 167; visits grandson in Kilkenny 168; disappointed at 1932 election results 177; horrified at dismantling of Treaty 178
AND MICHAEL COLLINS: hopes to meet MC 70, 74; MC sees HL as ally 72; makes MC feel comfortable in high society 76, 85-6; subject of MC-Birkenhead row 76; attracted to MC 76–7; attends Mass with MC 77; nature of relationship with MC 77, 87, 88–9, 91, 94, 95–6, 101–2, 105–6; political influence 79, 80–1, 84, 88–9, 90–1, 104; brings MC to Downing Street 81; MC recounts final negotiations 82; describes social round to MC 83; burns candle for MC 83–4; correspondence with MC 83–4, 85, 86–7, 89, 90, 94, 101, 102, 105–6, 107; dinner parties for political figures 85; fragments of letters and poetry from MC in HL's scrapbook 89; communicates with British officials on MC's behalf 90, 91; alliance with MC objected to 91-3, 103; prayer for MC 92; Kitty Kiernan suspects 'somebody else' 93–4; love poem from MC 94; shields MC from sniper 97; in ambush with MC 97–8; premonitions of MC's death 98–9; persuaded not to wear widow's weeds 99; flings rosary beads on MC's grave 100; writes 'To a Dead Lover' 101; assembles MC scrapbook 101; remains in contact with Hannie Collins 101; effects on MC's body attest to close attachment 101–2; advertises her grief 102; Shaw knew MC was 'Sunday husband' 102; mocked by Colefax and Cunard 102; remains in contact with MC's friends 102; mistaken for Kitty at cenotaph ceremony 106
AND KEVIN O'HIGGINS: letter from KO'H after MC killed 102–3; stays at O'Higgins home during Horse Show 111; focus of HL's affections 118; love letters

INDEX